KINSHIP CARE

Crystal Sanchez

KINSHIP CARE

A MEMOIR

TATE PUBLISHING
AND ENTERPRISES, LLC

Published by Tate Publishing & Enterprises, LLC
127 E. Trade Center Terrace | Mustang, Oklahoma 73064 USA
1.888.361.9473 | www.tatepublishing.com

Tate Publishing is committed to excellence in the publishing industry. The company reflects the philosophy established by the founders, based on Psalm 68:11,
"The Lord gave the word and great was the company of those who published it."

Book design copyright © 2013 by Tate Publishing, LLC. All rights reserved.
Cover design by Joel Uber
Interior design by Jomel Pepito

Published in the United States of America

ISBN: 978-1-62854-127-4
1. Biography & Autobiography / Personal Memoirs
2. Family & Relationships / General
13.10.30

For Boo

PROLOGUE

~~~~~~

*O*n December 31, 2006, I entered the hospital's intensive care unit and approached the nurse's quarters. I looked around but found no one to assist me. I cleared my throat in a loud and abrupt manner; still no one emerged. Fueled by the hatred and ill will consuming me, I turned toward the suspended row of curtains designed to give the unwell some measure of privacy and shamefully began to peek behind each one. As I rounded the nurse's quarters, a strong voice from behind startled me. "Can I help you?"

I turned to find a stocky, blond-haired female nurse positioned in what seemed to be a combat stance. With her well-rehearsed stern gaze sizing me up, it took a moment for me to answer. "I'm here to see Elaine Perez."

She looked at me suspiciously. "Are you a relative?"

"I'm her sister-in-law."

Looking a bit skeptical, she pointed at one curtain over from where we stood. "You'll find her in that room."

I thanked her and walked quickly over to the indicated curtain. I stood there for a long moment, then took a deep breath and moved the curtain just far enough back to look into Elaine's room. Elaine, was breathing through a tube and hooked up to various medical devices. She looked so frail, it was shocking.

A nurse who was attending to her looked over at me and asked in a pleasant voice, "Are you here to visit Elaine?"

I nodded.

"I'll be done in a minute, and then you can come over."

I awkwardly waited by the curtain, stifling the urge to plug my nose at the intense stench of illness coming from Elaine's bed. The nurse informed me that she was preparing to suction out her patient's breathing tube. I nodded my head as if I understood what was to take place, then watched in horror as Elaine launched into a frightening episode of gagging, coughing, and choking, all the while attempting, though feebly, to strike the nurse with the two strange pot holder looking things encasing her hands. The nurse, who patiently continued her painstaking task in spite of Elaine's resistance, repeated the words in a singsong voice, "I'm almost done. I'm almost done."

When the horrific business was over, I was overcome with shame as my only purpose for visiting on this day was to contentedly observe the much-deserved suffering Elaine, by her own hands, was now made to endure.

CHAPTER 1

The suffering parental substance abuse leaves in its wake is that of a child's.

—Crystal Sanchez

It was October of 2002 when I first met Andrew's mom, Elaine. My mom and I walked into the Adams County courtroom to attend my brother Adam's preliminary hearing, which was a result of a previous drug-related arrest.

Once we entered the courtroom, we stopped for a moment to look around and spotted him sitting in one of the middle rows of the spectator's seating. He was sitting next to a woman with long blond hair who I would come to know as Elaine.

Adam's drug-related arrest happened on September 4, 2002, after a search warrant was executed at a home he was renting. During the search, a meth lab was recovered as well as several meth lab components and chemicals along with a loaded nine-millimeter handgun. Consequently, Adam was charged with manufacturing a schedule II narcotic, possession of chemicals, supplies, and equipment with intent to manufacture and distribute a schedule II narcotic. In addition to these charges, due to the presence of two extraordinary aggravating circumstances, (Adam was in possession of a handgun, and he manufactured, or attempted to manufacture a controlled substance within a thousand foot perimeter of an elementary school) Adam was classified as a special offender x2.

At first glance, I noticed Elaine's long blond hair and her frequent need to run her hands through it. Although she was sitting down, I could see she was tall and dreadfully thin with the exception of her swollen belly.

Mom and I sat down on the bench directly in front of Adam and Elaine and turned to face them. Mom and Adam began to talk as Elaine and I looked on. Now at closer scrutiny, I noticed Elaine's gaunt face was covered with pockmarks, which even the zealous amount of makeup she managed to apply that day could not hide. Her teeth were slightly crooked and smoker stained, and her tired looking eyes were an indistinct shade of blue. Her swollen belly, a complete contrast from her emaciated body, looked as if it could burst at any time.

Adam, who had always been an attractive Hispanic man, was so thin and pale he was almost unrecognizable. Noticeably anxious, he was struggling through an introduction between me and Elaine, whom he referred to as Angel, when he was summoned by the judge. He rose from his seat and approached the bench. Annoyingly, from where Mom and I were sitting, it was impossible to hear what was being said. But after a few muffled words were spoken between Adam and the judge, the judge released him "on your own recognizant."

Adam thanked the judge and walked with haste toward his seat. He walked past Mom and I without even a glance in our direction. When we turned to look back, we were surprised to see that Adam and Elaine's seats were vacant. After our initial confusion, we decided Adam must be waiting for us outside the courtroom. But when we went out the courtroom doors, we found the hall to be coldly vacant, with Adam and Elaine being nowhere in sight.

Realizing that Adam had apparently left the courthouse without even saying a word to Mom made me fume. Yet Mom, brushing aside Adam's rude behavior, felt there had to be a good reason for his hasty departure. And she was right. There was a reason, but it was not by any means a good one nor an admirable one, as Adam would later convey to Mom that he and Elaine quickly left the courtroom that day because he was afraid the judge would discover his prior arrests in two other counties. If these arrests were discovered, the judge may have sent him straight to jail.

Even though Adam didn't reveal much about his prior arrests other than "they were drug related and really no big deal," Mom didn't make any further inquiries. She simply accepted his explanation as a reasonable one, which didn't surprise me since denial was often her way of dealing with the hard things. However, I would later discover that one of Adam's "no big deal" arrests was not so much drug related as it was violent. The police report revealed that Adam allegedly hit a woman in the face with a bat and tried to strangle her after an altercation over a car he previously sold to the woman's nephew. The recently pregnant Elaine, who was with Adam the day of the altercation, was identified as a witness. The arrest resulted in a second degree assault charge for Adam. Appallingly, Adam would later boast that he and Elaine were married months later, so she could not be made to testify against him.

After Adam's October hearing, I hadn't heard anything relating to him, Elaine, or the baby she was carrying until several months later when Mom dropped by my home on an unexpected visit. I felt uneasy as we sat in the living room across from one another making small talk. Finally wrought with anticipation, "What's going on Mom?" I asked.

She sighed. "Adam and Elaine had a baby boy, and I wanted to see if you would go with me to visit the baby this weekend."

I was worried that Mom's visit had to do with her on-going health concerns, so I was both relieved and surprised by her request. Even so, I didn't need any time to consider it. "I have no desire to get involved in Adam's new situation," I said adamantly.

Mom's immediate hurt look, which I believe she engineered for the sole purpose of making me feel guilty, made me feel guilty. Then she quickly rose to her feet and said as pleasantly as she could manage, "Well, I better get going. I have some things I need to get done."

We hugged good-bye and as if knowing something I didn't, she smiled at me. "Think about it," she said, "and call me if you change your mind." Evading any further response from me, she quickly walked to the door and let herself out.

Feeling guilty or not, I told myself I would not alter my decision as I knew seeing the baby would only set me up for the same kind of heartache my husband, Liam, and I had experienced for the past several years as we helplessly watched Adam's two older sons take a backseat to his drug addiction. In no way was I prepared to watch his newest son endure the same fate. Even so, now that I was aware of this new tiny being, I couldn't get him off my mind. I felt compelled to check on him to ensure he was in good health and being properly taken care of. "Damn it!" I yelled.

Consequently, on a sunny Saturday afternoon in February of 2003, I found myself driving south with Mom and Maria (my daughter) in tow, heading toward Elaine and Adam's provisional home; a hotel room, with the purpose of meeting my two-week-old nephew, Andrew.

It was a very long ride, and when we finally arrived at the hotel, I was suddenly stricken with a pang of anxiety. I felt totally unprepared for what may lie ahead. Would it be bleak and disheartening? What if I discover illegal activity? Would I then be duty-bound to report it, to report Adam? I considered these things as we got out of the car. My anxiety increased as we approached the door. I began to wonder if I should go back and wait in the car.

I was still on the fence when Mom's loud knock on the door startled me. Before I had any more time to think, Elaine opened the door and cheerfully waved us in, diminishing one's opportunity to do anything other than enter.

CHAPTER 2

Distrust and caution are the parents of security.

—Benjamin Franklin

Elaine was dressed in a red T-shirt and jeans and was dreadfully thin for someone who just had a baby. Her bright red tennis shoes appeared to be a couple of sizes too big, which curiously, made me feel sorry for her. As soon as I stepped into the hotel room, I was overwhelmed by the heavy smell of cigarette smoke lingering in the air of the remarkably cold room. As I moved in further, I could hear the air conditioner running, which was very odd for that time of year. Elaine walked across the room with her dog Chase, a boxer breed, at her heels and sat on the bed next to where little Andrew was lying and grabbed a cigarette from the pack that was next to her. Mom, Maria, and I walked over to the bed, and with no seating options available other than to sit on the bed itself, we just awkwardly hovered around it, looking down at Andrew, who was lounging on his back and looking up at us.

The little guy was wearing a blue and red baseball outfit. His head was tiny yet bursting with a considerable heap of dark hair, and his wrinkled skin was milky brown. Being so new, it was hard to determine which, if any, of Adam's features he possessed.

Since Adam was nowhere in sight I assumed he was working. "When will Adam be home, Elaine?" I asked.

She shrugged. "I'm not sure."

I wanted to inquire on his whereabouts but felt I should get to know her a little better first.

Mom and Maria focused their attention on Andrew as I briefly assessed the small room. It had the makings of a studio apartment, consisting of a tiny kitchen area located adjacent to the queen-size bed and a small separate bathroom located about four feet from the foot of the bed. The kitchen sink was piled with dirty dishes, and the curtain rod in the bathroom was being used as a clothes line.

Having reached an awkward silence, Mom encouraged Elaine to open the gifts we brought for the little guy, and soon we were all chatting and laughing. Elaine was very charismatic, seemingly intelligent, and had an awesome laugh. Yet oddly, I still found myself feeling unsettled in her presence.

Once the gifts were all opened and put aside, Elaine lit up the cigarette she had been holding as we discussed Andrew's belly button. The umbilical cord stump had not yet dried and fallen off, which seemed to be a concern to Elaine. However, I was more concerned about the cigarette dangling from her long painted fingernails as she made several attempts to feed Andrew a bottle. Andrew, seeming to have had enough of the force-feeding scenario, began to wail, so I instinctively picked him up and held him against me. His skin was very cold, so I covered him with the blanket he had been lying on and gently rocked him back and forth. Elaine seemed relieved by my actions, and as Andrew's cries subsided, she began to candidly convey to us the disturbing events that led up to her current situation.

She began, "I was doing real good. I had my own condominium, and I was working a good job, and then I met Adam. Adam told me he couldn't have children because of the likely exposure he encountered at Rocky Flats, and like a dummy, I believed him." (Rocky Flats was a US nuclear weapons production facility of which Adam was once employed.)

She paused to take a long puff of her cigarette, and after she blew the smoke out of her nose and mouth, she continued matter-of-factly, "When we found out I was pregnant I wanted to have an abortion, but Adam would have none of it. He said he wanted me to have the baby. He told me to quit my job and promised he would take care of my bills, and again I believed him. So I quit my job, and wouldn't you know, he didn't pay any of my bills, and I ended up losing my condo." She took a moment to consider this, and as she glanced about the room, she said, "Now look at me. I'm living in a hotel room, wondering if Adam's even coming back. If he doesn't come back, I don't know how I'm going to pay the rent or buy diapers." She looked up at the baby in my arms and said uneasily, "And the formula I have will only get him through Tuesday."

None of this was making sense to me as this self-proclaimed deceived woman was not a teenager or even a young adult. This woman was at least in her forties. "How long has Adam been gone? Did he say anything about you two breaking up before he left?" I asked.

She took another long puff off her cigarette. "He usually leaves for several days at a time and then just shows up to sleep, and when he's well rested, he goes out again. The last time he came back, I was so pissed off at him we ended up having a big fight, and now I don't know when or even if he's coming back."

I looked at Mom with raised eyebrow. She lifted her shoulders and slightly shook her head to let me know she didn't have a clue about any of this.

"I have WIC to get baby formula but don't have a way to pick up the card or get to the store." Elaine said. (WIC—Women, Infants, and Children—is a federal grant program provided to low-income women, allowing them to obtain formula and food for their children.)

"What about your family. Can they help?" I asked.

Elaine put her head down as if ashamed. "I come from a wealthy family. My mother disowned me because of the embarrassment I caused her with my appearance on *America's Most Wanted*. At that, she looked up at us and seemed pleased at the obvious shock and confusion on our faces. In explanation she said, "Yeah, I was wanted for check forgeries that amounted to millions of dollars in Las Vegas while I was on the run from some previous drug charges here in Colorado." She stopped for a moment to put out one cigarette and light up another while we waited with an uneasy impatience. After she exhaled, she picked off what seemed to be a loose piece of tobacco from her tongue, wiped it on her jeans, and continued, "Someone recognized me when the show aired and I ended up in federal prison. I was later extradited to Colorado to finish up my time in Cañon City." She took a long puff off her cigarette and glanced up at the infant I was holding in my arms. "I maxed out my sentence by doing my full eight years to avoid parole. I'm telling you, when you're in prison that long, you become institutionalized. When I was finally released, I was afraid to leave. Life is so much harder out here. I mean, when you're locked up, you don't have to worry about bills, food, or where you're going to sleep."

Even though I was convinced this woman's story was nothing more than a tall tale. I couldn't help myself from asking, "How long were you in federal prison?"

"Not long. I gave the feds everything they wanted, including the guy I was working with. Yeah, he beat me up, took all the money, and left me in some hotel room. I had to take a lie detector test to prove to the feds that I didn't know where any of the money was."

I looked over at Maria who had a "what the heck" look on her face to which I just shrugged. Mom, on the other hand, seemed unaffected by everything being said, so I had to wonder if she's already heard it all before.

I turned back to Elaine. "Do you have anyone else besides your mom?"

"I have seven brothers, but they all have their own lives to deal with. I also have a daughter, but she lives in Pueblo and doesn't have a car. I've called my uncle who is extremely wealthy to ask for some help but haven't heard back from him yet."

We all just stood there in front of the bed looking at the baby I held in my arms as we considered everything this bizarre woman had told us thus far. Then, without warning, Elaine began to cry. She looked up at me with an air of desperation. "I can't let social services take this baby away from me. They already took my other two sons. I just can't let them take this one."

I was stunned. "Why were your other sons taken?"

Between quick puffs of her cigarette and small bouts of tears, Elaine explained: "My ex-husband was an alcoholic, and when he drank, he would beat me. When I couldn't take it anymore, I decided to leave him. After I left, I got into drugs and ended up in some trouble. I knew I was going to get a lot of time, so instead of showing up for court, I left my daughter, who was three at the time, with my mom and fled to Vegas and, well, I already told you what happened there."

"Is this the daughter who currently lives in Pueblo?" I said.

"Yes, she's my first.

"And your sons..."

"My second child, a boy, was taken from me by social services when I went to prison and was put up for adoption." Her hand was shaking as she put out her cigarette. "My third child, also a boy, was born while I was in prison and immediately taken from me by social services and was also put up for adoption."

I couldn't listen to Elaine go on any further. Did she really want me to feel sorry for her when it was her children who were the true sufferers? And if she was making the whole thing up, what kind of person did that?

At this point, the only thing I was sure of was that this new baby sleeping in my arms needed help. So I placed Andrew back on the bed, covered him with the blanket, and turned to Elaine. "Where is the nearest grocery store so I can go get the baby some diapers and formula?"

Elaine wiped away her tears, and pointed her white bony finger towards the only window in the room. "There's a Super Kmart a couple of blocks down that way."

"All right, on the way back, I will stop and pay the rent that's due."

"Thank you so much," Elaine said with what seemed to be honest gratitude. "I didn't know what I was going to do."

"If Adam comes back, don't tell him the rent has been paid. Let him give you the rent money so you'll have a bit of a stash for emergencies," I said to Elaine under my breath.

Elaine agreed and thanked me again.

I asked Mom if she wanted to go with Maria and me to the store, but she chose to stay and visit with the baby longer.

On our way out, I picked up the half-empty can of formula sitting on the small shelf in the kitchen area and put the label to memory. On our drive to the Super Kmart, Maria and I discussed Elaine's bizarre story, trying to make some sense of it. Was it possible that what she conveyed to us was nothing but lies? Worse still, was it true? The only thing we were sure of was how concerned we were about Andrew.

After purchasing everything we thought the baby would need from the store, we stopped by the hotel's office and paid Elaine and Adam's overdue rent. When we returned to the hotel room, I informed Elaine that I would make myself available to drive her and the baby to the store, to any of their doctor appointments, and also to pick up that much needed WIC card. Maria chimed in to say that she too would be available if needed. I wrote down my number for

Elaine, and she thanked us as we said our good-byes and headed out the door with heavy hearts. I quizzed Mom in the car about Elaine, but she claimed that everything Elaine said was news to her. Silence filled the car on the drive home as we quietly contemplated the visit, which I had determined was even worse than I had anticipated.

Later that evening, unable to squash the feeling of unease pulsating through me, I telephoned Mom to discuss the disturbing visit we had that day. Mom assured me that she didn't know anything about Elaine's history and was just as surprised as Maria and me. However, she did convey that she was with Elaine at the hospital when Andrew was born.

"Adam was at the hospital for a while, then left saying that he had to go take a shower. While he was gone, the baby was born," she said.

"Adam wasn't even there when Andrew was born?"

"No, but Andrew was fine when he was born. He just didn't like the bright light they placed him under, so he screamed until the nurse finally turned it off, the little stinker."

"Mom," my tone serious, "I think we should call social services. Even though Elaine's story seems far-fetched, what if it's all true? If she's involved in drugs, which I don't doubt, it could all very well be true."

Mom, clearly in denial, ignored my allegation and asked me to hold off on calling social services. "If Elaine and Adam make up, between the two of them, Andrew will get the care and support he needs," she said with flawed reasoning.

"Not if they're on drugs, Mom. It's not just about her not having the essentials for Andrew. You heard what she said about her other kids?" I countered.

"Just give them some time to get themselves together. If things don't get better soon, I will call social services myself."

I knew very well that things couldn't possibly get better soon, but still I agreed to hold off on the call to social services even though my gut was telling me otherwise.

A couple of days after our visit with Andrew, Elaine called to thank me again for the visit. I was surprised to hear from her so soon but felt it was a good opportunity to get to know her better. As we talked, I asked how she and Adam met.

"We met through a mutual friend."

Though her answer was vague, I didn't ask her to elaborate as I got the feeling she was more than prepared to lie.

Further into our conversation, Elaine claimed that Adam had major anger issues. "He has hit me full fisted several times. In fact, just last month, he blackened both my eyes."

Unfortunately, I was quick to believe this about Adam because I'd witnessed his angry assaults firsthand and have even been on the receiving end at times. "Why didn't you call the police?"

"I was afraid they would take my baby from me," she said softly.

We were quiet for a moment as her odd statement lingered in the air.

"I know Adam is still seeing Angela, and if I ever see them together, I swear I'll kill them both!" She cried out without warning.

Confused by her sudden outburst, and change of subject, it took me a moment to grasp that Elaine was referring to Adam's ex-girlfriend. Once I realized this, I was alarmed by her threatening words and said with certainty, "Elaine, you really shouldn't say things like that."

With an obvious coldness in her voice, she said, "I know, but if I were to see them together, I wouldn't be able to stop myself."

For many years Adam and Angela had a very tumultuous on-and-off relationship. They were actually living together when Elaine entered the picture, at which time, both Angela and Adam were deep into their meth addictions.

We were both quiet again. "Elaine, you really need to start thinking about future plans for you and Andrew. You know it's possible you may be raising him on your own." I implored.

To my surprise, "I do have plans," she said. "I've made plans to go back to school."

Finally, I thought, *something that makes sense*. "That sounds like a very good idea," I said hoping not to sound condescending. Then we chatted for a few more moments about nothing in particular before hanging up.

Several days after our last phone conversation, Elaine called to ask if Maria would be available to babysit Andrew that next day while she and Adam attend court for a traffic violation she claimed Adam obtained a few weeks earlier.

"Is Adam living with you at the hotel again?"

"He stops by occasionally but doesn't live here." She said, sounding annoyed by the question.

I wasn't sure what that meant, but her tone indicated that I shouldn't pry any further, so I didn't. "I'll talk to Maria and call you right back." I advised.

I called Maria, who without hesitation, agreed to babysit Andrew, which I relayed to Elaine. Elaine informed me on the details, which I passed on to Maria.

When Maria arrived at Elaine's hotel room that next morning, she called to let me know that Adam and Elaine assured her they would only be gone for a couple of hours. "I'll call you when they return," she said.

When Maria, who was twenty-two years old at the time and perfectly capable of caring for Andrew, still had not called even though three hours had gone by, I decided to give her a call. When she answered, without preamble, I said, "Isn't Elaine and Adam back from court yet?"

"No, and they haven't even called to check on Andrew or to let me know they would be late."

Since it was past lunchtime, I asked if she had eaten lunch.

"There isn't anything here to eat," she said.

"Do you need me to bring you something to eat?"

"No, I'm fine. Don't worry, Mama, they should be back any time now."

"Call me as soon as they return," I said, before hanging up. Maria called a couple of times after that to let me know they still had not returned.

When dinnertime drew near, I began to worry that Elaine and Adam had abandoned the little guy. Finally, out of patience, I called Maria to inform her that I was going to stop by the store to pick up a car seat and would meet her at the hotel. She didn't oppose my plan, which made me believe that she too was out of patience.

Just as I was heading out, Maria called to inform me that Elaine and Adam had returned. Sounding relieved, "Mom," she said, "they just got back. I'm leaving in a couple of minutes. so I'll come by the house before I go home. I'll see you in a little while."

I hung up the phone feeling pretty relieved myself until my relief turned to anger.

When Maria arrived, she was quick to say that when Elaine and Adam finally walked in they were as happy as could be with their doggie bags filled with whatever was left over from their dinner. "Neither one of them asked about Andrew or even apologized for being late," she said with annoyance.

"Did they ask if you were hungry?"

She scoffed. "No, but them two seemed to have had a good dinner," she said with noted sarcasm. Then she grew quiet for a moment. "Mom," she said with noticeable concern, "I just wanted to pick up Andrew and run out the door with him. I hated leaving him there with those two."

I patted the chair next to me. She sighed and sat down. "Do you think they were on something?"

"When I was getting ready to leave, I watched Adam try to change Andrew's diaper. Poor Andrew kept crying because it was taking so long. I finally got so upset, I moved Adam out of the way to change the diaper myself." Maria drew a breath, and exhaled loudly. "Yes, they were definitely on something."

I tried to maintain my composure when I called Mom that next day to inform her about the babysitting fiasco. "Mom, what if Maria and I are right about Adam and Elaine using drugs? If they are, you have to know that vulnerable little baby could be in harm's way."

"Well, it sounds like Elaine and Adam are back together. Just give them a couple of weeks to work things out. Everything will work out. If not, I will call social services myself," she said ignoring my concern.

But we both knew she was not capable of doing anything that could be detrimental to Adam. Regrettably, I was not prepared to take on that kind of weight either. So for the time being, we shamelessly did nothing.

CHAPTER 3

But the hearts of small children are delicate organs. A cruel beginning in this world can twist them into curious shapes.

—Carson McCullers

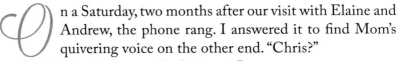n a Saturday, two months after our visit with Elaine and Andrew, the phone rang. I answered it to find Mom's quivering voice on the other end. "Chris?"

"Yeah, Mom, it's me, what's wrong?"

"Adam dropped Andrew off here earlier today and still hasn't come back for him."

"Why did Adam drop him off, and where's Elaine?"

"Adam said Elaine was pissed off at him because he left the hotel several days ago and hasn't called her. So I guess she finally got fed up with him. He said that this morning he was putting some of their stuff in a storage facility he rented, and Elaine showed up with some guy, apparently a friend of hers."

"What kind of stuff was he storing?" I interrupted.

"I don't know, but Adam said that Elaine and her friend drove past him as Elaine cursed at him, but he just brushed them off and finished putting the stuff he already unloaded into the storage area. When he was finished, he went to get in his car and was shocked to find that Andrew was in the car. Can you believe it? Elaine put the baby in the car without telling him."

I wasn't sure I heard her correctly. "What?" I said.

"Elaine didn't tell Adam that she left Andrew in his car," she said carefully.

I was fuming. "Neither one of them should be raising a baby, Mom. I can't believe a mother could be so reckless. How long was Andrew in the car by himself?"

"I'm not sure."

"Was it minutes, hours, or what?" I asked a little too loudly.

"Oh, I'm sure it was only for a few minutes," she replied sounding hopeful more than anything.

I was annoyed and baffled that it didn't even occur to her to ask Adam such an important question. "What happened after Adam found Andrew in the car?"

"Adam said he had to finish moving his stuff, so he took Andrew to your dad's house and asked if he could leave him there until he was finished at the storage facility. But your dad was home alone and told Adam that he couldn't leave Andrew with him because he didn't know how to care for an infant. So Adam brought Andrew here and asked if I could watch him for a while, but that was hours ago."

"Have you tried to call him?"

"I don't have a number for him."

"Adam didn't leave his number with you?" I said incredulously. "No."

As I considered this, sounding uneasy Mom sighed. "What if Adam doesn't come back for him? You know I can't take care of a baby. My health has not been good, and what am I suppose to do with him when I go back to work on Monday?"

Even though I too had a full-time job, in my concern for her I told her to call me in the morning, and if Adam hasn't picked up Andrew by then, I would go by and get him.

She sighed. "Thank you, honey, I'll call you tomorrow."

Late that same night, Mom called again. "Chris?"

"Yeah," I said sleepily, "it's me, what's going on?"

"I'm sorry to wake you, honey, but Elaine just called, and she was really pissed off. She said she would be here later to pick up Andrew."

"It's way too late to be picking him up. Can't she wait until tomorrow morning?"

"I told her that he was sleeping and asked if she could pick him up in the morning, but that just pissed her off more. She said she would be here to pick him up around 3:00 a.m." We discussed Elaine's outlandish behavior for a few more minutes, and before we hung up, Mom told me that she would call me in the morning.

As she said she would, Mom called that next morning. "Hi, honey, it's Mom," she said in a sing song voice.

"Hi, Mom. Did Elaine pick up Andrew?" I asked, already knowing the answer.

Yes, just like she said she would, she picked him up around 3:00 a.m."

"How was she when she got there?"

"She was totally pissed off from the time she got here until she left."

"What does she have to be pissed about?" I asked with disgust.

"I don't know, but she kept saying she couldn't believe how Adam could just dump Andrew off on me instead of taking care of him on his own."

"That crazy woman was the one that left Andrew in the car by himself! Adam should be the one that's pissed off."

Mom agreed.

"Mom," I said firmly, "I'm going to file a complaint with social services before something bad happens to Andrew."

"I think you should too," she said, "but I want Adam to think it was me that called because I'm not sure how he or Elaine will react if they find out it was you."

"I don't care if they find out," I said with conviction.

"But I do," she countered.

Eventually, I agreed to keep the truth from Adam and Elaine, but would not allow Mom to take the blame either.

On the following Monday, I contacted the Arapahoe County Social Service office to file a complaint. Because both Elaine and Adam had criminal records, the case worker I spoke with advised me that she, accompanied by two officers, would be checking on Andrew that next day.

In the meantime, I tried to remember that I was doing the right thing, no matter what effect my complaint would have on Adam.

I called the case worker again later that next day to inquire on my complaint. She conveyed that she and two police officers went down to the hotel room that morning to investigate. "Since the mother had formula and diapers and the child didn't seem to be in any distress, I found no reason to remove the child from the home."

"I purchased those diapers and formula. I even paid her rent because she was afraid she and the baby would be put out on the streets."

"It really doesn't matter how the mother obtained the items, the fact is that the home was equipped with the necessities to meet the baby's needs."

"And how do you think she plans on restocking the baby's necessities when those *I* provided run out?" I asked with disdain.

I'm guessing that the caseworker understood my question was a result of my frustration and really didn't require an answer since she didn't respond and instead said, "Although the child was not removed from the home, due to the mother and father's history with drugs, the police officers that escorted me to the home ordered both of them to appear at the office of the Department of Human Services in the morning to submit to a drug test."

"You know they're not stupid enough to show up for a drug test if indeed they're using drugs."

"Well then, let's hope they show up," she replied, a bit too chipper.

That next day, I called the caseworker to find out if Adam and Elaine showed up to take the drug tests. I wasn't surprised when she informed me that they were both no shows. "I called the hotel and was informed that the family moved out this morning," she added.

"What happens now?"

"There's really nothing further I can do."

"What about the police? Isn't there something they can do since they ordered that a drug test be taken?" The caseworker explained that it was more of a request than an actual order.

I felt sick. By filing a complaint with social services, I may have placed Andrew further in harm's way.

CHAPTER 4

If you always do what you always did, you'll always get what you always got.

—author unknown

It was early March of 2003 when Mom called to inform me that Adam was arrested on new drug charges and being held in the Adams County jail.

According to the police report, Adam and Elaine were pulled over on the report of a rolling domestic. The vehicle they were driving was a 1989 Grand Prix, yet their license plate was registered to a 1993 Buick. So even though Adam and Elaine claimed that they were merely having a verbal argument, the officers asked to search the vehicle and Elaine's purse, which was located inside the vehicle. Adam and Elaine gave their consent, probably believing the officers could easily be fooled. So both the vehicle and Elaine's purse were searched. Although it was carefully hidden, a small baggie containing methamphetamine was found in Elaine's purse. Elaine was immediately taken into police custody and transported to the Northglenn Police Department for processing.

At the same time, the police learned that Adam was wanted in Jefferson County on a felony warrant and consequently was also taken into police custody; however, prior to being placed in handcuffs, he was told to remove the gloves he was wearing. When he did, a small baggie containing methamphetamine fell out of one of his gloves and landed on the ground. Adam was then taken into police custody not only for the felony warrant but also for possessing methamphetamine.

While being processed, Adam initially told the police that Elaine knew about the drugs found in her purse, but then for reasons unknown, he recanted his statement and told the police that Elaine was not aware of the drugs found in her purse. He then wrote and signed a voluntary statement saying the same. Once processed, he was transferred to the Adams County Detention Facility. Elaine, however, was released from the Northglenn Police Department pending charges.

Mom went to visit Adam at the detention facility. It would be the first, but not the last, time she would see her son incarcerated. During the visit, Adam unfairly promised her that he would never use meth again. He claimed to have "learned his lesson." He vowed that Elaine was a good mother, and he planned on being a good father once he was released. Alarmingly, Mom seemed convinced that everything was going to work out for the new family of three regardless of the fact that Adam was sitting in jail as a result of a meth addiction, which would require a lot more than good intentions to defeat.

Not long after Mom's visit, Adam made bond and was released from jail; however, one month later, unsurprisingly and contrary to his promise to Mom, he was arrested on new drug-related charges and once again incarcerated. Mom was beside herself when she learned this, which annoyed me to no end. Did she really believe Adam could just will himself to stop using meth?

Adam was still in jail when, on June 2, 2003, Elaine was picked up on an outstanding warrant related to the meth found in her purse three months prior. I was surprised by this since Adam claimed that Elaine was released at the time of their arrests because she was innocent as the drugs all belonged to him. However, from an apartment she obtained through a government voucher program for low-income individuals, Elaine was taken into custody. Worse still, under the government voucher program, Elaine and Andrew were to be the only residents living in the apartment. However, at the time of Elaine's arrest, a man and a woman who both had prior felony convictions, the man for sexual abuse and the woman for child abuse, were also residing in Elaine's apartment. I was dumbfounded that she could actually have either one of these individuals living with her infant child.

Ultimately, Elaine was removed from the apartment in handcuffs and taken to the Jefferson County jail. A police hold was put on Andrew, and he was placed in a Jefferson County foster home.

Mom called me the day of Elaine's arrest to convey all that had taken place. Then without warning, she asked, "Would you and Liam be willing to care for Andrew until Adam or Elaine are released from jail? Otherwise, Andrew will have to remain in foster care." She remained silent for a moment, maybe to let her words sink in. "You know I would take him myself, but with my full-time job and all the problems I have with my health, I don't see how it would be possible."

How easy it was for her to ask so casually if Liam and I could completely change our current circumstances. How could she? Maria had recently moved out and started college, and Liam and I were settling into our empty nester's status, allowing ourselves to consider the dreams that were put on hold for those everyday life experiences and expenses that come with being a *responsible* parent. As I contemplated this, I realized Mom was on the other end waiting for an answer. But how could I just give her an answer? Didn't she realize how crucial it was for something this important to be given a great deal of consideration?

Feeling the pressure, I said, "Mom, I don't think it's a good idea. I really don't think Liam and I can handle such a huge responsibility, economically or emotionally. I mean, it hasn't even been determined how long either of them will be incarcerated. It could be years, and I don't think I could care for a child long term and ultimately return him to drug-addicted parents should that still be the case."

Mom, knowing very well that I was a person of deep empathy, said, "I understand how you feel, and we will cross that bridge when we come to it, but for now, Andrew is in foster care and that should be our first concern."

With her words came the self-reproach and the surrendering. Andrew needed help, and if Mom was not up to it, how could I in good conscience say no? However, I informed her that I needed to discuss it with Liam and Maria before giving her a definite answer. At that, Mom informed me that a dependency and neglect petition was filed by the county attorney and the preliminary protection hearing was to be held that next day, so I needed to make a decision that evening.

Hence, aware of the limited time I had to make such a crucial decision, I called Maria and asked her to come over after work for a family meeting. When Maria arrived, Liam and I had already been discussing the possibility of caring for Andrew. Maria sat with us at the kitchen table and listened attentively as I brought her up to speed on the conversation. Once she was caught up, I informed her and Liam of all the responsibility, hard work, and sacrifice that's required when taking care of an infant. However, I didn't have any wisdom or clarity to offer on caring for someone else's infant.

We also discussed Liam's position. Since he worked for himself, he didn't receive employer-provided benefits such as paid vacation, so missing work wasn't an option for him. With this reality, we both understood that since I had vacation time built up and was lucky enough to have an employer that was understanding when it came to family matters, I would be the one missing work to attend the necessary court hearings, meetings with social services and any other parties associated with the case as we cared for Andrew. Therefore, an actual vacation would be off the table. When everything had been thoroughly discussed, ultimately we all agreed that the responsibility of caring for Andrew was now ours.

That next morning, I attended the preliminary protection hearing and proposed to the court that Andrew be placed with me and Liam as I was Andrew's paternal aunt. After the hearing, I met with Andrew's court-appointed attorney, Kirk, also known as the guardian AD litem (GAL), and the caseworker, Jaime, from Child Protection Services. I gave them the requested information required for Kirk's office to initiate a home study and to also conduct a criminal background check on both Liam and me.

The next morning, Kirk's paralegal called to schedule an appointment for the home study. We agreed she would come by that next week. Consequently, on June 9, 2003, the home study commenced. After the paralegal inspected our home while informing me what changes needed to be made, we sat down at the dining table, and in a matter-of-fact way, she said, "The GAL and the caseworker intend on recommending Andrew be temporarily placed in your home."

I really thought I was prepared for this, but once I heard the paralegal's words, a pang of fear rose up in me as the realization of being responsible for an infant again was nothing less than terrifying. I must have looked unwell because the paralegal asked, "Are you all right?"

I forced a smile. "I'm fine, just feeling a little overwhelmed at the moment."

"Trust me," she said reassuringly, "what you're feeling is completely normal." Then she stood and asked if I had any more questions.

"I don't think so," I said with uncertainty.

She gave me a moment to think about it, and when she was convinced that I actually didn't have any more questions, she offered me her hand. I took it and thanked her for her time and walked her out.

Before going back into the house, I took a moment to consider the little guy who would soon be living in our home, and no matter how terrifying it seemed, the very thought of him made me smile.

Three days after the home visit, Maria and I drove down to the Jefferson County Human Services' office to visit and get reacquainted with Andrew, who was now four months old. Andrew's foster mother greeted us with a smile as we made the necessary introductions. She then handed Andrew over to us, and we were taken aback by the little guy's appearance. He looked completely different from when we first met him as a two-week-old. At that time, his tiny little head was covered with an abundance of black hair and his skin tone was at least three shades darker. Yet now, Andrew's once-abundant black hair was so thin and light in color, it made me think of peach fuzz. And his once dark skin, with the exception of his bright pink cheeks, was now milky white. The change was so significant, Maria and I wondered if maybe they gave us the wrong baby.

After a brief meeting with Andrew's foster mother, Maria and I were left alone in the facility's lunchroom with the little guy. Even though we were strangers, he didn't show any wariness toward us. He was barefoot and dressed in a blue-and-white-striped onesie that snapped across his chest and around his diaper. His cheeks, legs, and arms were chubby while his torso was long and thin. He had the smallest little nose, full, butterfly-shaped lips, and the most beautiful big blue eyes imaginable. He was absolutely breathtaking! Soon he was gurgling and smiling as we talked to him, walked with him, sang to him, and danced with him. Nearing the end of our time together, Maria and I watched in awe while the beautiful baby boy's battle to fight off the sandman came to a gentle end.

CHAPTER 5

Today is the first day of the rest of your life.

—author unknown

$\mathcal{O}$n June 19, 2003, Maria and I quietly sat on a bench outside the courtroom waiting for the adjudicatory hearing to commence. The purpose of the hearing was for the court to determine if Andrew was indeed dependent and neglected; even though with both his parents incarcerated, it was obvious he was at least dependent.

I heard footsteps coming down the hall, and when I looked up, I noticed Dad and Bianca, dad's third wife, approaching. I knew their presence that day was to state their position as Andrew's paternal grandparents to the court and to formally request to be his caretakers as Adam informed me of this somewhat in an earlier letter he wrote me from jail. Within the letter, he not only asked me to care for Andrew but also informed me that Dad and Bianca expressed an interest in caring for Andrew—to whom they would express such an interest, he didn't say—and that he was totally against it.

I understood his resolve as I had experienced firsthand Dad and Bianca's lack of good or even adequate parenting skills. Even so, as Dad and Bianca quickly approached, I realized my stupidity in allowing myself to be put in such an awkward position. Uncertain on how or what to say, before they could address me, I simply turned on my heels and darted into the courtroom with Maria following close behind. As we took a seat, as close to the podium as possible, the guilt washed over me. Regardless of our estranged relationship, I still had no desire to hurt my dad. As we waited for the hearing to begin, I continued looking back at the courtroom doors, unnervingly waiting for Dad and Bianca to enter, but they never did.

After a couple of cases ahead of ours were continued or settled, a door just left of the front of the courtroom opened and Adam, escorted by a deputy, shuffled into the room. He was wearing a bright orange jumpsuit and was bound by handcuffs and leg shackles. My eyes welled up with tears as I made an effort to smile his way. While the proceedings commenced, I struggled to fight back the tears as my gaze kept falling upon him. It was painful to see him this way. What led him here? He was always very popular in school with his peers, being that he was handsome, athletic, and very intelligent. The girls were crazy about him, and the guys were envious of him. When he was granted a college scholarship for his diving skills, he seemed to have such a bright future, yet here he was.

During the hearing, as anticipated, Andrew was adjudicated a dependent child as to Adam. I, the paternal aunt, was joined to the case as the special respondent, and it was ordered that on agreement of the caseworker and guardian AD litem, temporary legal custody of Andrew would be vested with me under the protective supervision of the Department of Social Services.

As the hearing concluded, since Elaine didn't appear even though a writ (a written order from the court) was issued for her to be produced, a continued hearing was ordered for her and a treatment plan hearing was ordered for both Adam and Elaine, both to be held on July 9, 2003.

Upon leaving the courtroom I met with Jaime and Kirk. Jaime advised that she would arrange to have the foster parents drop Andrew off at my home that next Saturday. Feeling a bit overwhelmed by the quick pace of all that was happening and all that needed to be worked out prior to the little guy's arrival, I asked, "Will social services be helping out with Andrew's daycare expenses?"

I was surprised when Jaime shook her head and said resolutely, "There is no money in our budget for kinship care." Seeing the concern on my face, she informed me that if Liam and I chose to take all the required training courses to become certified foster parents, we could then be reimbursed approximately four hundred dollars a month to cover food, clothing, and any other items Andrew may need. However, if daycare is required, it would be at our own expense and would have to be with a licensed daycare. "What about medical expenses?" I asked, trying not to appear as alarmed as I felt.

"Medicaid is available for Andrew." Jaime said. "I'll have his foster mother bring his current Medicaid information with her when she drops him off. Unfortunately, you will need to have the Medicaid changed to the county where you reside."

I nodded my head in agreement, and to let her know I was listening as I'm sure I looked preoccupied with my own thoughts. Then recognizing that I may need some guidance with the change in Medicaid, she added, "Call me if you have any questions." Realizing their busy schedules, Jaime and Kirk said their good-byes and headed for the elevators. On my way home, I wondered what daycare for an infant costs these days.

As Andrew's "drop off" date quickly approached, Liam and I scrambled to prepare for his arrival. Fortunately, a friend gave me a crib and changing table that she no longer needed, and I was able to borrow a car seat and stroller from a coworker. Yet even with these major items checked off, there were still so many things an infant required.

As Liam and I were feeling overwhelmed in our preparation efforts, I was surprised with a baby shower arranged by several fellow coworkers and friends. I received so many much-needed items, I couldn't have been more appreciative or feel more blessed for knowing such wonderful people.

Feeling well equipped and reasonably certain in our capabilities, on June 21, 2003, Liam, Maria, and I waited eagerly for Andrew's arrival. We scurried to the door as Andrew's foster parents and several other children, including another infant, arrived with Andrew in tow. After our initial greetings, the foster mother handed me a small plastic bag and explained that the bag and the infant car seat, which Andrew was sitting in, were his belongings. She then informed me about Andrew's Medicaid as she handed me his card.

We all made small talk for several minutes until the foster dad advised that they needed to be on their way. After the good-byes and well-wishes, we all walked out to the front porch. The foster mother told the others to go ahead and get in the car and she would be right there. I offered her my hand and thanked her for taking such good care of Andrew. She shook my hand and said she was going to miss him.

When our hands parted, she hesitated a moment, then looked at Andrew. "I have a couple of concerns about him."

"What kind of concerns?" I asked, once I realized she was referring to Andrew.

"Well, the back of his head has an unusually deep indention, which makes me suspect that his mom left him in his car seat for long periods of time, maybe even used it as his bed. And it's the weirdest thing, but he acts as if he doesn't know he has legs." In answer to the puzzled look on my face, she said, "You'll see what I mean."

After the family departed, Andrew sat quietly in his car seat, looking up at us seeming totally unaffected by his new surroundings, and it made me wonder how many new situations he has already been made to endure. I unstrapped him and lifted him out of his car seat, and as I held him close to me, I said softly, "Don't worry, little guy, we will take very good care of you."

Later, when I looked over the bag of contents his foster mother identified as his, I found two baby shoes, not a pair as they were two completely different shoes, a couple of onesies and an adult-size hair brush that had long blond strands of hair entwined within the thistles. The meager and unusual items made me feel sad for Andrew.

That same evening, we understood the foster mother's concern about Andrew's legs. When we would pick him up, his legs would just hang there as if he was a ragdoll. When we held him under his armpits and placed him in a walking stance, he still had no desire to place his feet on the ground and instead would just let them hang loosely or even allow them to almost roll underneath him. It was very strange.

I discussed this with my friend Dolores as she often had her young grandchildren about her, and she suggested we try a doorway bouncer. She said, "I think I still have one at home. I'll look around for it. If I find it, I'll bring it to you tomorrow."

Dolores brought the doorway bouncer to me at work that next day and demonstrated how it should be used.

When Liam arrived home from work that evening, he hung the bouncer thing in the doorway and we placed Andrew in it. We had to suppress our giggles when he just kind of hung there looking up at us. In an effort to make it more appealing, Liam moved the straps a bit to achieve a slight bouncing motion. This resulted in the cutest toothless grin we had ever seen. Still it took several days of trying before Andrew felt comfortable enough to let his feet fully touch the ground. But when he finally did, the awareness took hold, and soon he was pushing his feet off the ground, achieving the bouncing motion on his own.

CHAPTER 6

~~~~~~

Sacrificing your happiness for the happiness of the one you love is by far the truest type of love.

—author unknown

With Andrew's recent arrival, I understood this was a critical time for him to get to know all of us and to acclimate to his new surroundings. I took two weeks off from work, but with the two-week mark quickly approaching, I was in no way prepared to just drop him off at a daycare facility when, really, he was still just getting to know us and his new scheduled routine. So with Maria being on summer break from college, Liam and I offered to pay her living expenses if she would quit her job and take on the task of caring for Andrew while we were at work and until her classes started up again. This would allow him some consistency for a while longer and offer me and Liam some peace of mind. Maria, already in love with Andrew, agreed wholeheartedly.

Having an infant in our home was both joyful and eventful. Though we already loved the little guy, Liam and I were still learning how to share time and space with him and each other.

I was also sporadically adjusting my full-time work schedule to accommodate the requested meetings with social services and the GAL and keeping both of Andrew's incarcerated parents updated on the little guy through biweekly letters and pictures.

Regardless of all that was going on, I knew getting Andrew's Medicaid changed was paramount as I assumed he was in need of a checkup and possibly some vaccinations. In an earlier conversation I had with Jaime, she advised that I needed to reapply for Andrew's Medicaid in the county where I reside. However, when I called the Medicaid office, they informed me that in order to reapply, they would need Andrew's social security card and birth certificate, yet I had neither. Consequently, in an effort to obtain these items, I wrote to Elaine to inquire on their whereabouts and also to inquire on Andrew's vaccination record.

While I was waiting for Elaine's response, I asked the human resource supervisor at my place of employment about putting Andrew on my insurance. But because I only had temporary custody of him and not legal guardianship, which was required, it couldn't be done.

Several days after writing to Elaine, I received a letter from her responding to my inquiries in which she informed me that Andrew's documents were in a storage facility she leased before she was incarcerated. She asked that I contact Kate, a friend of Adam's, as she had the key to the storage facility. She also stated that Andrew received his medical care at Rose Medical, so they would have his medical records, and Denver General would have the records from when he was born. She provided Kate's number at the end of the letter, and I placed the call.

Kate, aware of Elaine's and Adam's incarcerations, agreed to obtain the paperwork from the storage facility and meet me in a couple of days. The scheduled meeting was to take place in a parking lot near her home. Assuming she was choosing the particular location for my benefit, I offered to pick up the paperwork from her home so that she would not be inconvenienced. However;

she declined, which made me think she simply didn't want me to know where she lived.

A couple of days later, I arrived at the parking lot. I was a few minutes early, and since waiting in a deserted parking lot for a complete stranger was not the norm for me, I felt a little uneasy when a car drove onto the lot. As the car drew near, a woman offered a slight wave out of the window, offering me some relief. Then she pulled up next to me, "Are you Crystal?

"Yes, you must be Kate."

She nodded, parked, and got out of the car. Now facing me, she handed me the paperwork. "This is all I could find. I hope it has what you need." "Me too," I said, nodding in agreement.

With the sun in my eyes, I had to squint to get a good look at her. She had a light complexion, short, blondish red hair, and a figure that was small and thin. Though her smile seemed genuine, her eyes revealed her disenchantment with life. We spoke of Adam, whom she apparently held in high esteem and even seemed to be indebted to him. Then the conversation turned to Elaine. "I don't know if you are aware that Elaine lived with me for a short time." Kate said.

The surprised look on my face made it evident that I didn't know.

"Adam is such a good person," she continued, "he has done so much for me, so when he asked if I could take Elaine in while he was locked up, I couldn't say no. But I ended up throwing the lazy, deceitful bitch out. She couldn't even manage her dog. I mean he was constantly up on my furniture."

"Yeah, I noticed the lazy part myself," I said, trying to include myself in the conversation.

"That deceitful bitch claimed that my boyfriend tried to make it with her. I was so sick of her lies I finally threw her out and haven't heard from her since."

She went on about how she never trusted Elaine and that she even warned Adam about her, but he wouldn't listen.

Still unaware at this time how Elaine and Adam met, I continued to seek out an answer. "Do you know how the two of them met?"

I wasn't sure if Kate didn't hear my question or just didn't care to answer. Regardless, she didn't answer, and since I was anxious to get home and look over the paperwork I held in my hands, I didn't press any further. Instead, I listened to her go on about Elaine for a few more minutes before telling her that I had to be on my way. I thanked her for the paperwork and her time and offered her my hand. She shook it and said it was no problem. We said our good-byes, and she turned to leave. I started to get back in the car when I heard her call out, "Hey, Crystal."

I turned to look at her.

"Just know that anything Elaine says, I guarantee is one big fat lie."

I raised my hand to let her know I heard her, and waved good-bye.

Back at home, I reviewed all the paperwork I received from Kate. Most of which was irrelevant. However, I did find Andrew's social security card, immunization information, and a document relating to his two-week exam, but there was no birth certificate. I reviewed the immunization information and found that the only time Andrew had visited the doctor in his five months of life was on his two-week checkup, which actually took place when he was seven weeks old. I wrote to Elaine to substantiate this as I didn't want to make the mistake of over-vaccinating him. Elaine responded in a letter I received a couple of days later in which she stated, "Andrew hasn't received any vaccinations other than those given to him at his two-week checkup."

But according to his paperwork, Andrew only received the hepatitis B vaccination when he was born, which meant Elaine didn't even remember when the shot was given to him. Worse still, Andrew was already five months old and had not received any other vaccinations. I couldn't understand how Elaine and

Adam could be so irresponsible. It couldn't have been an issue of money since Elaine had Andrew on Medicaid.

Knowing that Andrew was way behind on his shots, I felt it would be quicker if I tried to order his birth certificate as his temporary custodian rather than taking the time to hunt down one that may not even exist. So I completed the necessary paperwork, submitted it to the proper authorities, and to my surprise, I received the birth certificate a few weeks later. I immediately applied for Andrew's Medicaid, and thankfully, because he was currently on Medicaid in another county, the wait for approval was brief.

Once Andrew's Medicaid was approved, on July 7, 2003, a week after Andrew turned five months old, Maria and I took him to have a checkup and begin the process of catching up on his vaccinations. Because Andrew only received the hepatitis B vaccine, the doctor informed us that he was currently nine vaccinations behind. The unsettling "catch-up schedule" the doctor placed him on required Andrew to have five shots on that first visit and four shots a month later, and because he was seven months old by the time he received his second dose of shots, two months later he received five more shots, which would include the first half of the influenza vaccine.

Andrew's checkup revealed that he was merely in the five percent range of his age group in weight and only twenty percent in height. I was stunned. I knew Andrew was small, but I had no idea his weight range was so deficient. On the doctor's way out, noticing my concern, she placed her hand on my shoulder. "He'll catch up in no time," she said warmly. "I'll send in the nurse to administer the vaccinations."

I feigned a smile and thanked her, and within a couple of minutes, the nurse entered the room. Andrew was gazing quietly at her while she positioned and readied herself. She began by speaking to him in a calming voice, and then a piercing scream filled the air and Andrew's quivering lips turned a poignant shade of blue. My eyes welled up with tears as I held him close. His screams eased into weeping, and the weeping softened into somber sniffles. When he was certain he wouldn't be receiving any further pokes, he looked up at me with what seemed to be distrust, and my heart broke. I wondered how this little guy would ever learn to trust me when these numerous vaccinations were going to continue for the next three months.

Although I was on Andrew's bad guy list, Liam had become his trusted pal. Later that afternoon, I went out back to check on the two of them. Andrew was arranged comfortably in Liam's lap as Liam, sitting in a rocking chair under the pergola, read softly to the little guy. And even though Andrew was too young to understand the words, he gazed up at Liam in awe as if he was hanging on to every word.

CHAPTER 7

The truth is rarely pure and never simple.

—Oscar Wilde

On July 13, 2003, I went to see Adam at the Jefferson County Detention Facility. After the required preliminaries took place, I was instructed to take a seat in front of a window and was informed that the inmate should arrive within a couple of minutes.

As I waited anxiously, I thought about what I wanted to say and needed to ask. Then Adam entered the room. I was shaken by his appearance. He was extremely thin and awfully pale, and when he looked at me from behind the glass, it was obvious he felt very uncomfortable.

He picked up the phone, and I did the same. Trying to hold back the tears, I made an effort to speak but only managed a small cry. He too was trying to keep it together. My heart ached as my lips tried to form the words that I was unable to say. Aware that our thirty-minute visit was ticking away, "How is Mom doing?" he asked in a hoarse voice.

"She's hanging in there," I said, sounding a little too cheerful.

He nodded in agreement. "She's been a real trooper through all of this."

"Yes, she has."

He asked about Andrew, and I updated him on the daily activities of his son. He thanked me for keeping Andrew from falling into Dad and Bianca's care and went as far as to say, "I would rather have Andrew stay in foster care than let Dad and Bianca care for him."

His harsh but understandable words lingered in the uncomfortable silence for a moment. "I want to ask you something," I said.

He looked at me carefully, then nodded his consent.

"Did Elaine use drugs during her pregnancy with Andrew?"

He looked at me with uncertainty. Realizing his hesitation, I added without reproach, "I need to tell Andrew's doctors everything I can about his history, and I need to be prepared for any ill effects his history may have on his health."

Adam lowered his eyes, and his shoulders slumped submissively. "Yes, Elaine used coke while she was pregnant with Andrew."

I went cold. Even though I had already suspected this, hearing the words out loud rattled me just the same. Then Adam's eyes met mine. "I really want to thank you for taking care of Andrew," he said softly.

"I love you and all your sons, what else would I do?" He smiled at that.

After some more small talk, a guard informed us that our time was up. I managed a smile as we said our good-byes, and turned from the window with a heavy heart.

As I walked to my car, I considered Andrew's prenatal drug exposure and what it could mean for him. Then a frightening thought came to me: *was Elaine exposed to Adam's meth lab while she was pregnant?*

I went straight home after my visit with Adam because Jaime was coming over for a home visit. I was able to clean up a bit before she arrived. During the visit, I informed her of Adam's admission that Elaine used cocaine during her pregnancy with Andrew. Jaime winced at my words.

"It seems that Andrew is behind on a few things according to a book I've been reading, but I could just be overreacting as a result of Adam's admission. Even so, I feel we should remove all doubt and have him see a specialist. Don't you think?" I said with a bit of uncertainty.

Jaime was genuinely concerned for Andrew and found this news was cause for alarm. She immediately began to search for something in her folder, then handed me a card. "Tomorrow, contact Adams County Early Childhood Connections to schedule an appointment for Andrew." She said with a high degree of importance to her voice, "What they do is send a specialist to your home to administer an evaluation that will cover all aspects of Andrew's development."

"I'll call them first thing in the morning."

When our visit ended, I walked Jaime out to the front porch, and when she was half way down the sidewalk, she turned toward me. "Call me as soon as you get a scheduled date for the evaluation."

"I will," I said as I offered a slight wave good-bye.

I called Early Childhood Connections that next morning and made an appointment for Andrew through a service coordinator. The earliest appointment available was on August 25, 2003, that next month. The coordinator advised that the specialist would screen Andrew at my home on the scheduled date.

On the long-awaited morning of August 25, 2003, the motor skills specialist arrived. She played with Andrew for a long time and asked me and Maria several questions before the screening part of the appointment ended. The results were upsetting. Andrew was behind in several areas. However, with the knowledge that he quickly mastered the doorway bouncer, the specialist assured us that he would soon be on target. Before the appointment ended, she demonstrated some games we could play with the little guy and some exercises we could do with him to help speed up his progress. She then advised that I make another appointment so he could be seen again in a month's time.

With much determination and in spite of our daunting schedules, which included Maria having started her fall classes, we all made time to continually work with Andrew. And thankfully, our efforts paid off because by his next screening, he was at the appropriate level for someone his age, and that tight knot that had taken up residence in the pit of my stomach finally loosened up.

Although Maria's fall classes commenced, her new school schedule allowed her to care for Andrew two days a week. Liam, who was already taking care of Andrew on Mondays since the day the little guy came to live with us, continued doing so. Still, for the two remaining days, we had no other option than to place Andrew in a licensed daycare. I would have liked having the option of placing him with a private daycare provider for the two days, but in order to comply with the Department of Human Services (DHS), I was to place him in a licensed facility.

Prior to doing this, Liam and I talked about the possibility of me staying home to care for the little guy, but with all our expenses, which now included a baby in diapers and a daughter's living expenses, and because both Liam and I received our medical benefits through my employer, it was not an option. Unfortunately, we found no other alternative than to place Andrew in a licensed daycare facility for two days a week.

Andrew, who was almost seven months at the time, had a very hard time adapting to daycare. Since moving into our home, he was finally beginning to trust me, and now here he was suddenly thrown again into unfamiliar surroundings full of unfamiliar people. When his daycare teacher spoke to me about his slow progress in adapting to his new surroundings, I informed her on the instabilities he was previously made to endure—being removed from his mom and placed in foster care, then being removed from foster care and being placed with Liam and me and now this new situation. She listened empathetically and said that she would continue to help make this a smooth transition for Andrew. Yet we both knew the overly zealous teacher to infant ratio permitted in a licensed daycare would not make it possible for her to give Andrew the special attention he deserved.

CHAPTER 8

Good people do not need laws to tell them to act responsibly, while bad people will find a way around the laws.

—Plato

*O*n July 31, 2003, the continued adjudication hearing and disposition was held. During the hearing, Andrew was adjudicated a dependent child as to Elaine, his mother. Temporary legal custody of Andrew was continued with me and the treatment plans for Elaine and Adam detailed in social services' family services plan were adopted as an order of the court. Elaine's request that she be allowed visits with Andrew at the jail was denied, and a permanency plan hearing was scheduled for October 9, 2003.

On August 28, 2003, Elaine's bond hearing regarding her criminal case took place. At which time the judge released her on her own recognizant regardless of, or maybe unaware of, Elaine's extensive criminal history, which included being a fugitive of the law and several FTAs (failure to appear).

Now out of jail, Elaine requested parenting time with Andrew through social services. She was given supervised parenting time, and the visits were to commence on September 3, 2003. I argued that because the visits would be taking place on a weekday, I would have to take time off from work to facilitate them. But my words were for none since the facility at which the visits were to take place was only open during the week.

So on the afternoon of September 3, 2003, I drove Andrew to the Jefferson County Department of Social Services' office to have his first two-hour visit with Elaine. When we arrived, we met with a staff member who directed us to the visitation room where Elaine was already waiting for us. As soon as we entered the room, Elaine imperiously took Andrew from my arms and smothered him with overwhelming kisses. When this seemingly put-on and over-the-top display finally ended, she managed to make the rest of the visit about her. She talked nonstop about herself and her current situation as she attempted to feed Andrew something orange from the baby bottle she brought for the visit. Andrew finally decided to give the bottle a try, and as I watched in horror, she said, "Under the advisement of my public defender, I'm planning on entering a residential drug rehabilitation program called CiCore. Entering into a long-term treatment program would more than likely mean a reduced sentence for me, but the best part is, once I've been in the program for three months, Andrew will be able to live there with me."

Uncertain I heard her correctly, I ran her words back through my mind. Once I fully understood, I thought, *Not while I'm alive.* I will never consent to Andrew living in a drug rehabilitation center. But did I really have a say-so? I told myself to remain calm.

The visit ended with another installment of overwhelming kisses showered on a startled-looking Andrew, as I struggled to mask my disgust.

As soon as I got home from the visit, I contacted Jaime and Kirk to discuss Elaine's plan to eventually have Andrew reside with her at CiCore. I conveyed my concerns and was relieved to know that they too did not agree with Andrew being moved out of a safe and happy home only to be made to live in a drug rehabilitation facility.

Subsequent to that first visit with Elaine, it was agreed that the supervised visits would continue to take place at my home under my supervision, and in accordance with the Jefferson County Social Services treatment plan, Elaine was to provide her own transportation to and from each twice-a-week two-hour visit and provide diapers and formula for Andrew during each visit.

The visits at my home commenced and continued onward as every seedy character from Elaine's criminal existence showed up at my doorstep to either drop her off or pick her up, which managed to make both Liam and I more and more uncomfortable with the situation. Even so, because we acknowledged that Elaine was making somewhat of an effort where Andrew was concerned, we allowed the visits to continue in our home along with Elaine's excuses on why she was frequently late and unable to provide diapers or formula during the visits. Then just as quickly as they started, the visits would stop—that is to say, temporarily.

As advised by her public defender, Elaine entered the CiCore program on October 7, 2003. Her first month in the program was defined as the orientation period. During the orientation period, Elaine was not allowed any visitors, so her visits with Andrew temporarily ceased. However, I sent her a weekly update on Andrew along with any recent pictures taken of him.

While Elaine was looking at a two-year sentence in a rehabilitation program, according to her, Adam was looking at a twenty-eight-year prison sentence. Yet as a result of his attorney's exceptional plea bargaining skills, or perhaps more simply a result of the overcrowded and underfunded prison system, ultimately he received a seven-year prison sentence. Still, a seven-year prison sentence was hard to take.

Even though Adam and I hadn't had a real relationship for the past several years, I still had faith that with the appropriate drug rehabilitation program, not prison, he would triumph over his lengthy drug addiction. Believing this, prior to Adam's sentencing, I wrote a letter to Judge Tina Olsen, pleading with her to place Adam in a drug rehabilitation facility rather than sending him to prison. However, my efforts were unsuccessful, and Adam's prison sentence commenced in October of 2003 at a minimum security facility in Cañon City, Colorado.

CHAPTER 9

~~~~~~~~~~~~~~~~~~~~~~~~~~~~~~

Disappointments are to the soul what the thunderstorm
is to the air.

—Friedrich von Schiller

*O*n October 9, 2003, the first permanency plan and review
hearing was held as the next step in the dependency
and neglect case. Adam did not appear at this hearing.
His public defender, Ben Wills, who appeared on Adam's behalf,
claimed that Adam's absence was due to problems relating to
his writ.

During the hearing the recommendations of the family
services plan were adopted and made an order of the court.
The court found that reasonable services were being offered by
the Jefferson County Department of Social Services to reunite
Elaine, Adam, and Andrew—the family. The court authorized an
expansion of visitation between Andrew and Elaine at CiCore
upon agreement of all parties. Then due to Adam's continual
nonattendance, the court advised that Adam's public defender
contact Adam and find out if he wished to attend any future

court hearings. As the hearing came to an end, a permanency plan and review hearing was scheduled for January 29, 2004.

In response to the court's advisement, Adam's public defender contacted Adam, and unfortunately, Adam advised that he did not wish to receive any more writs to attend any future court hearings involving his son.

Soon after the October 9 permanency plan and review hearing, I received a speed letter from the Jefferson County Department of Social Services stating, "Effective October 13, 2003, your new caseworker will be Donald Malone. Thank you." It was signed by our current caseworker, Jaime. I was devastated. Jaime was very much involved and empathetic to Andrew's case. She was unmoving when it came to Elaine's needs when they eradicated Andrew's well-being. I had learned to trust that her decisions concerning Andrew were based on his best interest. Now essentially, that learned trust was obliterated with only uncertainty lingering in its place.

Three weeks after the new caseworker, Donald, entered the case, Elaine was sentenced for the charges pending from her March 2003 arrest. As she and her public defender anticipated, entering herself into a drug treatment program proved to be beneficial to the outcome of her sentencing, which resulted in four years of intense supervised probation (ISP) along with an order to complete the two-year treatment program at CiCore.

With her orientation period complete, Elaine's two-hour visits with Andrew at the CiCore facility began the second week of November but were not yet expanded. After the first few visits, the social worker that had been transporting Andrew to and from the CiCore facility advised that she was having a hard time fitting Andrew into her already daunting schedule. Realizing this was an opportunity for me to not only look over the facility but also keep an eye on Elaine's progress, I offered to transport Andrew to and from the visits. Contentedly, the social worker accepted my offer and later advised that Elaine's treatment counselor at the facility, Julie Stevens, would be supervising the visits.

CiCore was several miles from my home and located in a seedy part of town, off of West Colfax Street. Ironically, Colfax Street had a nasty reputation for drug dealers and prostitution.

As we drove to CiCore for Andrew's next visit with Elaine, I peered in the rearview mirror to find Andrew happily playing with the toys connected to his car seat, and I had to smile. As I approached the unappealing CiCore facility, I was filled with anxiety. After parking the car, I removed Andrew from his car seat and gave him a big hug and kissed him on one of his fluffy cheeks. He looked up at me with his beautiful big blue eyes, and my heart sank at the thought of having to leave him in such a strange place.

I entered the front door with Andrew in my arms and noticed a cafeteria just beyond the reception area where two women were sweeping the floor. I informed the young lady who greeted us at the makeshift reception area that Andrew is here for a visit with Elaine Perez. While she took a moment to recall who Elaine was and where she was located, I requested a tour of the facility and sleeping quarters. She looked at me with raised eyebrows, obviously surprised by the request.

"Is that a problem?" I asked.

"You are not permitted to go beyond this reception area," she said, drawing an imaginary square around the makeshift reception area with her index finger.

"Couldn't I just take a quick look at the family sleeping quarters?"

"You are not permitted to go beyond this reception area," she repeated.

Now a little annoyed, I said, "And why is that?"

"Resident's privacy," she said curtly.

Just then, Elaine approached us, and without regard to me, she grabbed Andrew out of my arms and exclaimed in her annoyingly raspy voice, for all to hear, "Hi, my little love bucket." Andrew seemed shaken at first, then stared up at her in awe. Upon hearing Elaine's loud, attention-seeking voice, a couple of women came over to meet the little guy. While Andrew seemed engaged in the considerable amount of attention being showered upon him, I announced my departure to no one in particular and, with much trepidation, exited the building.

I sat in the car agonizing over whether I should just sit there and watch the building for two hours or find somewhere to hang out. I didn't want to leave, but I knew staying would only make me more anxious. So I decided to drive around and see what was in the area. I ended up at a coffeehouse, and as I sat there drinking a latte, I thought about CiCore.

How could Andrew possibly thrive in a place like that? The knowledge that stood behind the program had to do with drug and alcohol rehabilitation for adult addicts. Why throw vulnerable children into the mix? It didn't make sense to me, but maybe I didn't want it to.

Not long after the two-hour visits at CiCore commenced, Elaine requested unsupervised weekend visits with Andrew. Although I understood this was the next step in the reunification process, I wasn't prepared to leave Andrew overnight in an environment that was predominantly managed by a staff of individuals who were once drug addicts themselves, an environment where relapse was always a possibility. Things were just moving too fast in Elaine's favor. Andrew didn't break the law. He wasn't arrested on drug charges, yet if Elaine had anything to do with it, he would have to leave the only home he has ever known and be made to live under the same confinement and restrictions as her. It seemed the only way to put a stop to this lunacy would be for me to obtain primary custody of Andrew.

After two months at CiCore, Elaine was promoted by her treatment counselor, Julie Stevens, to an internal job. "It usually takes six months to earn an internal job," Elaine proudly stated when I arrived to drop Andrew off for a visit. I wanted to be happy for her as she seemed to be doing so well, but everything in me was saying something wasn't right. Maybe it was the obvious budding friendship between Elaine and Julie, her treatment counselor. In fact, they would become such good friends, later Elaine would be in Julie's wedding. I had to wonder if the promotion was actually a product of preferential treatment, rather than an earned status.

On December 31, 2003, I woke to find that Andrew wasn't feeling well. In fact, he wasn't even interested in getting out of his crib. I picked him up and held him in my arms and noticed his breathing was rapid. Alarmed, I immediately took him to the doctor. After checking in, I paced in the waiting room while holding a practically motionless Andrew in my arms eagerly waiting to be called. Once we were in the examining room and all the necessary questions were asked and answered, the doctor took great strides in examining the sick little guy. When the examination was complete the doctor advised that Andrew had been infected with respiratory syncytial virus (RSV), which causes infection of the lungs and breathing passages. Andrew's infection was so severe that the doctor ordered him to receive nebulizer treatments every four hours, day and night. Consequently, the doctor ordered the nebulizer kit, which we picked up on our way out of her office that day along with a prescription for albuterol, the medication to be used in the nebulizer machine.

Liam and I together administered the treatments as Andrew adamantly opposed each and every one. The evening treatments were the most difficult as the unkind effects of the medication, which included tremors, anxiety, and restlessness, made it nearly impossible for the little guy to get back to sleep.

Due to the RSV, Andrew did not attend his next visit with Elaine, which only made her angry. She couldn't grasp that Andrew was very sick and that I needed to comply with the doctor's instructions, which included keeping him away from other children until he improved. Knowing this, Elaine still contacted Donald, the new caseworker, and claimed that I was keeping Andrew from her. Donald then contacted me, at which time I informed him of Andrew's latest illness. Without concern for Andrew, as he didn't even inquire on his condition, Donald advised that I needed to ensure the missed visit is made up. Assuming that Donald's lack of empathy was due to him thinking that I was being deceitful about Andrew having RSV, I informed him that I had a prescription from the doctor and an order for the nebulizer kit and offered to send him a copy of both as proof of Andrew's illness. He just scoffed and insisted that sending him copies would not be necessary.

CHAPTER 10

The farther backward you can look, the farther forward
you are likely to see.

—Winston Churchill

In an effort to prepare for the permanency hearing, I felt it
would be wise to learn everything I possibly could about
Elaine and the two boys she claimed were taken from her
when she went to prison.

My first task was to order a criminal background check on
her through the Colorado Bureau of Investigation's website. As
directed, I input all the required search information and paid the
small fee. In a matter of seconds, a match was found, and the
information was downloaded. I was staggered by the extensive
criminal record and the vast amount of aliases crammed on the
first page. After reviewing the record in full, I had to wonder, *Who
in their right mind would return a vulnerable child to this woman,
natural mother or not?*

My second task was to seek out someone who could possibly
corroborate or contradict Elaine's claims as to what happened to
her two other boys. It took me a while to consider this, but then

the answer was so obvious; I had to try to locate her mother. I knew her mother's maiden name was Jacobs from one of my earlier conversations with Elaine. I began calling all the Jacobs on the Internet's white pages, beginning at the top of the list and working my way down. With my full schedule, I had been making calls for a couple of days when on January 10, 2004, I actually found her.

I was at the Cs of first names, and a woman answered the phone. "Hi, my name is Crystal," I said, "and I am trying to locate the mother of Elaine Barela." Barela being Elaine's previous married name.

I was surprised when the woman said, "Yes, Elaine is my daughter."

In my effort to approach the reason for my call as gently as possible, I let the woman know that I had temporary custody of my nephew, Andrew, who is also Elaine's son.

"I am aware of the situation." The woman interrupted. This surprised me, but was also a relief because I didn't want to be the first to inform her of Elaine's current run-in with the law. "I am close with my granddaughter Becky, who is Elaine's daughter. Elaine has been in contact with Becky since she returned to Colorado and keeps Becky somewhat informed on her goings on," she said.

The woman spoke softly with a slight German accent. She introduced herself as Claudia, and confessed that she wished Elaine would just leave Becky alone. "Becky is in school and doing well. I don't want Elaine to mess things up for her."

I understood her concern.

"What has Elaine done now?" Claudia asked wearily.

"I'm not sure how much you are aware of, but as part of a sentence she received on some drug related charges, Elaine is currently living in a drug rehab facility. She has requested to be reunited with Andrew, and if she gets her way, he would be made to live in the drug rehab facility with her."

Claudia heaved a sigh. "How can they let her do that?"

Not sure who she meant by *they*, I said, "My husband and I are in the process of trying to keep it from happening and plan on trying to obtain primary custody of Andrew."

"Let me know what, if anything, I can do to help."

"I will. Thanks."

"I can't believe that any judge would be stupid enough to give that baby back to Elaine," she said firmly.

"I know it seems like an unlikelihood, but since she is the biological mother, there's no telling what could happen."

Claudia let out another sigh.

"The reason why I called you is to find out what *really* happened to Elaine's other children," I said.

"Oh, those poor children," she said. "Becky was abandoned by Elaine when she was just three years old. Elaine was leaving her with me more often than usual, and one day she just dropped her off and never returned for her. Then about six weeks later, Becky's father picked her up from my home and took care of her until she was old enough to be on her own."

"What about the boys?"

"Oh those poor boys. I learned about Elaine's second child, Kenny, from a detective in California where she was apparently living at that time with some drug dealer. The detective wanted to know if I could go down to California and pick up Kenny. " Claudia was quiet for a moment. "I am old and have been ill. I was not a suitable caretaker for Kenny, so I had to tell the detective that I could not care for this child."

"Where was Elaine?"

"The detective said that Elaine left the child with some woman while she and this woman's husband ran off together. When Elaine didn't return for Kenny, the woman dropped him off at the welfare department."

"Elaine abandoned Kenny?" I asked incredulously.

"Yes, she left him with some woman and ran off with the woman's husband." Claudia gave me a moment to consider this before she divulged the unthinkable. "The detective also told me that before Elaine left Kenny with this woman, while Kenny was still strapped in his car seat, her boyfriend, this drug addict, dumped him in the street and just left him there. Thankfully, a maintenance man found him and took him to a child haven facility." Claudia sighed. "Can you believe it? Those people at that child haven place let Elaine pick up that baby the very next day after he was dumped in the street. Elaine should have never been able to have children. I don't know why she even picked Kenny up from that place because she just ended up leaving him with that woman."

"Was Kenny ever adopted?"

"I don't know," she admitted.

We were quiet for a moment.

"What about the other boy?" I asked.

"Jacob was Elaine's third child. He was born while Elaine was in prison, then was taken by social services to be placed in foster care. The Thompsons were his foster parents and seemed to be a real nice couple. They told me that Jacob was born addicted to drugs, and as a result, his heart would race and he would have seizures. They really wanted to adopt Jacob, but Elaine refused to voluntarily terminate her rights. And can you believe it, after Elaine got out of prison, she got Jacob back."

"How is that possible?"

"I don't understand it myself and will never know why she even wanted him back because it didn't take long for her to just drop him off at the welfare department because she no longer wanted to care for him." Claudia took a moment, then said, "He ended up going to a new foster home, and after he turned four years old, Elaine voluntarily terminated her rights, and Jacob was eventually adopted." Claudia sighed heavily and added, "Jacob had it the worst of all of Elaine's children."

Knowing how Jacob suffered from being born with a drug addiction, later I would ask Elaine if she wanted to hold on to Andrew in an effort to atone for what Jacob was made to endure. Without the least bit of remorse, she said with a shrug, "Maybe." Her sheer and utter heartlessness made my blood run cold.

After we discussed Elaine's children, I asked Claudia if she would confirm a few things that Elaine conveyed to me.

Claudia agreed and sighed wearily, "What stories has she told you."

"Well, she told me she came from a rich family and has a very wealthy uncle," I said feeling a bit foolish.

Claudia immediately let out a little chuckle. "Elaine comes from a bunch of poor hillbillies, most of who live in Tennessee, but I'm not surprised by her tale because she has always been dramatic and likes making up stories."

"Yeah, I'm starting to get that."

She chuckled again. "It took me a while to figure it out too."

Feeling a bit less foolish, I smiled. "She also told me that she was on *America's Most Wanted* for stealing millions of dollars from casinos."

Claudia scoffed. "Elaine wasn't on *America's Most Wanted*. I don't know why she tells people that when she was actually on a show called *Unsolved Mysteries*. That's how the FBI in Colorado finally found her. After the show aired, several people called the tip line and turned her in."

"Did she actually steal from casinos?"

"I don't know about that, but the *Unsolved Mysteries* episode showed her character using counterfeit cashier's checks to buy expensive things." "You should have seen the way they portrayed her on that show. The actress was in a fur coat and driving a convertible Mercedes." She sighed. "And here was her daughter with almost nothing."

Later I would locate on YouTube.com the *Unsolved Mysteries'* episodes exposing Elaine's unlawful activity. The name Beth

Maguire was one of the many aliases she used to hide her identity. At one point during the program, the detective who was referring to con artists stated, "Beth was one of the best."

I let Claudia's unsettling words sink in for a moment. I took a deep breath and exhaled. "Elaine claimed that she was physically and mentally abused by you, her dad, and Becky's dad." I waited a moment to see if she wanted to respond, but she remained silent. "So in an effort to escape the pain from the abuse, she turned to drugs."

Anger rose up in Claudia's voice. "Elaine has been in trouble since she was a little girl. I used to tell her that she should be an actress because she was so good at making things up. Once she told some people at her school that I had all kinds of men sleeping at the house, and when I had sex with these men, she would have to sleep on the floor." She chuckled nervously. "Can you believe it?"

Not knowing how or even if she wanted me to respond, I remained quiet. "Of course this never happened," she said firmly.

"Of course," I said.

"Elaine's stories were so disturbing, I had to take her to see a therapist. After that first session, the therapist told me that Elaine was going to marry the first man she met. I didn't really understand this, but that is exactly what she did. She married the first man she met."

"It's odd that a therapist would make that kind of prediction, don't you think?" I asked, trying to make sense of it myself.

Disregarding my statement, Claudia chuckled, "She married him because he had a car."

The therapist thing was baffling to me, but it was evident that Claudia didn't wish to add anything further regarding what came out of that session or even if there were any further sessions, so I withheld my desire to pursue it any further. At this point, the only thing I was convinced of was that the ambiguity surrounding all things concerning Elaine was relentless.

"Elaine married someone for a car?" I said in an exaggerated tone of amazement.

Claudia chuckled again. "Yes, she married her first husband just so she could have a car to drive."

I thought for a moment about Elaine's seemingly continuous misfortune when it came to cars. "Elaine must be unlucky when it comes to cars because Adam told me that she managed to wreck a couple of his vehicles."

"She wrecked mine too," she said with reproach.

I began to wonder if any or even all of Elaine's car accidents were intentional, including the one that resulted in Andrew's birth.

"Do you think Elaine meant to wreck your car?"

"Yes," she said with certainty.

"Why do you think she would do something like that?"

"When Elaine didn't get what she wanted, she would have these uncontrollable bouts of anger. When she got that way, she would become very destructive with no concern for anyone's well-being, including her own." In Claudia's effort to corroborate this, she spoke of an unpleasant incident that occurred when she locked Elaine out of the house: "Elaine kept knocking and knocking like a crazy person, and when she realized I wasn't going to open the door, she started pounding on it with her fists and kicking it with her feet until she actually managed to break down the door. After busting down the door, as if that wasn't bad enough, she turned around and busted out the front windows of the house."

Disturbed by her story, "Did you call the police?" I asked.

"Oh yes, and they arrested her." Then Claudia went on to inform me of Elaine's further criminal activity, which she claimed included shoplifting, prostitution, and identity theft. "Elaine opened a credit card in my name, charged it to the limit and never paid a penny of it," she said.

"That's awful."

"Oh, that's nothing. She also managed to con me out of my life savings. Yeah, when she was still living at home, that girl had me convinced she was going to college. Then one day, she came home crying and said that she needed money for tuition or she would be kicked out of school. Of course I didn't want her to get kicked out of school so I emptied all my savings and gave her the money she said she owed to the school. Then I found out she wasn't even attending college."

I gasped and said incredulously, "Really?"

"Oh yes, really. And can you believe it, she used the money I gave her—my life savings—to get her car fixed, and believe me, I have never been a rich lady."

As our conversation dwindled, Claudia advised that I should speak to her son, Wayne. She said she talked to him about Andrew, and he was disgusted by the whole thing. I agreed to give Wayne a call and wrote down the number she recited. Before our conversation came to an end, I asked if she would be willing to speak to Andrew's GAL and his caseworker and maybe even testify in court if it were to come to that.

"Yes, of course," she said.

"Is it all right if I give the GAL and caseworker your number?"

"Yes, of course," she repeated.

We spoke briefly about Andrew. Then I thanked her for all the information she provided and left her my number in case she needed to get a hold of me. After hanging up the phone, I felt overwhelmed by all the new unpleasant information I now needed to consider.

CHAPTER 11

Come away, O human child! To the waters and the wild with a faery, hand in hand, for the worlds more full of weeping than you can understand.

—William Butler Yeats

During my earlier phone conversation with Claudia, I asked if she knew if Kenny, Elaine's second child, was ever adopted. In response to my inquiry, Claudia later sent me a short note stating, "These people might have the Thompson's address or phone number." The Thompsons were Elaine's third child's foster parents. Along with the note were two letters concerning Jacob and Kenny. The letters were from Jacob's guardian AD litem in Charlotte, North Carolina, which were written to Elaine, who was in custody at that time in the El Paso County Criminal Justice Center in Colorado Springs.

April 6, 1994

Dear Elaine,

Thank you for your warm letter. I enjoy hearing from you. Your cheery letter from a bad situation is most heartening to me.

Enclosed are another couple of (not so hot) pictures which were taken last week. Jacob's foster brother, James was quite sick with chicken pox, and Jacob was upset that he was sick and wanted to stay with him. I met both foster grandmothers, who were there to rock and comfort the boys. The boys were eating up all the attention, and Jacob was not interested in leaving his comfortable rocking lap. The foster mom did not need me there in the midst of all that, so I didn't stay but a minute.

I called this morning to see how everyone was getting along. James is still sick, covered with spots, but feeling a little better. Jacob still wanted to be near him but as yet doesn't have the chicken pox. Jacob is twenty-five and a half inches tall, weighs thirty-four pounds, and has sixteen teeth (we think)—he wasn't too keen on having us peer into his mouth. At any rate, his next teeth to come in will be his two-year molars. He has a while for those.

Court went very well on March 15th. Jackie Simpson did very well for you. We got copies of all the tests you passed while in Nevada (Good for you!). Jackie explained that since you are not in a federal facility, you will get two on one time and could expect to be out in October of 1995.

The judge asked Judy McDonald to look into an interstate compact, which is how Jacob could be sent to Colorado. I saw Ms. McDonald at court on Monday, and she said that she too had gotten a nice letter from you. Also, that she had looked into interstate compact and, though very complicated, could be done.

Also the judge told Jackie that she must find out about Kenny. You do not mention Kenny in your long-term plans. Can you tell me what has happened with him? I know that you told me that you were fighting for him when we spoke on the phone.

You must live almost from Saturday to Saturday for your visits with your daughter, Becky. If you haven't seen her in about five years, you have a lot of ground to cover, getting to know each other. Bittersweet, I should imagine, for you, a dream coming true.

Do be honest with Becky when sharing your dreams with her about all the hard work and determination it's going to take on your part for everyone's dreams of family together to come true. Ten-year-olds are still young enough not to be very realistic, and you don't want to disappoint her expectations of you or what you say—so be sure to cover yourself.

That's about it for now, blew two kisses and love to Jacob from his momma and sister Becky (he didn't want to be touched this time). Look forward to hearing from you.

Jacob's GAL

May 28, 1994

Dear Elaine,

Thank you for your very lovely card. I certainly enjoyed your making it for me. You are a good artist!

Your notes to your boy are crumbled, shredded, and sucked on. Is he eating your words, who knows, he does enjoy them, but not in a manner that you might expect.

Your letters are always welcomed, and I appreciate your straightforward answers to my prying questions. Thank you for the GAL information. I will call Mr. Atkins to see how things are handled in Colorado.

I've not seen Jacob in a couple of weeks but have talked on the phone with his foster mom. He still has a few pox marks, but they are fading, and no scarring is expected. He is a very active little boy, beginning to put two and three words together, *mine* and *no* used frequently and something that means *James* that I can't begin to spell. His hair is cut like a boy's with tight curls in the front. He is losing his baby look fast. He and James are great buddies. He no longer wears diapers and is busy doing what James does, so toilet training was a snap.

Jacob is in such an ideal situation that I don't feel the need to check on him very often anymore. If anything comes up, his foster mom will call; otherwise, I phone once a week and just drop by now about once a month.

Elaine, I do thank you for answering my questions. Your answers fill in a lot of my mental blanks about how things are, might be, etc.

My heart goes out to you as you mourn the loss of your Kenny. Perhaps it will ease your ache somewhat to know that he is in a loving home with warmth and security that is every child's birthright. I wonder if you had thought when he was TPR (termination of parental rights), to voluntarily give him up, saying that you wanted him to know growing up that his mother loved him enough to give him up to a good home, which he deserves and you are unable to provide, for a very long time. This would be the ultimate gift of love to him. How nice and comforting to him to know this one day when he is grown enough to seek you out.

I should think your mind would rather think of him in a warm, loving family than in who knows what kind of limbo, waiting his young life away because in spite of him, his mom made mistakes that cost him a secure childhood. If you can think of Kenny as secured and loved rather than just out there somewhere, it would help ease your loss.

Becky is so fortunate to have had her daddy and grandmothers, no substitute for mommy, but at least family who love her. I'm so happy to know that your visits are going well and that you are taking advantage of counseling. You are doing all you can to make amends.

I will keep trying to get a photo for you and will give Jacob your love notes. Thank you for keeping in touch.

Cordially,
Jacob's GAL

PS. Sorry your appeal was denied. Better luck next time...

After reading the letters, I sent an e-mail to the GAL's office in North Carolina to make inquiries on Andrew's half brothers, but of course the GAL's office would not give out any information on the boys or the closed dependency and neglect case.

CHAPTER 12

The first faults are theirs that commit them, the second that permit them.

—author unknown

Not long after my conversation with Claudia, I spoke with Kirk's paralegal and the new caseworker, Donald, to inform them of the conversation I had with Claudia and to leave them her phone number. The GAL's paralegal advised that she would contact Claudia and thanked me for the information.

Donald, who I had not yet met in person, also agreed to contact Claudia, but added, "Since Elaine and her mom have been estranged for so long, I don't see how any information from her would be relevant to the case." Obviously, he had already met with Elaine and they spoke about her mother.

I was irritated by his resolve. "Wouldn't it be best to actually speak with Claudia before making that kind of determination? Claudia told me that Elaine's other three children where either abandoned or removed from her through social services. She also said there was some neglect and abuse toward two of those children. I can't see how this kind of information would not be relevant to the case."

"I said I would give Claudia a call," he said with a tone of indignation.

When our conversation ended, I considered if a reprisal from this disturbing individual was imminent, and what it could mean for Andrew.

The Division of Children and Family Services claim to be dedicated to ensuring the safety of children and achieving permanency as quickly as possible for every child, giving paramount consideration to the physical, mental, and emotional conditions and needs of the child. Sadly these claims are not what they seem. The trust given to these individuals to make crucial and life-changing decisions on behalf of a child could prove to be devastating when the decisions are made without a meticulous and thorough investigation by an incompetent, inexperienced, and above all, narcissistic individual.

On January 29, 2004, the second court review and permanency plan hearing took place. Adam, who did not appear, had his public defender appear on his behalf.

For this hearing, Donald generated the family services plan, and within the plan, he stated, "Mrs. Barela-Perez has been in compliance with her treatment plan. The CiCore Program appears to be an appropriate setting for her. However, she has a long history of leading a criminal and unstable lifestyle and has lost custody of other children as a result of this."

These statements left me with the false impression that the Department of Social Services was no longer in favor of reunification. After all, it seemed unlikely that a child protection agency would allow a vulnerable child to be cared for by not only a chronic offender in the criminal arena but also someone who has already lost or abandoned three of her children.

The hearing went the same as the previous hearing; the recommendations of the family services plan were adopted and made an order of the court. The court found that reasonable services were being offered by the Jefferson County Department of Social Services to reunite the family and that Andrew's placement with me continued to be in his best interest. Unfortunately, at Elaine's request, with the backing of Julie, Elaine's counselor at CiCore, and Donald, the court also ordered an expansion of visitation for Elaine.

Although Kirk and I did not specifically object to an expansion of Andrew's visits with Elaine, we joined in objecting to a continuation of a permanency plan of reunification for Andrew with Elaine and instead recommended a permanency plan of long-term permanent placement with me and Liam. And as an added precaution, I requested that Elaine submit to a psychological evaluation, which, in light of the information I obtained from Claudia, seemed to be a valid request.

In opposition, Elaine objected to a psychological evaluation and long-term permanent placement for Andrew and instead recommended that the court continue with the permanency plan of reunification.

In the end, under the weight of social services, the court found that there was insufficient evidence to support my and Kirk's request to modify the permanency goal, so the matter was set for a permanent allocation of parental responsibility hearing to be held on April 5, 2004.

In accordance with the court order, Elaine's two-hour visits with Andrew, who turned a year old two weeks prior, were extended to weekend visits at the CiCore facility. Consequently, on February 6, 2004, a social worker from the Jefferson County Department of Social Services came by to pick up the little guy and drive him to CiCore for his first overnight weekend visit.

Trying to put aside our uneasiness and apprehension, Liam and I decided to make that first night without Andrew a date night. We made plans to go out for dinner and afterward take a walk through the mall. We managed to enjoy our dinner; however, our walk fell short.

With all the families about us, I began to begrudge all the happy parents for having the freedom to ensure their children were safe and secure, when I, a mere special respondent, didn't have such luxuries. That's when the ache that had been mounting in my heart came to roost. It began with that nudging "I feel like I forgot something" feeling, and as I considered this, the obscurity became clear; Andrew was notably and painfully absent. The pungent clarity triggered the heartache, and those fickle tears of mine began to fall. Liam moved me toward a bench, and as I sat down, he attempted to console me, yet the despondent look that plagued him made it clear that he too was feeling the loss. We sat for a while just holding one another, painfully aware that Andrew would not be sleeping in his own bed tonight and not daring to speak of an unthinkable future without him.

An hour or so after Andrew was returned from that first weekend visit, he started having loose bowel movements that persisted until the next afternoon. Though I managed to keep him hydrated, still worried, I left a message at CiCore for Elaine to call me.

By this time, I knew that the sleeping quarters or private rooms at CiCore consisted of three to four families to one room, with each family being divided by a mere curtain. After several of his prior visits at CiCore, Andrew would often become ill within a day after returning home. The illnesses included RSV, projectile vomiting, pink eye, bronchitis, the flu. I believed he was infected with all of these illnesses at CiCore since his daycare did not report any outbreaks of any of these illnesses.

I reported Andrew's illnesses to Donald, who seemed to think they were all simply a result of normal childhood illnesses. "Yes, they are normal childhood illnesses, but for one child to be infected with almost every single one within a matter of months is not normal." I argued.

Elaine returned my call late that afternoon, and I asked her what Andrew had eaten and drank during his visit with her. "Is something wrong?" She asked.

"Andrew has had diarrhea since he was dropped off yesterday, and I'm trying to figure out the cause in case I need to take him to the hospital." I said impatiently.

"Oh," she said matter of factly, "that first whole day Andrew was here he didn't have a bowel movement, so I gave him an enema."

I was dumbfounded. "An enema? Where did you get an enema?"

Elaine explained that a nurse stopped by the facility a couple of times a week, and she obtained the enema from her.

"Is this nurse a pediatric nurse? Was the enema meant for Andrew, or did she give it to you for your use?"

Elaine didn't answer.

I was livid. I couldn't grasp the idiocy in giving an underweight child an enema. "The next time Andrew is not feeling well, you need to take him to see his regular pediatrician or to a hospital." She tried to interrupt, but I wouldn't allow it. "No one should advise you medically on Andrew without the proper training if that indeed is what happened in this case."

She remained quiet for a moment, then asked if Andrew was feeling better. "No, Elaine, he is not feeling better. No one should give a child an enema after one day of not pooping, or ever for that matter," I yelled before hanging up on her.

With the allocation of parental responsibility (APR) hearing quickly approaching, social services felt that due to the complexities of the case, the observations of a CASA (court-appointed special advocate) volunteer would be helpful. So the case was referred to the CASA staff for review. The CASA staff reviewed the case files and assigned an appropriate volunteer and forwarded an order to the court for approval. Consequently, on February 24, 2004, the court found that it was in Andrew's best interest to utilize all community resources available to the Court to investigate the circumstances affecting his welfare; thus, the CASA order was approved.

I was pleased that a CASA volunteer was going to administer an independent investigation as I too understood this was a complex case. Consequently, I met with an attorney, and on February 25, 2004, Sandra Voigt, attorney-at-law, filed an entry of appearance with the court as she was now representing me, the special respondent in the APR hearing.

Also taking note that the APR hearing was quickly approaching, Donald Malone made it a point to finally administer a home visit and actually meet Andrew and speak to me in person. It was March 29, 2004, when I answered the door to find a thin-framed, medium-height young man who appeared to be in his early thirties. His hair was jet black, and his light skin paled in comparison giving him an under the weather appearance. He introduced himself, and I found his attempt to portray himself with confidence came off as cockiness. I welcomed him into my home, and we made small talk for a moment. Then he asked to visit with Andrew for a bit. Afterward, he looked around the house a bit then met me back in the living room. We sat at the dining table to talk.

"After my last meeting with Elaine and her counselor at CiCore, I am recommending reunification for Andrew," Donald said without warning.

I was horror-struck at his resolve. "What about Elaine's extensive criminal past and the fact that she abandoned two children and lost custody of another? What about the CASA investigation? Don't you need to review the findings before you make such an important decision?" I was desperately searching my brain for something more to add, but before I could say another word, he advised that Elaine informed him that her other two boys were placed in foster care due to her incarceration and even though he was unable to thoroughly check on it, as it took place in another state, he believed her.

"If you speak with Elaine's mom, she can tell you what *really* happened to those other children," I said.

"It's been several years since Elaine and her mom have even seen each other, so her input is irrelevant to the case."

Not willing to back down, I said, "Those children are her grandchildren, surely what she has to say is relevant."

I grabbed the folder that I put on the dining table prior to Donald's arrival and pulled out the two letters written to Elaine by Jacob's guardian AD litem and a letter Elaine wrote to Claudia in 1992, all of which I received from Claudia a couple of months earlier. I passed the letters over to Donald, who was sitting across from me at the dining table. He looked at the letters, but when he noticed the dates that the letters were written, he immediately determined that because they were written so long ago, they too were irrelevant. In the end, Donald disregarded all that I had to say as he was incapable of acknowledging even the most obvious issues concerning Andrew's best interest and definitely failed to notice the most crucial. The very notion that this inept individual could very well have the power to dictate Andrew's future left me with a keen awareness of what true injustice really is.

The day after meeting with Donald, I wrote to Claudia to inform her of the rescheduled upcoming court hearing and to update her on any new developments in the case.

March 30, 2004

Dear Claudia,

I am returning the original letter, written by Elaine in 1992, that you sent me of which I made a copy for myself. I want to thank you for sending it to me.

I am not sure if you have heard anything from the courts so far. Originally the hearing was scheduled for April 5, 2004, although that date has recently been changed to April 26, 2004. You should be receiving a subpoena in the next couple of weeks.

I was hoping that the attorneys and caseworker would come to an agreement prior to the next scheduled court date that would allow Andrew to stay with me rather than live in the rehab center with Elaine. Then neither you nor my mom would have to be a witness to the case and undergo that heartache. Though after visiting with the caseworker (Donald Malone) last night, I do not believe this will happen.

The caseworker advised that he spoke with Elaine regarding her other three children. Elaine stated that she never abandoned any of her children including Becky and went on to say that Kenny was taken from her after she was incarcerated, and when she got out of prison, she tried to get him back. The other child, Jacob, was taken at birth because he was born while she was incarcerated. The caseworker said he could not get all the details but feels Elaine is telling the truth.

The caseworker seems to have reservations about Andrew living with Elaine at CiCore, but he is still going to recommend that Andrew be returned to her care. My heart aches at the thought.

Andrew's attorney, Kirk, (the GAL) believes strongly that Andrew should stay with us. We also hired our own attorney, who also believes that Andrew should stay with us. However, the bottom line is that the judge on the case has to make the final decision as I am sure Elaine is not willing to do what is best for Andrew.

The caseworker informed me that he tried on several occasions to contact Elaine's daughter and ex-husband, but they never returned his phone calls. He said that Elaine is having them both subpoenaed as witnesses to her case and believes that they will corroborate everything she has conveyed to him. I am not sure what their take is on this, but Elaine is counting on them to help her get Andrew back. I hope she does not plan on causing Becky any more pain.

Please call me when you get your subpoena so we can arrange to pick you up. Thanks again for the letter. I guess all we can do now is wait and pray.

Sincerely,

Crystal Sanchez

CHAPTER 13

We must never be afraid to go too far, for truth lies beyond.

—Marcel Proust

*P*rior to the APR hearing, which was changed from April 5 to April 26, 2004, due to Elaine's public defender having a scheduling conflict, a case management conference was set. The conference seemed to be a last ditch effort for all the parties involved in the dependency and neglect case to reach some kind of agreement, rather than continuing with the half-day hearing.

Prior to the case management conference, I felt I should speak with Wayne, Elaine's brother, in an effort to leave no stone unturned. I punched in the number Claudia gave me, and a woman whom I assumed was Wayne's wife answered. I introduced myself and asked to speak to Wayne. She placed me on hold, and then Wayne answered.

Again I introduced myself.

"I'm glad you called. My mom updated me on Elaine's latest trouble."

I began to ask him a question, but he boldly interjected. "Elaine is out for Elaine. She will lie, cheat, and steal to get whatever she wants, and if any judge thinks that some program Elaine's been involved with is going to change her, he's sadly mistaken."

In an effort to substantiate this, Wayne revealed some cruel things Elaine subjected him and their stepbrother to when they were young boys, one being; making them fist fight each other for her enjoyment.

Wayne also spoke of the heartless behavior Elaine showed toward Becky. "After abandoning her, Elaine would call Becky at my mom's and promise to be over to pick her up in fifteen minutes or so. Becky, filled with anticipation, would wait at the door all day, but Elaine would never show," he said.

Wayne then corroborated all of Claudia's claims concerning Elaine and maintained that Elaine was truly a deceitful and untrustworthy individual. As our conversation came to an end, Wayne asked if he could write a letter to the court stating his concerns for Andrew should Elaine regain custody of him. I was surprised and appreciative of his request and asked that he e-mail the letter to my attorney, Sandra, which he agreed. Consequently, I gave him Sandra's e-mail address and advised that I would notify her of the upcoming letter. Then amiably, Wayne thanked me for caring for Andrew, and we said our good-byes.

I hung up the phone wondering if it were possible that Elaine was actually as emotionally bankrupt as she was being portrayed; someone only capable of leaving destruction, broken people and broken hearts in her wake. I prayed she wasn't, for Andrew's sake.

The CASA report was complete and distributed on April 20, 2004. Initially the report stated the issue at hand, "Should the permanency plan be changed from reunification to long-term permanent placement with the paternal aunt and her family through an allocation of parental responsibility?" After that,

Elaine's unsettling criminal and drug history information was revealed along with the factual information on how her chosen lifestyle negatively impacted her children, which basically covered most everything Claudia had already shared with me. In addition, the report shared Claudia and Wayne's input and concerns, of which the CASA volunteer deemed *relevant*. Next, Andrew's current situation and Elaine's current situation was described, and the fact that Adam was incarcerated and unavailable to parent was stated. Lastly, the CASA volunteer's recommendations were stated: "The CASA volunteer supports the allocation of parental responsibility to the paternal aunt and uncle, Crystal Sanchez and Liam Wallace, for the following reasons: They will provide a very good permanent home for Andrew. They have maturity, commitment, a family relationship, and a strong affection for Andrew." In contrast, it addressed how Elaine's latest arrest for possession and association with a criminal element placed Andrew in an injurious and corruptible environment. It also acknowledged that Elaine's successful participation at CiCore is not a sufficient duration to evaluate her potential for success beyond the highly structured program.

Six days after receiving the CASA report, I drove downtown to the GAL's office for the case management conference feeling both pleased and optimistic by the CASA report. Sandra was waiting for me in front of the building when I arrived. We walked in together and were greeted by a receptionist who asked us to take a seat at the round table in the next room. We did as she requested and conversed while the other attendees began to show.

Elaine and her posse were the last to arrive. She sauntered into the room and flamboyantly flung her long blond hair back to one side as if she didn't have a care in the world. She was accompanied by her ISP officer, Sheila Day, her case manager from CiCore, Julie Stevens, and their driver. I had to stifle a chuckle when Elaine looked directly at me and flashed a sardonic smile. She wore an olive green dress made of a lightweight material, and as she turned to sit down, I noticed that her bunched-up panties had created an unsightly lopsided rumple to her behind. The contradiction between her haughty attitude and those bunched-up panties made me grin.

The meeting commenced, and many issues were argued by each side. Ultimately, all parties involved agreed to move forward with a stipulated APR rather than continuing on with the APR hearing, meaning that Elaine would have to meet a list of conditions in six months' time to gain primary custodianship of Andrew, and I would obtain parenting time for three days a week. If the conditions were not met, I would maintain primary custodianship, and Elaine would obtain parenting time.

I myself agreed to the vacating of the APR hearing and moving forward with a stipulation because even though the GAL and the CASA volunteer maintained that Andrew should remain with me and my family on a permanent basis, social services still wanted to move forward with reunification. If I were to continue with the APR hearing and the court decided to comply with social services' recommendation of reunification, which was a real possibility, seeing that not only is Elaine the natural mother, but also because the court seemed to be most receptive to social services, not only would Andrew be made to reside at CiCore for the next two years of his life, but parenting time for Liam and I could terminate altogether. If that were to happen, our ability to keep a protective eye on Andrew would also end. With the stakes being so high, I agreed to the only other option given to me, a stipulated allocation of parental responsibilities.

With the discussion of the stipulation now in motion, I requested that Elaine leave CiCore and instead enter herself into an outpatient drug rehabilitation program as I was totally against Andrew *ever* residing at CiCore but still felt that Elaine should be made to complete a drug rehabilitation program.

Elaine, as anticipated, was not against leaving CiCore but would not agree to enter an outpatient program as she stood by her original story—that she has maintained her sobriety since 1990. I knew very well this was a lie, but still I acquiesced since one of the already agreed-upon conditions was that she remain in compliance with all the terms and conditions of her ISP probation, which included continual drug testing.

With everyone finally in agreement on all the terms of the stipulation, Elaine's public defender was asked to generate the document, and the meeting concluded.

A few days after the management conference, Mom came by for a visit. I was in another room when the phone rang in the kitchen. Being closest, Mom answered it. Since she didn't yell for me, I went to the kitchen to see who had called. Mom had the phone to her ear, apparently listening to someone on the other end. After a couple of seconds, Mom's uneasy look convinced me to take the phone from her. I put the phone to my ear, and Julie Steven's voice gave me pause. She was in midsentence as I tried to understand what she was talking about. Then the purpose of the call became clear. Choosing to believe all of Elaine's lies about Mom and I, Julie took it upon herself to express the disapproval and dislike she had for both of us. As I continued to listen, Julie claimed that Mom and I wanted Elaine to fail in her sobriety so we could steal Andrew away from her.

I believed that was a good time to interrupt her fruitless babbling. "Elaine has declared on many occasions that she has been clean for several years. She has argued time and time again that she was wrongly accused when she was arrested with Adam, even claiming that he put the meth in her purse without her knowledge. So how is it possible that Elaine's sobriety would be at risk if she left CiCore?"

Possibly struck dumb by my question, Julie remained quiet for a moment. I began to wonder if she hung up, but no such luck. "You and your mom are nothing but baby thieves," she bellowed, then hung up.

I turned to Mom and said with disbelief, "Julie just called us baby thieves." Mom, who was apparently as shocked as I at Julie's unprofessional and unethical behavior, looked uneasy. Trying to lighten the situation, I smiled at her and said lightheartedly, "We are not baby thieves, Mom." She grinned at this.

Ten days after the case management meeting, Elaine left CiCore. I questioned her decision to leave when the stipulation hadn't even been approved by the court yet. Even so, as soon as Elaine received the premature approval from her ISP officer, she made a mad dash to freedom. With CiCore's help, authorized or not, Elaine moved into an apartment she referred to as a transition home. Since the transition home had a firm policy that prohibited children of overnight stays, her unsupervised visits with Andrew would exclude nights.

It was a day away from Elaine's first unsupervised visit with Andrew, and I still had not heard from Donald regarding any arrangements made for that following day. With the 2:00 p.m. hour closely approaching, it seemed to me it was no longer prudent to wait to hear from Donald, so I made a call to his office instead. I was expecting to get his voice mail, so I was a bit taken aback when he answered. Without preamble, I informed him that I was calling about the arrangements for Andrew's visit with Elaine that next day. "Have you visited Elaine's new apartment?"

Donald advised he had not visited the apartment but assured me that Andrew would be fine as he had talked with Elaine earlier, and she planned on taking Andrew to the park near her apartment.

"What about food? Are you certain she has something to feed Andrew?"

Donald sighed. "Elaine assured me that Andrew would have everything he needed and would be fine."

Provoked by his continued indifference, I laid into him. "Elaine's assurance that everything will be fine does not by a long shot put me at ease. Then again, should you decide to make an effort to competently perform your job and administer a home visit prior to Andrew's first unsupervised visit and assure me yourself that everything will be fine, I may at that time, be put at ease."

With apparent disdain, Donald said, "Elaine will call you tonight to discuss the time frame of tomorrow's visit." His tone hurled me into instant regret. What was I thinking? He was the one with all the power no matter how inept and lackluster I found him to be. I recognized that I had to do something to smooth things out before he hung up the phone. "Donald," I said as calm as possible, "I can transport Andrew to and from Elaine's apartment tomorrow for the visit and also any or all the visits thereafter if need be."

This seemed to take the edge off as Donald sounded relieved and even genuinely appreciative while accepting my offer. We said our good-byes, and I hung up, not really clear on how I felt about my newfound pretense: butt kisser.

Elaine called early that evening and asked if I could drop Andrew off downtown, "at Colfax and Grant," instead of her apartment claiming she had an appointment in the area that next morning.

I wasn't comfortable with her last minute request. "How are you going to get back to the apartment after the appointment?" I asked.

"We are going to take the bus home."

"What about a stroller? Do you have a stroller for Andrew? It would be hard to lug him around without one."

"I don't have one yet, but I plan on getting one next week."

At that, I told her I would bring one from home for her to use. She thanked me. "I'll see you tomorrow," she said a bit too cheerfully.

Andrew was not feeling well that next morning, and I was reluctant to drop him off in the middle of downtown but knew I didn't have a choice. When I reached the corner of Colfax and

Grant, I pulled over. Elaine and a shorter red-headed woman were waiting for us on the corner. I got out of the car, and Elaine introduced me to her friend, who she referred to as Lily. I said hello and opened the trunk to remove the stroller. Elaine opened the back door, and began to remove Andrew from his car seat. "Lily is going to drive us back to the apartment after my appointment," she said.

I tried to not look as concerned as I felt. "I thought you were taking the bus home."

Elaine looked at me smugly. "Yeah, well, Lily offered to take us home."

"Does she have a car seat for Andrew to use?" I asked, but what I really wanted to know is if Lily had a valid driver's license.

Elaine shook her head. "But I'm going to buy one today."

Knowing Elaine was more than likely being untruthful, I pulled Andrew's car seat out of the car and handed it to her. "How about you use this one for today," I said.

Being parked in an area that was clearly a no-parking zone, I briefly explained to Elaine how to use the car seat and open and close the stroller, kissed a confused Andrew on his fluffy cheek, and got back in the car to leave. Feeling sick to my stomach, I watched Andrew disappear from my rearview mirror as I drove away.

The following visits continued in a manner of irregularity and last-minute changes on Elaine's part. But worse than that, Andrew began objecting to the visits by screaming and making every effort to hang on to me when I dropped him off at Elaine's apartment. I did everything I could to make the transition easier for him, but he was having none of it.

As Andrew's objections to the visits continued, his behavior at home with Liam and me began to change. He started having unusually aggressive temper tantrums, which included, cussing, screaming, hitting, biting, kicking, and at times banging his head against the wall or floor. Concerned, I spoke to Elaine about this. "He doesn't act that way when he's with me," she said in a patronizing manner.

I found this to be quite amusing since we both witnessed firsthand Andrew's steadfast reluctance to simply go to her when I dropped him off at her apartment.

CHAPTER 14

In any moment of decision, the best thing you can do is
the right thing. The worst thing you can do is nothing.

—Theodore Roosevelt

On April 26, 2004, the stipulation was presented to
Magistrate Sanderson, and to everyone's surprise, the
magistrate was not only adamant in his unwillingness
to approve it, but he was also very upset by it and made it known
to all concerned. "Permanency should be taking place, not a
stipulation. Six months to see what progress the respondent
mother has made would violate state and federal law regarding
permanency timelines," he advised.

Elaine's public defender objected to Magistrate Sanderson's
jurisdiction and requested that the district court hold the
APR hearing. As a result, the APR hearing was moved to the
district court, at which time Judge Jackson vacated Magistrate
Sanderson's orders and found good cause to extend the EPP
(expedited permanent placement) guidelines due to the pending
stipulation. The court set the matter for review/status on May 27,
2004.

On the morning of the review/status hearing, the Rocky Mountain News revealed that CiCore's license was suspended that previous day after an investigation found alleged substance abuse and inappropriate intimate relationships among staff and clients, food stamp fraud, and financial improprieties. I wasn't surprised by CiCore's demise, but I was definitely blown away by the unfortunate timing of it.

Upon arrival at the courthouse that afternoon, I crossed paths with Donald. He was wearing that smug smile on his face I had grown to hate. Aware that once the stipulation was approved, I would no longer have to deal with him I turned to him. "So," I said with reproach, "did you hear that CiCore's license was suspended yesterday?"

"What?" he said looking puzzled.

"You know," I flashed him a wry smile, "that drug rehab facility you wanted Andrew to live in for the next two years of his life, their license was suspended."

"I haven't heard that."

"Well, now you have," I said spitefully.

He didn't comment, or even ask why CiCore's license was suspended. He merely shrugged his shoulders and proceeded ahead of me through the metal detectors.

When I arrived at the courtroom, I was asked to sign the stipulation that had already been signed by all the other parties involved. I hesitated, wondering if my chances of gaining custody of Andrew have improved now that CiCore had closed its doors. I discussed this with Sandra, but she felt that the risks haven't changed since Elaine already left CiCore and because social services, in spite of everything, was still recommending that reunification with Elaine was in Andrew's best interest. I was torn. Yet I eventually signed the stipulation, believing that if Elaine was going to relapse in her sobriety or get into any trouble, it would more than likely happen before the stipulation expires. On the other hand, if she was to prove herself to be a worthy mother, this would allow Andrew and his biological mother to be together sooner than later.

I wasn't surprised that Adam didn't appear at this hearing. However, I was surprised to find that his public defender was also absent though he did manage to sign the stipulation on Adam's behalf.

As the hearing commenced, Judge Jackson found that the stipulation was in Andrew's best interest, approved it, and made it an order of the court. Judge Jackson then authorized the dependency and neglect case be certified into a domestic relations (DR) case and advised that the court will not close the dependency and neglect case until a DR case has been opened.

The May 27, 2004, Stipulation follows:

STIPULATED ALLOCATION OF PARENTAL RESPONSIBILITIES AND PARENTING TIME

Andrew currently resides with his paternal aunt, Crystal Sanchez. Upon meeting the following conditions, Elaine will become the primary residential custodian for Andrew and a parenting time schedule will be agreed upon giving Crystal Sanchez parenting time with Andrew. The change in the primary residential custodian shall occur without further court order and upon agreement of the parties. The conditions include:

1. Elaine will leave CiCore and establish a track record of stability and sobriety in the community for six (6) months. Her probation officer has applied to the court to have this requirement removed from her terms and conditions of her probation. Elaine has left CiCore as approved by her ISP probation officer and she has established a private residence.
2. Elaine will establish a stable residence during the six-month period and she will provide proof of a lease to Crystal Sanchez. She must be current on her rent during this six-month period and at the end of it when Andrew moves in with her.

3. Elaine will obtain and maintain a stable job during the six-month period. She will provide proof of lawful employment to Crystal Sanchez.

4. Elaine will be current on all her household utilities during this six-month period and at the end of it when Andrew moves in with her.

5. Elaine will comply and be in compliance during the six-month period with all terms and conditions of her ISP probation with Adams County. Specifically, Elaine will comply with all UAs (Urinary Analysis) required by probation and all UAs will be negative for all substances. Missed UAs will be considered positive UAs. Elaine will sign a release so that Crystal Sanchez can receive proof of negative UAs.

6. Elaine will obtain insurance for Andrew through private insurance or Medicaid.

All parties agree that it is in Andrew's best interest to be raised by his biological mother. The parties further recognize that this can only be accomplished if the mother meets the above-mentioned requirements within the six-month period.

If the above conditions are not met by Elaine Barela-Perez, then Crystal Sanchez shall be the primary residential custodian and the sole decision maker for Andrew. If Elaine has violated the terms of her probation, then she will be remanded to prison to finish her sentence. If Elaine fails to maintain her sobriety, then she will have only supervised visits with Andrew, the cost of those visits to be borne by Elaine. If Elaine fails to meet the above mentioned conditions, but she does not fail to maintain sobriety and she does not violate probation, then she will have unsupervised, liberal and reasonable parenting time with Andrew.

With no objections to the stipulation, the dependency and neglect case was eventually terminated, and Jefferson County Social Services was relieved of their so-called protective supervision over Andrew as the case was now certified into a domestic relations case.

Three months into the stipulation, Adam was kicked out of the Colorado Department of Corrections' TC (therapeutic community) program. He claimed that the part of the TC program that required inmate peer groups to provide feedback was crap. He felt the inmates were made to criticize and squeal on one another, which only managed to generate hostility between them. Unfortunately, in accordance with the DOC (Department of Corrections), because Adam was no longer in a program, he was reclassified and transferred from a minimum security prison to a medium security prison.

I worried that this news would have an ill effect on Elaine's efforts regarding the stipulation. If Adam continued to create obstacles for himself, how could he ask her to make every effort to meet the conditions of the stipulation?

CHAPTER 15

You may delay, but time will not.

—Benjamin Franklin

ow with the stipulation signed and approved, the clock was ticking. Elaine was adamant when she declared she wouldn't have any problem finding a job, a condition of the stipulation. Knowing she had such an extensive criminal record, I was a bit skeptical but surprisingly, a month into the stipulation, she began working. She claimed her job consisted of cleaning offices in commercial buildings, such as dentist's and doctor's offices. During the first couple of weeks of her employment, she seemed to be working pretty hard—that is, until she broke her hand or rather claimed that her roommate broke it.

I never met Elaine's roommate from her transition home; however, Elaine advised that the woman was an alcoholic, and that her broken hand was a result of her roommate's drinking problem. "Why is a woman with a drinking problem living in a transition home, which I assume is for those individuals actually recovering from addiction?" I asked. Elaine just shrugged. "I hope you're not allowing Andrew to be around her when she's been drinking." I added.

At that, Elaine insisted that wasn't the case and, without elaborating, advised that they were no longer roommates.

Regarding her broken hand, Elaine claimed that she and her roommate were engaged in an argument. She claimed that her roommate was drunk, and when Elaine made her way to the front door to leave, the roommate slammed her hand in the door and broke it. Elaine then claimed that the break would require therapy at least three times a week and that her doctor advised that she should refrain from using her hand in any way until it was completely healed, which could take up to a month.

When Elaine told me this, I reminded her that she still has not signed a lease, which is a condition of the stipulation. "You have to work to get money to lease an apartment."

She rolled her eyes. I ignored her juvenile behavior. "If any individual raising a child broke their hand, they would still have to find a way to support their child."

"But I won't be able to keep my job if I have to leave work three times a week," she whined.

"I understand your frustration," I said, "but you are going to have to figure this out." Silence hung in the air as she considered this. "How do you plan on paying your rent at the transition home if you're not able to work?"

Sounding a bit rehearsed, "My ISP officer is going to pay it through victim's services," Elaine said.

I had half a mind to contact her ISP officer to corroborate this but decided against it as I knew this would only manage to enrage her.

Once Elaine was past the broken hand drama, she managed, although in the eleventh hour, to accomplish all the conditions of the stipulation with the exception of obtaining medical insurance or Medicaid for Andrew. But because Andrew was already covered under child-only Medicaid and Elaine would merely need to change the Medicaid to the county in which she resided, as she herself was indigent, the court could very well review an attempt on my part to fight the stipulation as frivolous.

As an alternative, I thought about trying to get the stipulation amended for another six months, which would allow Elaine some more time to improve her situation and develop her parenting skills, but that would mean Andrew's bond with us would only grow stronger, thus making the transition over to Elaine that much harder for him and for us.

At that point, I had to ask myself if I was merely being arrogant in thinking that I needed to be the one caring for Andrew even above his own mother. What gave me that right? Then again, has Elaine *really* changed? If I succumb to this belief and later discover I was wrong, what would that mean for Andrew? Still, Andrew was no longer objecting to his visits with Elaine. Whether that meant he realized resisting was pointless or that he wanted to be with his mom, I had no idea.

Torn as I was, a month before the stipulation came due, I wrote to Adam to express my concerns. Adam and I had been writing to one another since May of 2003, when he was still in county jail. Even though I felt that he should have taken more of an interest in Andrew's court proceedings, I also realized that he was trying to adapt to prison life. In response to my concerns, he wrote me the following letter:

November 1, 2004

Dear Crystal,

Hi, I got your letter. It's always nice to get mail in here. Also I thank you for the money. It means a lot. In response to your concerns about Andrew living with Elaine full time, I really don't know what to say except you have gone above and beyond when I asked you if you would take Andrew as Elaine and myself get our lives together. I can't even put into words how much I appreciate what you have done for Andrew, all the love you and your family have given him. I am proud of you and glad to call you my sister. I am not going to sit here and tell you what I think is best for Andrew because I'm not in any position to do so right now. I can only show you once I get out. I do know one thing though. I think I figured out why Andrew might not be feeling too well when he leaves Elaine's house. The women can't cook a lick. Betty Crocker, she is not. She cooked for me once and that's all it took. I wasn't tripping though because Pizza Hut delivers.

Anyway, here's what I suggest. You should ask her to take some child nutrition classes and, at the same time, mention culinary arts. I am not kidding. I really do think this could be the problem. I'm not taking your concerns about Andrew lightly. I just think there is no way she would hurt Andrew on purpose, and it might be something as simple as her cooking.

Look, I know I have a lot of responsibilities and obligations to meet once I get out. Don't you think it's time Elaine starts meeting those obligations now? I feel your concerns about Andrew's safety and happiness, but it's not like you are going anywhere as I would hope you would still be interested in seeing him all the time. I hope this letter makes some kind of sense to you as I'm still trying to make sense of things as to why my life has to always be so complicated.

Love you, sister!

Your brother, Adam

CHAPTER 16

~~~~~~

All our final decisions are made in a state of mind that is not going to last.

—Marcel Proust

The reasoning behind my decision to yield and have Elaine take primary custody of Andrew is murky at best. I know I agonized over the possibility that I could be doing Andrew an injustice if I were to prevent him from being raised by his natural mother. And I wanted to believe that if any child could inspire a woman to be a good mother, Andrew was that child. No matter the reasoning, choosing not to fight for Andrew would prove to be a dire mistake.

On November 29, 2004, after having Andrew living in our home for the past seventeen months, I stepped aside while Elaine took over primary custody of Andrew.

When Elaine rang the doorbell, Andrew must have sensed the finality of it because as I held him in my arms, he clung on to me with both hands. Liam and I glanced at one another as I answered the door, and I invited Elaine in. Without taking a seat, we all chatted in the living room for a moment before Elaine put her arms out to Andrew, "Come see Mommy, my little love bucket," she said in a raspy voice.

Andrew pulled back and began to cry. Liam and I were trying to soothe him when Elaine reached out and pulled him from me. Liam, in obvious distress himself, reassuringly placed his hands on my shoulders as Andrew began to scream and desperately reach out for me. I held Andrew's little hands in mine until he finally managed to calm down. Once he was quiet, Elaine was suddenly eager to leave. She put her free arm around me and in an attempt at sincerity said, "I know this hurts, but you will be seeing him every week, and I'll take good care of him."

I knew prolonging the inevitable would only make it harder for Andrew, Liam and I, so I kissed the salty tears on Andrew's sad fluffy face and walked him and Elaine to the door. I stood at the door, smiling and waving for Andrew's benefit, until they drove out of sight.

Back in the house, I became overwhelmed with sorrow, and those fickle tears of mine poured down my face. Liam held me to him. "It has always been you and me and will always be you and me. I promise we'll get through this," he said.

Even so, the pain on his face was so raw, I knew it wouldn't be that easy. How could it? Elaine and Adam had the luxury of knowing Andrew was safe and secure while in our care. Sadly, we didn't have that same luxury. All we did have was emptiness and relentless worry.

A little over a month after Elaine took primary custody of Andrew, as Liam and I were living in a state of grief, Adam wrote me the following letter. His sincerity may have been genuine, but his words offered no comfort.

January 8, 2005

Dear Crystal,

How are you doing? I hear Elaine is doing pretty well and loves having the baby back. I'm so glad you're staying involved in his life, and again thank you for all you do for him. I also want to thank you for your letters and the money you send me. I really appreciate it; every little bit helps, and I thank you. What a year, huh? I'm sure glad it's over. How was your Christmas and New Year? Things here are the same. Nothing changes. I wouldn't wish this hell hole on anyone. OK, enough crying, at least I'm clean and sober, huh?

I know I have put you through a lot, but when all this started, I had no idea all the bull we would have to go through. I just felt you would be the best for Andrew as you proved me right. I know you got pretty attached to Andrew, and it must have been a hard day when you gave him back to Elaine. But I want you to know you will always be a part of his life as you are with my two other sons. Man, you're a great sister. I love you, Crystal, and I pray for you and yours.

Your brother,

Adam

Elaine and Andrew eventually moved out of the terrible apartment they leased to move into a nice condominium. When I asked how she was able to lease such a nice place without a criminal background or a credit check as I knew neither would work out well for her, she said her boss's friend bought the condo to lease it out and that's how she found it. She added that because her boss vouched for her, his friend felt a credit or background check was not necessary.

Now that Andrew seemed to have a more permanent residence with his very own room and because we wanted to make his transition as easy as possible, Liam and I took the toddler furniture and television that we had at home for him to the condo. Before leaving the condo, for Andrew's safety, Liam added cabinet and drawer safety locks where needed and placed caps over all the unused electrical outlets. Then we would later return with some swivel chairs and a couch to occupy their bare living room. Ultimately, the condo looked like a real home.

Not long after moving into the condo, Elaine called to inform me that Adam got into some trouble in prison and was now spending time in "the hole." Apparently, the trouble had to do with him bartering and or selling contraband. The contraband turned out to be coffee. Elaine seemed to be very upset and asked if I would speak to Adam and try to reason with him as he was now filing a lawsuit against the involved hearing officer. "Adam's claiming that the hearing officer denied him proper procedure," she said.

I promised to speak to Adam, but first, I wanted to review the lawsuit he filed. Elaine sounded overly pleased as she thanked me, so I was compelled to add, "I can't promise that talking to him will make a bit of difference."

Prior to contacting Adam about his alleged lawsuit, I called the Huerfano County Records clerk to first establish that a lawsuit was indeed filed and, should that be the case, to establish if the complaint had standing. The clerk put me on hold for a moment, and when she returned, she said, "Yes a lawsuit was filed by Adam Perez."

Since the courthouse was so far from my home, I asked, "Would it be possible for you to read a couple of pages of the suit to me over the phone? I wouldn't ask if it wasn't important or if your office wasn't so far away from where I live." The clerk was good enough to read me a couple of pages, which was all it took for me to establish that the lawsuit needed to be dropped.

That next weekend, I went to Elaine's condo to pick up Andrew, and as Elaine and I were talking, her phone rang. She answered it, and without preamble, she said, " Crystal's here, do you want to talk to her?" I looked at her with confusion as she handed me the phone.

I took the phone and said warily, "This is Crystal." I was taken aback when I heard Adam's voice on the other end. The call was so unexpected and it had been so long since I last heard his voice, I didn't know how to react. When I finally found my words, they seemed contrived. Our conversation only lasted a couple of minutes. Even so, I felt nothing but relief when it ended, and I was able to hand the phone back to Elaine.

On February 7, 2005, Adam wrote me a letter in response to our earlier and somewhat odd, phone conversation.

February 7, 2005

Dear Crystal,

I received your letter the other day. It was good to hear from you, and I want to thank you for the $100. When I talked to you on the phone, you seemed surprised. Why was it so weird to talk to me? Anyway, in your letter, you said you talked to Elaine, and it would be in my best interest to reconsider. My question is, what did Elaine tell you?

I am so glad you, Liam, and Maria are still and hopefully always will be involved in Andrew's life as he has grown so close to you guys and needs you all in his life. He is lucky to have you guys. I know this whole experience has been very hard on you and yours, but you will always be Andrew's aunt, and he will always be in your lives.

Crystal, I could never thank you enough, so I guess I will just keep thanking you. Anyway I hope things are going good for you guys, and I hope to hear from you.

Love you, sister.

Your brother, Adam

February 11, 2005

Dear Adam,

I hope this letter finds you well. I received your letter, and it is always good to hear from you. You asked me what Elaine told me. She told me about the suit you filed. I feel it is not in your best interest since you should be taking responsibility for your actions in order to get back into the TC program. Filing a suit would only make you look like you are blaming others.

I had a clerk at Huerfano County Courthouse read me some of your five-page complaint letter, and it read as if you didn't have a legitimate complaint because you were caught in the act. Maybe you didn't receive due process, but no matter whom the coffee was for or how they went about reprimanding you, the truth is that you were still breaking the rules, and for that you are responsible. I know I am on the outside looking in and could not even fathom the world you are now in, but I feel my interpretation of the whole scenario is objective.

Your goal should be nothing more than to do your time as quickly as possible and return home to the children who need you as a father and the wife that needs you as a husband. Nothing else should matter or be as important to you at this point. Try and consider that.

Love you.

Your sister, Crystal

Fortunately, in Adam's next letter, he advised that he dropped the lawsuit.

CHAPTER 17

~~~~~~~~~~~~~~~~~~~~~~~~~~~~~~~~~~~~

Opportunity may knock only once, but temptation leans
on the doorbell.

—author unknown

laine seemed to be doing well until June of 2005 when
she called to ask me if I could alter my parenting time
schedule, (Saturday morning to Tuesday morning) to
include Friday nights. She explained she needed to start working
double shifts at her place of employment through the remainder
of the summer months as she recently borrowed some money
from her boss to not only purchase a new car, but also to pay off
the thirteen hundred dollars she owed in restitution. She claimed
that her probation officer advised that since she was doing so well
in her probation, if she were to pay off her restitution, she could
be off probation two years early.

Elaine caught me off guard with the prospect of her early
release from probation; still I agreed without hesitation to the
proposed change as it meant Liam and I would be able to spend
more time with the little guy, and even though Elaine claimed
that the change would only continue through the summer

months, the topic to revert back to the original schedule was never again discussed, so the modified schedule remained and that suited Liam and I just fine.

Soon after the new schedule commenced, Elaine had become steadily and increasingly late in picking up Andrew on her scheduled nights. She had an elaborate excuse for every time she was late, but no matter how off the wall and ill prepared they were, in an effort to maintain some degree of civility with her, Liam and I played along—probably seeming like a couple of chumps to her.

Through the fall months, Elaine's peculiar behavior steadily increased. She no longer invited me into the condo, but instead she and Andrew began waiting for me outside, even on the chilliest of nights. When I questioned her about it, she simply said, "Oh, Andrew wanted to take a little walk while we waited for you."

After months of picking up Andrew from outside of Elaine's condo, she began asking me to meet them at various fast food or retail store parking lots and pick him up from there. It was apparent she was spiraling down, which made me believe she was using again.

Along with Elaine's transformation, Andrew's behavior began to regress. He was having several temper tantrums a day, using inappropriate language and talking often about someone named Frank. In an effort to find out what was going on with Andrew, the next time I picked him up, I walked straight up to Elaine and asked, "Who is Frank?" It was obvious she was caught off guard because she just looked at me for a moment. In order to clarify, I said, "Andrew has talked about a Frank on several occasions. I just want to know who he is."

"Oh, Frank is Andrew's little friend," Elaine said matter-of-factly.

I knew immediately that she was being untruthful, but I pretended to believe her by nodding my head and acting as if it made sense. I then asked if Andrew was still in daycare. She claimed that she's kept Andrew out of daycare for the past couple of weeks because she hasn't been working days lately, but she planned on taking him back that next week. Her answer was quick and spoken with confidence, still I knew she was lying about this too and understood if I wanted the truth, I needed to look elsewhere.

As the Christmas holiday of 2005 quickly approached, Elaine and I agreed that Andrew would stay overnight at my house on Christmas Eve, and she would come by and spend time with him on Christmas morning. Knowing how unreliable she could be, I didn't convey any of this to Andrew and rightly so as Elaine turned out to be a no-show. However, she called later on that day and asked me to take Andrew to my dad's house so she could visit with him there.

Even though I was unhappy with her, because it was Christmas, I agreed to take Andrew over to Dad's house that afternoon. Elaine wasn't there when we arrived; however, she showed up shortly thereafter. But, even though she was physically present, she wasn't connected or engaged where Andrew was concerned. In fact, she spent the whole visit whispering on the phone to someone.

When Andrew and I decided it was time to go home, Elaine followed us out to the car. While I was strapping Andrew in his car seat, she asked to use my phone. I found her request odd since she obviously had her own phone. Still, I handed her my phone. She punched in a number and waited a moment. "Hi, Mom, it's me, Elaine," she said to my surprise.

I don't know what Claudia said to Elaine or if it was even Claudia whom she spoke with. In any case, after the short call, she handed me the phone and began to cry. I understood a mother's resolve to keep her disturbed daughter out of her life. Still, in that moment, I felt sorry for Elaine.

A couple of weeks after the Christmas holiday, Adam wrote me the following letter to inform me, amongst other things, that he had been returned to the minimum security prison where he was initially incarcerated, prior to being kicked out of the Department of Corrections' therapeutic community program.

January 6, 2006

Dear Crystal,

I wanted to let you know that they moved me back to Arrowhead yesterday. I'm glad about it, and now I can finish the TC program and get on with it. I hope you had a good Christmas and New Year. I thank you for the Christmas card and money; it helps out a lot. Over here in Arrowhead, you can't mail money orders any more. So when you mail money, you have to send it by Internet www.jpay.com or by a toll-free phone payment 1-800-574-jpay or by Western Union 1-800-634-3422 or at any Ace cash express under JPay. I hope this is convenient, and I'm keeping track of all the money you sent me because I plan on paying you back every dime.

There are a lot of other things you do for me and my boys that money could never buy, and I will never forget it. Don't even trip though because I know it was in God's plan for me to go through this so I can get back on the right path. God bless the broken path that brought me straight to him. Also, he knew I had to get saved myself before I could be any good for my kids. Anyway, I'm excited about the future, and I look at what I'm going through as a radical goodness restored to my soul. I try not to dwell on the past, but I just want you to know I realize I am lucky to be alive by God's grace. I will never let him or my family down again. I love you, and you and yours are always in my prayers. I hate asking, but if you can, could you send a few dollars? Because my money off my books in Walsenburg won't reach me for a least a month.

Thank you.

God bless you.

Adam

Regardless of Adam's plan to pay me back every dime I sent him during his prison sentence, it would never happen.

A month after Adam was moved back to Arrowhead, Liam and I drove down to Elaine's condo to drop Andrew off after our visit. When we arrived, Elaine was waiting for us outside. As I unstrapped Andrew from his car seat, she informed us that she found a new place for her and Andrew to live and explained that they had to be out of the condo by February 13, 2006 because her landlord found a buyer.

This was not surprising to me as Elaine told me sometime earlier that her landlord was planning on putting the condo up for sale, so she was in the process of looking for a new place. I asked for her new address, but she claimed she didn't have it on her. However, she advised that she would call me later with it. Feeling like something was amiss, I asked for her new phone number. She recited a number, and Liam jotted it down.

Three days later, I answered the phone and was surprised to hear Bianca's voice on the other end. She said that she was calling to inform me that a guy named Pete contacted her, claiming he was concerned for Andrew's safety. Apparently Pete was given Bianca's phone number from a mutual friend of his and Elaine's.

According to Bianca, Pete informed her he was in the process of evicting Elaine from his condo. He claimed he bought the condo so Elaine and Andrew could have a place to stay as he felt sorry for them having to live in the apartment on Yarrow Street, which was somewhat of a slum. He also claimed he bought Elaine a cell phone and a car and that Elaine agreed to make the payments on the condo and the car and reimburse him for her cell phone bills, which she had not done for some time.

Since I was aware that Bianca had a knack for stretching the truth, before she could say anything further, I asked her for Pete's number so I could speak to him directly. Bianca read me the number; I thanked her and immediately phoned Pete.

The voice on the other end, which sounded old and maybe even intoxicated said, "This is Pete." As I introduced myself, he interjected. "I'm aware of who you are and know that you help take care of Andrew. That's why I wanted to get in touch with you. I've been worried about little Andrew."

"How do you know Elaine?"

He said that he met Elaine in a park, and they had become good friends.

"Why are you worried about Andrew?"

"Elaine started dating a guy named Frank this past summer. Since then, she has neglected Andrew and neglected to pay her bills. I'm having her evicted from my condo on the thirteenth of February, so if you want, you can go by and pick up Andrew's things."

While our discussion progressed, I began to feel like I was talking to a boyfriend scorned rather than someone concerned about Andrew. Trying to understand the depth of their relationship and remembering what Bianca said earlier, I said, "Did you purchase the condo just so Elaine and Andrew would have a place to stay?"

"Elaine had been crying that she couldn't find a place to rent with her felonies and all, so I finally just bought the condo and gave her a lease for half of the monthly payment, five hundred and fifty dollars."

"Wow, you're a good friend," I said.

Ignoring my comment, Pete continued. "Then she was crying that she needed a car to take Andrew back and forth to daycare and for the traveling that her job required. So I ended up buying her a car too, a Saturn. Well then, the Saturn wasn't good enough for her, so I ended up trading it in for a Pontiac Grand Am."

"I've seen the Grand Am. It's a nice car."

"You know, she was keeping up on all her payments until she met Frank. Then no matter how much I asked about the payments she owed me for the car and the rent, she just had one excuse after another on why she didn't have the money. After a while, she even stopped answering my phone calls, and I'm the one who bought her the damn phone."

Thinking a bit ahead, I half-asked and half-stated, "Her cell phone is in your name?"

"Yes, she said she needed one for her job."

I thought about this for a moment, wondering whether or not I should ask him for a copy of Elaine's phone records, but before I could make up my mind, Pete continued: "It got to the point where Elaine wasn't making any of the payments we agreed on. Her latest excuse was that she was paying off her court costs and restitution because she was being released from her probation early."

"She told me that too, do you think it's true?"

"I don't know if it's true or not, but I finally got fed up with her excuses and had a friend pick up the Grand Am without telling her," he said, sounding pleased with himself.

Unfortunately, even though Pete had the paperwork proving that he purchased the vehicle, because Elaine convinced him to put the title in her name, the authorities made him return it to her.

"So that's what happened," I said, recalling a time when Elaine came by to drop Andrew off, and I noticed one of the windows in the Grand Am was completely broken out. "When I asked Elaine about the broken window, she said the car was stolen, and when it was returned to her, I assumed by the police, the window was broken out. She even mentioned that she found some cigarette burns in the carpet, maybe in an effort to make her story sound more authentic. Anyhow, I can't say I believed her, but because I was concerned about Andrew riding around in a car without a window during those cold winter months, I had my husband price the window, then gave her three hundred dollars to get it fixed."

Pete scoffed. "Well, you wasted your money because I went to the condo this past week and found a note on the door that said, 'Elaine, call your bondsman immediately,' so I wrote down the name and number and gave Jerry from American Bail Bonds a call. Jerry, who said his business is located in Pueblo, informed me that Elaine put up the title to the Grand Am as collateral to secure Frank's bail bond, at which time she also promised him some cash, cash he never received. So now he is trying to track down Frank because he owes him a lot of money, especially after skipping bail."

"So, you're saying Elaine signed over the Grand Am to bail Frank out of jail?"

"Yes, and unfortunately I'm still making the payments on that car," Pete said sounding embarrassed.

Now I understood what fueled Pete's initial phone call to Bianca. Elaine deceived and defrauded him, and now he wanted to settle the score. I felt sorry for this elderly man; still, it sickened me to know that I live in a world where a child's ill treatment is only revealed as an act of vengeance. Needing time to consider all that Pete conveyed, I thanked him for the information and asked if I could call him again at a later time. He agreed that I could call again but advised that when he's resting he doesn't answer the phone.

Immediately after my conversation with Pete, I attempted to call Elaine only to find the number she gave me was not in service. I tried again, thinking it may have been a mistake, but to no avail. I kicked myself for not trying the number earlier. I then called Liam to see if maybe I had misread one or any of the numbers he wrote down, but he confirmed that the number I called was what Elaine recited to him. At that, I worried that maybe Elaine ran away with Andrew.

Liam, also worried, said, "I'll call Sandra, then drive over to the condo to check things out."

Upon Sandra's advisement, Liam called the sheriff's office to see if a police officer could meet him at Elaine's. They agreed to send someone out.

When Liam arrived at the condo, he could hear Elaine's two dogs barking. Liam knocked on the door, but no one answered. Because the dogs, both pit bulls, shredded the blinds, Liam was able to look in the window. A police officer arrived, and he too looked in the window. They were shocked to see that everything in the living room was chewed to pieces, including the couch and chairs, with their stuffing strewn about.

Elaine's upstairs neighbor came down to address the barking. After introducing himself, Liam asked him if he knew Elaine and Andrew. The neighbor, who introduced himself as Stephen, said he did know them but hasn't seen them for a couple of days. Then he went on to say that he heard the dogs barking that previous day and wondered if they had been fed. Concerned by their relentless barking, he decided to let himself in to check on them. When he entered the condo, not elaborating on how he entered, he found that the dogs were so hungry they were actually eating the walls.

Liam explained our situation to Stephen and the officer and also the concerns we had for Andrew. Stephen said that he too had concerns for Andrew. "One night when Elaine and I were both outside smoking and talking, out of the blue, she told me that she would kill me if I ever snitched on her. I still have no idea what she was talking about and just figured she was on something."

CHAPTER 18

No greater grief than to remember days of gladness when sorrow is at hand.

—Friedrich von Schiller

The police officer went on his way after advising there wasn't anything he could do without speaking to Elaine. Then Stephen and Liam exchanged phone numbers as Stephen agreed he would give us a call if or when Elaine showed up at the condo.

On his way home, Liam called to inform me on everything that happened that evening. Consequently, I called Sandra to convey the information to her. "Since Andrew is now under Elaine's custody, you should get a hold of social services and file a complaint. Let them know that Elaine is being evicted and that several individuals have told you she may be using again," she advised.

With uncertainty, after speaking with Sandra I contacted Jefferson County Social Services to file a complaint. The caseworker I spoke with advised that child protection services would look into my complaint, which offered me some relief.

I was uneasy when Bianca called again that next day to inform me that Lily, who was apparently one of Elaine's estranged friends, wanted to meet with the two of us to divulge some information about Elaine, as she too was concerned for Andrew's safety. I agreed to the meeting, which was to be held that next morning at a Denny's in Lakewood. For the remainder of the evening, I was on edge, eagerly waiting for Elaine to call as she knew I was expecting my parenting time to begin at 7:00 p.m. that evening, but she never called.

Where are they? Is Andrew safe? These were the incessant questions running through my head, making it impossible for me to get any sleep. Thankfully, the long and arduous night came to an end as the sun came up. And though I was sleep-deficient, with great expectations, I jumped into the shower and got dressed for the upcoming meeting with Lily, who may possibly have information on Andrew's whereabouts.

I arrived at Denny's just before noon. Under the impression that only Bianca and I would be meeting with Lily, I was surprised to see Bianca, Dad, a friend of theirs, and my sister Anna all sitting in a booth ordering breakfast. The scene was very unsettling to me as the joyous family breakfast left me feeling alone in my concerns for Andrew. I sat at the booth adjacent to theirs and looked out toward the door, ready to run after Lily lest she was to look upon the family gathering and decide against having the meeting.

When a red-headed woman walked into the restaurant, I knew immediately that she was Lily as she was the same woman waiting with Elaine when I dropped Andrew off downtown soon after Elaine left CiCore. I walked over to greet her and also to caution her about the family gathering. We approached the booth where my family was having breakfast, and I cringed as hot sauce was being passed from one person to the other. I introduced Lily to everyone, then ushered her to the adjacent booth.

Lily was fair in complexion, shorter than average in height, and was built like a gymnast. Her hair was cut short in a bobbed style and was red in color. She was cute, but not beautiful, and talked in a nonchalant fashion no matter the topic.

As we sat down, Lily immediately started fiddling with her cell phone. She explained that the battery died, so she needed a place to charge it. As we were looking for an outlet, Bianca and Anna joined us in the booth. I asked Lily for her consent to tape the meeting. She shrugged. "That's fine."

I removed the small tape recorder from my handbag and placed it on the table. Before we began the discussion at hand, Lily advised that she was aware that Pete had spoken to both Bianca and me about Frank. In turn, I advised that since learning of Elaine's eviction from the condo, I had no idea where Elaine had taken Andrew and finding him was my main objective.

Once we were all situated, I turned on the tape recorder, and the allegations or perhaps enlightenment began. "When Elaine moved the stuff out of Frank's house, I located the storage place they were using, and their stuff was still there," Lily said.

I wanted to ask why she was looking for their storage place but refrained. "How long ago was this?" I asked.

"November 21, 2005," she said, then claimed that the storage unit was rented in Frank's brother's name.

I would later find that the storage unit was necessary because the house in which Frank was residing was raided by the police. Consequently, Frank was unable to return to the house to obtain his things. So Elaine obtained them for him and moved everything into the storage unit.

Looking around, Lily said, "I need to plug in my phone because there's some numbers on it, such as Julie Stevens, who may still talk to Elaine."

We all got to our feet and began looking for an outlet. After finding one, Lily plugged in the phone, and we all sat down again.

Lily turned to face me. "How can she (referring to Elaine) keep Andrew away from you? Don't you have a court order?"

"Yes," I replied nodding my head.

"So then, are they (referring to the court) going to press anything on her?"

"I don't know what's going to happen. Right now, I'm kind of at a loss."

"Well, I know Elaine is definitely on drugs."

"Do you know what she's on?"

"Crack cocaine. She smokes crack."

"Yeah, I heard that's her thing," I said, trying to sound hip.

"Remember when Elaine lived on Twelfth and Yarrow? That apartment belonged to Rita first. And the management is on site, so that would be an easy way to find out Rita's last name," Lily said changing the subject.

"What? Can you say that again?" I said confused.

Lily said slowly this time, "Remember when Elaine lived on Twelfth and Yarrow?"

I nodded in response.

"Well, she took that apartment over from her friend Rita because Rita moved out to move in with her boyfriend. Anyhow, the management is right on site. They're a young couple, and I don't think they would have any problem giving you Rita's last name."

The apartment that Lily was referring to was the apartment Elaine leased prior to moving into the condo, the apartment Pete referred to as a slum. Seeing the place myself, slum was a fair description.

In an effort to understand what Lily was trying to convey, I considered her words for a moment. "Rita may know where Elaine and Andrew are staying," Lily explained.

Finally getting it, with raised eyebrows, I nodded in comprehension.

"I never met Rita. I know that Elaine has been friends with her for a long time and that she's a hair dresser." Lily took a moment to tinker with her phone, then looked up at me. "Do you know where I think Elaine may have gone?"

Without waiting for a response, "To Frank's mom's house," she said.

Lily explained that Elaine was very close to Frank's mom, and with Elaine being on drugs, it was hard to tell who she would have kept in contact with other than Frank's family. "And like I said, I know Elaine went and got all of Frank's stuff out of his house, and he had some pretty valuable stuff."

"And where was his house?" Bianca said.

"On Elliott Circle. In fact, they (referring to the police) did a search there. They actually did surveillance on it for a long time before they caught him."

"So was he manufacturing meth and selling it?"

"He was just selling it, and he sold cocaine too."

"Because I seen that he has a rap sheet," Bianca added.

Lily nodded. "I was the one who got arrested with Frank this last time. I worked for an escort service on and off with Elaine for years. I can't remember if Frank called the service. I think he did. No, I can't remember where I met him, and I don't know why since he tried to destroy my life. But anyway, I had a boyfriend at the time and Frank was like, 'I would like to take you out.' And I was like, 'Here is my business card, but I'm not available like that.' He called me a couple of times, and so I picked him up one night at that Valley Inn Hotel right at the Boulder Turnpike. He was like, 'I need to run by somewhere.' And he had his guitar with him and whatever. So I took him to Alameda and Stuart, and he had me drive down an alley and park."

Without being specific on Frank's purpose or destination, whether it was a residence or a business, Lily said, "He walked in, came back out, and got in the car. I started driving down the alley, and of course when you get to the end of an alley, you should stop, so I did, and there was a Denver police car right there, and he motioned for me to go. I was like, 'You have the right of way, so you go.' But he wouldn't go, so I went ahead of him, and I was like, 'They are going to pull us over because my plates are from my other car.'

"So Frank started freaking out, and I'm not stupid, I know he didn't work a nine-to-five job and he wore more gold then Mr. T., but what exactly he had on him I really didn't know. So the police pulled us over, and Frank right away said, 'I'm screwed.' I myself had a weapons charge, so right away they pulled us out of the car, and they were like, 'Do you have any weapons?' I was like, 'No sir.' So then they searched us and put us back in the car. Frank had been drinking a beer before we got pulled over, and he was like, 'Tell me what they are doing.' I was looking in my rearview mirror, and I was like, 'Why? You aren't doing anything, are you?' He was like, 'Well, I want to put this beer can under the seat.' Then the cops came back and said they were going to search our car, and I was like, 'Of course you are.'

"So we were escorted and placed into two separate police cars. They started searching the car, and all the sudden, this cop pulls out like a half of pound of coke and meth from underneath Frank's seat. I was like, 'Can't you guys take fingerprints? Because honestly it's not mine.' Well, I already have three escapes from chopping off ankle bracelets [electronic ankle monitors], and I have a menacing with a deadly weapon's charge from when I was eighteen, and so that's like four felonies, and I knew that if I tried to get on the stand and say I didn't have a clue of what was going on, it wouldn't be believable.

"My public defender was like, 'You know it doesn't take a rocket scientist to figure out that you weren't the drug dealer. It was all under his feet. He had three thousand dollars in cash on him, but it's not like you are completely innocent—I mean you did know or you had an idea of what was going on.' So the DA's office came to me and made me an offer of two years probation if I would testify against Frank. So that's what I did. I took drug court probation."

Dad, who had been listening in, said, "Who is this Pete guy? Is he the retired guy?"

"Yeah, his wife died about six years ago, and he, I guess, had called the escort service. I don't know how many people he's seen through the service," Lily replied.

I chuckled because Pete told me that he met Elaine in a park, and I believed him. "What escort service did you and Elaine work for? Is she still working there?"

"Elaine was on the Internet for a service in Pueblo. It's called Suite Time Services. A guy named Clay runs it out of a Holiday Inn, but he directs calls up here," Lily said.

"Do you know Clay's last name?"

"No, I don't, but he has an Internet site," she said handing me a business card. "Here's the Internet address that links to the escort service."

Knowing Elaine had many aliases, I asked, "What name was she using?"

"Angel." Lily chuckled. I wasn't surprised by the name since Adam used it when he first introduced me to Elaine. Lily went on to say that she knew Elaine was currently on drugs and claimed that she relapsed on her last birthday, which I knew would have been in August of 2005, just two months after Elaine informed me that once she paid her restitution, her probation would be terminated two years early.

Lily acknowledged that Elaine had actually cleaned up her act for some time, but after meeting Frank, she went back to her old ways. "I even saw Elaine smoking a crack pipe while Andrew was sitting on her lap." The thought of this immediately brought me to tears.

Lily took a moment to allow me to compose myself, and then she spoke of Frank. She claimed that Frank was Elaine's new love interest. "I met Frank first, and we became somewhat of a couple, but when I introduced Elaine to Frank, around May of 2005, the two of them hit it off, and soon after, Elaine was giving everything up for him. I can't believe it. I've known Elaine for a lot of years, and she has done a lot of things, but she gave up everything for this guy. Pete bought that condo and car for her, and she gave it all up for Frank."

I chimed in, "I asked Elaine who Frank was because Andrew had mentioned him, and she told me that Frank was Andrew's little friend."

Lily chuckled. "Frank is a drug dealer," she said with certainty, "who walks around with a semiautomatic weapon."

"Do you know why Elaine has kept Andrew out of day care?" I said.

"Since Frank was always using her car, she wasn't able to take him to day care, so she eventually lost her CCCAP (the Colorado Child Care Assistance Program). Afterwards, she just had Frank watch him during the day."

"Great, the drug dealer with the semiautomatic weapon," I said sarcastically. "What about Elaine's job? Isn't it legitimate? She did give me a few of her pay stubs."

"Elaine was actually doing web cam porn for this guy named Kenny who owns the janitorial service she claimed to be working for."

Hearing this, I recalled a time when I went to pick Andrew up at the condo and a tall Hispanic guy was in Elaine's living room idly fiddling with a newly placed computer. Knowing I'd be curious, Elaine had said hastily, "Yeah, this is a coworker that my boss sent over to install the computer."

"You have a new computer?" I said.

"Actually, my boss wanted it installed, so I can start doing some bookkeeping for him," Elaine replied.

I looked over at Lily and said, "I took a long look at her so called coworker who was dressed all in black. He looked like a night club owner in his silk shirt, perfectly pleated cuffed pants, and wing-tipped shoes. There is no way that guy cleaned office buildings."

Lily nodded at me as if to say, "So you're finally catching on."

Our meeting was coming to a close when Maria called to let me know that Stephen, Elaine's upstairs neighbor, called and said Elaine and Andrew were at the condo. "I'm on my way there now," I told Maria.

I thanked Lily for the information and hurried out the door. Everything that Lily said was running through my mind as I drove to Elaine's condo on autopilot. As soon as I drove into the parking lot, I ran to Elaine's front door. Trying hard to maintain my composure, I knocked, perhaps a little too hard. Elaine was on the phone when she came to the door. She was obviously annoyed by my visit, but still moved aside, stepping over some packing boxes piled next to the door, to allow me into the condo. As I entered, I was hit with a strong odor of urine. I looked around and was shocked to find the place in complete shambles. The couch and chairs were chewed to pieces and the stuffing was scattered everywhere.

Trying to hold back my tears, I turned to her and asked, "Where's Andrew?"

Before she could answer, I spotted the little guy in her bedroom. He was quietly playing with two action figures among chewed-up toys, remnants of chewed-up furniture, and piles of dog feces. The tears welled up in my eyes as I stood watching him for a moment. Then softly I said his name, "Andrew."

He looked up at me with the biggest smile and put his arms out to me yelling, "Auntie." I picked him up. "Are we going to your house, Auntie?" he said.

"I don't know, sweetie. I just came to check on you."

I walked over to Elaine who was now off the phone and leaned into her to prevent Andrew from hearing. "You should be ashamed of yourself. How could you let everything go to hell like this?" I said with disgust.

Elaine tried to reason that she was moving, and she couldn't help what the dogs had done since there was no place to take pit bulls, and she didn't want them put to sleep.

"They would be better off being put to sleep than slowly starving to death," I said maybe a bit too harshly. She began to dispute my words, but I didn't allow her to. "Your neighbor Stephen told me that these dogs have been barking so much for the past couple of days that he decided to check on them. And when he did, he found that they were so hungry they were actually eating the walls." I looked at one of the living room walls, which was chewed up, and said wryly, "Looks like he was telling the truth." Elaine just looked at me coldly. Unmoved I said firmly, "You know very well I have parenting time on Saturdays, so I'm taking Andrew home with me."

I went to move past her with Andrew in my arms but was jerked back when she grabbed a hold of Andrew's arm. "I will pull his little arm right out of the socket if you don't put him down," she swore. Andrew began crying and even though he was crying for me, I knew I had to put him down.

I realized she wouldn't stop at anything, even hurting Andrew, to keep him from going with me. Crestfallen, I looked at his little face as I put him down. "I'm sorry, buddy, I have to go, but I will see you soon, okay?" Even though I was leaving, Elaine was cursing at me and yelling for me to get out of her house. Then oddly enough, once I walked out the front door, she starting yelling for me to come back so she could "kick my ass". Having heard enough of her harsh words, I turned and did exactly what I shouldn't have done—I yelled back at her, telling her to shut her ugly mouth, among other things. When I turned back around, I practically ran into the Lakewood Police officer who had just arrived.

The officer asked me to explain what was going on. I informed him of Elaine's eviction situation, the state of the condo, and the fact that Andrew has parenting time with me on Saturdays. "I tried to leave with him, but she stopped me by grabbing his arm and threatened to pull it out of the socket, so I had to let him go," I said. The officer asked if I had the court order confirming the parenting time schedule. Not wanting to get him too confused by trying to explain the stipulation agreement, I told him that I didn't have anything with me, and what I did have, referring to the stipulation, does not include a written parenting time schedule as our schedule was agreed upon verbally.

The police officer looked at me with uncertainty. So idiotically, I then made an effort to try and explain that when custodianship was moved from me to Elaine, in accordance with the stipulation, it was done without a court hearing, and so my parenting schedule was agreed upon verbally and not part of a court order.

Saying I didn't have a court ordered parenting schedule out loud made me realize how foolish I've been to ever believe a woman such as Elaine could be trustworthy enough to honor a verbal agreement or any kind of agreement for that matter.

Noticing that the officer was looking truly baffled, I finally stopped talking to his relief. He then advised that I get the parenting time schedule written down and into a court order to avoid any further altercations or confusion. Then he turned from me and said he was going to speak to Elaine and asked me to wait outside. When the officer went in to talk with Elaine, I turned to the second officer, Officer Morales, who informed me that he was one of the officers that picked up Frank that prior Sunday on a warrant. He added, "Elaine was with Frank at the time."

"Why didn't Elaine get locked up too? Wasn't she harboring a fugitive or something like that?" I said. But before Officer Morales could answer, the other officer returned.

Whatever Elaine said to him managed to change his demeanor toward me. "Since you don't have any court papers or a court order proving your parenting time, you and your family will have to leave the premises," He said coldly. I thought to myself, *How can I leave? I'm already half out of mind with worry. Worried Elaine may leave town with Andrew and I will never see him again. What if I never see him again? How can I leave?*

"That place is not suitable for a child. Did you at least make that determination?" I said desperately. Astonishingly, the officer said that there wasn't anything wrong with the place. "What about the dog feces?" I retorted.

"I didn't notice any dog feces," he said smugly. I could see that I was fighting a losing battle with this guy, so I turned to Officer Morales and asked him if he could please take a look for himself.

Officer Morales looked over at the other officer and then back to me and said, "I have to go with what he says."

I could feel my face go flush and the tears well up in my eyes. "Please, just take a look," I implored. But my words fell on deaf ears. Filled with disenchantment and anguish, I looked back at Andrew, waved, and said with false merriment, "I'll see you soon, buddy."

Once I got home and pulled myself together, I thought about those poor dogs. Worried they may be left in the condo to starve, I contacted the Jefferson County sheriff's office to inform them of the neglected dogs. The lady I spoke with advised that someone would be out to take a look. I offered to take the older pit bull temporarily should they need an interim home for him as we were familiar with one another.

I never received a call back from the sheriff's office, but later learned that Elaine had moved the dogs out of the condo. Where they were being kept was unknown to me. However, Elaine would later inform me that the puppy ran away.

The morning after the incident at the condo, I called social services to check the status of their investigation. The same caseworker I spoke to just days before, who was all set to pursue an investigation, now seemed annoyed by my call. She said that her office didn't plan on taking any further action regarding my complaint as my claims were unfounded. I began to question her resolve when she advised that she could not discuss the case with me any further and actually disconnected the call. I could not believe it. Did that woman actually screen out my complaint then hang up on me?

I immediately contacted Sandra to inform her of my brief interaction with social services. As if already expecting nothing more than apathy from them, Sandra wasn't surprised and said she would file a motion with the court to restrict Elaine's parenting time. The motion was filed on February 15, 2006.

To my relief, the court found that the motion established that unsupervised parenting with Elaine would place Andrew in imminent physical or emotional danger and ordered that any parenting time between Elaine and Andrew be supervised, pending a hearing on the motion, which was set for February 22, 2006.

CHAPTER 19

~~~~~~

Three things cannot be long hidden: the sun, the moon, and the truth.

—Buddha

There were so many conflicting stories and information I'd been given that I wasn't sure what or who to believe. My instincts were telling me that Andrew was not safe, but at this point, I wasn't even sure if I could trust my own instincts. Was I mistaking heartfelt aspirations for instincts? Regardless, I felt I owed it to Andrew to get to the truth.

Consequently, I decided to conduct my own fact-or-fiction investigation using the taped information I obtained from the meeting with Lily and the information I received from Pete, Claudia, and Stephen. However, first and foremost, I had to locate Andrew because even though her parenting time was restricted by the court, Elaine still had Andrew in her care and hidden from me as she, being a career criminal, didn't take things like court orders too seriously.

Beginning my investigation, I took Lily's advice and drove down to Elaine's old apartment on Yarrow Street to meet with the couple that managed the apartments. With my court documents in hand, I explained the situation. They seemed empathetic to my painful dilemma and without hesitation informed me that Rita's last name was Sands. I graciously thanked them and went on my way.

As soon as I arrived home I got on the Internet and made a search on Rita Sands. All I could come up with was her address, so I went to one of those sites that charges a fee for unlisted phone and cell numbers and was surprised to find that it worked. Mom, who was helping to locate Andrew, called the cell phone number and left a message with Rita to call her. I then called Rita's home phone, but there was no answer. Desperately, I tried several more times, and fortunately, Rita finally answered. Overjoyed to finally get an answer, I said without reproach, "Rita, this is Crystal, Elaine's sister-in-law. I just want to know if Elaine and Andrew are staying there with you and if Andrew's all right."

"How did you get my number?"

"Does it really matter?" I said gently.

She seemed to soften at that. "Andrew is here and he's fine, so don't call me again," she said before disconnecting the call. Even knowing that she could have been lying, I was still overwhelmed with relief.

My next order of business was to find out what I could on Elaine's so-called employer. I checked the Colorado Secretary of State Business website and found the company's mailing address, phone number, and owner's name, which was Kenny, just as Lily said. As I wrote down the information, I realized the company's mailing address at that time was the same as the condo Elaine was recently evicted from. Confused, I decided to give Kenny a call. I was expecting someone to answer with the company's name, but instead a man's voice said, "Hello."

I asked to speak to Kenny Simms, and the man's voice said, "This is Kenny." Trying to remain calm, I managed to introduce myself and added that Elaine Perez was my sister-in-law. Kenny remained silent for a moment and then asked in an overly friendly voice, "What can I do for you?" From his tone, I could tell he knew exactly who I was.

"Hi, Mr. Simms, I'm calling to see how Elaine is doing in her position." Instead of saying something like, "All employee information is confidential," he told me that Elaine was doing quite well in her position. Realizing that he was willing to talk, I decided to catch him off guard. "Can you tell me why your company is registered under Elaine's address?" I said.

He was obviously taken aback as he remained silent for a moment. "I don't know, maybe because I had the Internet installed at her condo," he finally said.

I knew that couldn't possibly be the reason, but I went along with it. "Why does Elaine need Internet service for a janitorial position?"

"So she could get e-mails I suppose," he said in a none-of-your-business tone.

"E-mails from whom?"

Sounding annoyed, he said, "I don't get involved in my employee's affairs."

None of what he was saying was making sense. In an earlier conversation about her new computer, Elaine said that it was installed so that she could do some bookkeeping for her boss. Yet this man, who I assume is her boss, has yet to mention anything regarding Elaine administering his bookkeeping. I took a moment to consider this. "Did you also have a web cam installed at Elaine's condo?" I said.

"No, I did not install a web cam in Elaine's condo. I don't have that kind of business," he said in a defensive tone.

I thought to myself, *Then why jump to the assumption that I'm implying that a webcam would be used for something unscrupulous? After all, don't legitimate businesses use webcams for meetings?*

In an effort to keep the conversation going, I apologized for whatever he felt I was implying. The apology seemed to pacify him, so I continued, "Elaine told me she borrowed money from you to buy a car and that you have been allowing her to work double shifts so she can pay you back as soon as possible."

He took a moment to respond. "Yes, Elaine did borrow money from me and quickly paid me back," he said hesitantly.

I took a calming breath, then said, "I thought you didn't get personally involved with your employees?" Before he could respond, I said, "Since Pete bought Elaine the car, why did you lend her money?"

I must have hit a nerve because he was no longer able to compose himself. "Who is Pete?" he said angrily.

I ignored his question. "Has Elaine really been doing janitorial work for you and has she actually been working double shifts or any shift for that matter?" I pressed. At that he said he didn't wish to talk to me any further and slammed the phone down. I was shocked. Not from how he slammed the phone down, but because it took him so long to do so.

Moving forward in the investigation, I looked over Elaine's cell phone records, which Pete mailed to me earlier upon my request. I punched in one of the frequently called numbers and found it to be the number to the escort service of which Lily claimed Elaine and she both worked for several years off and on. Then I looked up the website information I obtained from Lily and quickly found a disturbing webpage. The webpage had a seductive picture of Elaine and a heading that read "Massage by Angel" and advertised one-hour hot oil massages. Within the webpage, Elaine introduces herself as Angel and states that she works out of her cozy downtown apartment. The bottom of the webpage provided the booking information.

I called the booking number, and a man, who introduced himself as Clay answered. I recalled Lily saying that a guy named Clay owned Suite Time Services. I introduced myself as Angel's friend and said that I've been trying to get a hold of Angel for some time now. "A mutual friend of mine and Angel's thought she may be working for you."

"Angel did work for me over the summer, but then she took off without paying the money she owed me, and I haven't heard from her since," Clay said with obvious irritation. I assumed the money he was speaking of was his booking fee.

"Well, she owes me money too." I lied.

He warmed at that and said, "Well, good luck getting it."

"Yeah, you too," I said. Then I thanked him for his time and hung up.

Unfortunately, every disturbing thing that was conveyed to me about Elaine had checked out thus far. However, I still had one more person to contact, and that was Jerry Law, who Pete claimed was Frank's bonding agent. I wanted to contact Jerry to see if he could corroborate Pete and Lily's claim that Elaine put her Pontiac Grand Am up as collateral for Frank's bond.

Sadly, Jerry did corroborate their claim and also claimed that Frank still owed him a lot of money. He explained that when Frank and Elaine handed over the car, they agreed to give him an additional five thousand dollars in cash since that would have met and secured Frank's bond. However, they didn't follow through. So Jerry tried to get a hold of them on several occasions, but apparently, they didn't want to be found, so he ended up having to sell the car and only got six thousand dollars for it, which evidently didn't meet the amount Frank owed him.

At the end of our conversation, Jerry was adamant when he expressed that he felt nothing more than pure loathing for Elaine and Frank. "I have never known anyone who could lie as much or as well as them two," he said.

I hung up the phone wearily. I found no comfort in knowing that my instincts regarding Andrew's safety were correct. In fact, with Elaine's troubled lover thrown into the mix, my concern for Andrew had intensified.

CHAPTER 20

What we anticipate seldom occurs; what we least expected
generally happens.

—Benjamin Disraeli

The hearing on the motion to restrict Elaine's parenting
time took place on February 22, 2006. Stephen, Lily, and
I were all signed on to testify; however, Lily was a no
show. Regardless, Stephen and I testified that we believed Elaine
was using illegal narcotics and that such beliefs were based on
our direct observations of Elaine's physical appearance, her odd
behavior, and even odder statements.

Elaine, who appeared at the hearing pro se, said that she met
with the Department of Social Services that very morning and
voluntarily submitted a urinalysis drug test, which came back
negative. She then claimed she hasn't used drugs in four years,
which even contradicted the statement she made on the Family
Social History and Assessment Summary of 2003, in which she
states that she hasn't used since 1990. However, with Elaine
voluntarily submitting a drug test that morning, which of course

came back negative as it was preplanned, the magistrate seemed to be leaning in her favor.

Also discussed was Elaine's total disregard for our agreed parenting time schedule. Sandra requested that the parenting schedule be put in writing and be made an order of the court of which the magistrate agreed.

In the end, as Sandra recommended, I agreed to vacate my motion under the conditions that Elaine transports Andrew to me on February 24, 2006 for makeup parenting time and continues submitting UAs at the Department of Social Services. I also requested that Elaine agree to submit to a hair follicle drug test, which are considered to be more accurate than urine for pinpointing long-term and low-level drug use as they are not affected by brief periods of abstinence as urinalysis tests.

Aware that refusing to submit to a hair follicle test would make her appear like she had something to hide, Elaine advised the court that she would not agree to a hair follicle test until she consults with an attorney. The court informed her that the consultation should occur forthwith. The case was then continued to March 31, 2006, for a review hearing.

As ordered, Elaine dropped Andrew off at my house on Friday, February 24, 2006. Andrew was happy to see both Liam and I; however, he seemed distant. When I asked him what was wrong, he shrugged and said, "Nothing."

"Are you mad at me?" Again he shrugged.

"You know you can tell me or Uncle Liam anything that's troubling you because no matter what it is, we will never stop loving you or caring for you."

He looked up at me. "My mom said you went to jail because you were bad when you tried to take me."

I was stunned by his words. I got down on my knees to be eye level with him, and looked at him reassuringly. "I was not in jail, and I'm sorry that you thought I was because that would be a pretty scary thing for a little boy like you to think."

He smiled at me. "Auntie, I'm glad you didn't go to jail."

Although he seemed to believe that I really didn't go to jail, he asked several questions relating to jail and bad people and things of that nature throughout his visit, sadly, the kind of things a three-year-old shouldn't be concerned with.

Two weeks had lapsed since the last hearing, and Elaine still had not consulted with an attorney regarding my request for her to take a hair follicle test. So on March 8, 2006, Sandra filed a motion for Elaine to submit a hair follicle drug test.

The motion definitely hit a nerve because on March 30, 2006, Elaine filed a four-page response, which was not only lengthy but way on the ugly side. It included my alleged lack of standing stating, "Special respondent appears, from the research of this respondent, to be a nonentity, as there appears to be no such authorization by statute to such an individual to file, litigate, and waste judicial resources with frivolous, time stale, and inappropriate claims."

Then she requested that I be barred from any further custodial visitation forthwith and even revisited the complaint I made to the Jefferson County Department of Social Services after learning she was being evicted from her condo, stating, "Further, it is a matter of record that the alleged special respondent has made claims to the Department of Social Services regarding this matter, and the department, after a full investigation of the several and numerous complaints of the special respondent, have closed their investigations and continue to refuse to litigate or bring any action or actions to judicial attention of the court simply because that department has, in each instance, determined that the natural mother is not acting inappropriately, that there are not any concerns that the minor child is at any risk, and agree that the child's best interests are being served by the natural mother and the court's present placement of the minor child with the natural mother, who is the respondent in this case."

A letter written by Tony Marino, MSW (masters of social work), of Early Intervention Services, Jefferson County Division of Children, Youth, and Families was attached as an exhibit to Elaine's response to my motion with a section of the letter stating:

> On February 9, 2006, Jefferson County Child Protection Intake received a report alleging that Andrew Perez is living with his mother, Elaine Perez, in an unsanitary and unsuitable environment and that she has a history of drug use. The reporting party believed Ms. Perez has relapsed. The Colorado Trails system indicated Ms. Perez had a previous case with Jefferson County in 2004. These allegations were investigated by Intake Worker Tonya Gonzales. Ms. Perez submitted a urine screen on February 17, 2006 which tested negative for all substances. Caseworker Gonzales stated the following in her report:
>
> Ms. Perez was very cooperative during the investigation and met all the requirements asked by the department. Ms. Perez was also willing and interested in participating in voluntary services.
>
> No safety concerns were identified on the Colorado Safety Assessment during the investigation and the allegations of abuse/neglect were determined to be unfounded. Ms. Perez, however, requested voluntary services through our program: Early Intervention Services.

The following note written by the social service intake worker was also attached as an exhibit to Elaine's response to my motion.

Elaine,

Hang in there! You're doing all the right things to take care of Andrew!
I believe in you!

Tonya

For me, the note had established that the intake worker, Tonya Gonzales, was biased toward Elaine and consequently predisposed to doubt my claims. Tonya had not met with Lily or spoken to Pete or interviewed me for that matter. So how could an investigation have taken place? How did Ms. Gonzales come to the determination that my allegations were unfounded? By speaking to Elaine and her social network? Or maybe the negative urine test had something to do with it—the urine test that Elaine took eight days after I filed the complaint with Ms. Gonzales's department, giving her ample time to get clean. In any case, I had to question if Tonya Gonzales or Tony Marino possessed even the slightest amount of social perceptiveness because Elaine truly had them fooled.

Tonya's note was so troubling to me that Sandra and I met with an assistant county attorney, Jeff Edwards, at the Jefferson County attorney's office to discuss it. We sat across from Mr. Edwards, a white haired, Caucasian man who seemed to be in his early sixties as he looked over the information we presented to him. He hummed and hawed, cleared his throat and occasionally looked up at us as we eagerly waited for a response to our complaint. Though his tone was indifferent, he managed to agree to the inappropriateness of the note, and that was it. No words suggesting that he was even going to have a small chat with Ms. Gonzales or that some kind of reprimand was on the horizon. He just thanked us for bringing it to his attention and walked us out.

I was appalled. I started to complain, but Sandra interrupted by shaking Mr. Edwards hand and thanking him for his time. Then she looked over at me with her well-known (don't say a word) look, and I winced.

When Mr. Edwards went back into his office and closed the door behind him, Sandra smiled at me apologetically. "What a jerk," she said.

"What was that?" I asked.

Sandra shrugged. "We have to tread carefully when it comes to these people," she warned.

"So that's it? That's all we can do?"

"Yes," she said. "Unfortunately, that's all we can do."

CHAPTER 21

To be trusted is a greater compliment than being loved.

—George MacDonald

*P*rior to the March 31 review hearing, Adam wrote me the following letter:

March 19, 2006

Dear Crystal,

I hope this letter finds you well. Just a short note to let you know my parole hearing is May 2nd, I know you're pretty busy with the things you're doing for Andrew—by the way I'm behind you one hundred percent—I'll never be able to trust her again. Anyway, let me know how all that goes. My prayers are with you.

Like I said my parole hearing is May 2nd, and it would be nice to be able to hand them some support letters. I was hoping you would write one for me. I'm asking Mom and Dad also. I'm planning on paroling to the New Hope Rehab Program. I think it will help me so I will be able to be there one hundred percent for my kids. The Lord has put it in my heart to do this so I have been talking to Mom about it, and she thinks it's a good idea also. I'm just tired of hurting everyone around me, and I feel this program will not only help me but give me the proper tools to help others in my similar situation.

Like I've been saying all along, meth is a runaway epidemic and one of Satan's worst tools for ruining lives, and I just want to do my part to help the Lord in this battle, but first I'm smart enough to know I can't help anyone (especially my kids) unless I first help myself. Satan's a smartsome beach, but he's not smarter than God, and as long as I have God on my side, I could win this drug battle I'm in. If I can just keep my boys away from drugs, everything I've been going through will be worth it. Let's keep praying and please send me that letter as soon as you can. Thank you.

Sincerely,

Your brother, Adam

PS. How are you at resumes?

Adam's affirmations in his letter, "I'm behind you one hundred percent," and, "I will never be able to trust 'her' again." I assumed were related to the upcoming hearing and my request that Elaine submit to a hair follicle test. I wasn't surprised by the anger and distrust he had for Elaine, given that she cut off all contact with him six or seven months prior without explanation. But I hoped his newfound support also had to do with his concern for Andrew as Elaine's deteriorating behavior should have been a clear indication that she had once again given in to her drug addiction, consequently placing Andrew in an unsafe situation.

On March 31, 2006, as scheduled, the review hearing was held to visit my motion requesting Elaine to submit to a hair follicle test and also Elaine's lengthy response to my motion. During the hearing, the magistrate denied my request for Elaine to submit to a hair follicle test. He simply said, "I can't make her take a hair follicle test." And that was the end of it. The magistrate also denied Elaine's request to terminate my parenting time along with her motion to dismiss my pleadings as he found that I had standing in the case and my motions were properly filed. The court then adopted my current parenting time plan: every week from Friday at 7:00 p.m. until Monday at 7:00 p.m. and made it an order of the court. The hearing concluded with the magistrate ordering Elaine to continue administering random drug tests through the Jefferson County Early Intervention Services.

A week after the review hearing, on April 6, 2006, I received a short note from Adam stating that he was leaving prison that next day to go to a forty-five-day drug treatment program in Colorado Springs, and after that, he would be moved to the Williams Street halfway house in Denver. I was happy for him, but I was also concerned as he seemed so adamant about being paroled to the New Hope Rehab Program, but now that's obviously been dropped.

I also had concerns about his new locations, Colorado Springs and Denver, which would be too close and too convenient for Elaine, should she decide to visit. Since Pete cut her off and Frank got locked up, I knew Elaine was hurting for money. With Adam being located close enough for her to visit, she may again begin to pursue him, seeing that working and earning a paycheck was to be part of his treatment program.

Since our meeting with Lily, I resolved to regain my relationship with Dad and Bianca and agreed that Andrew and I would accompany them on their drive to Colorado Springs to visit Adam at the rehab facility. When we arrived, we were asked to sit down at one of the four or five tables in a room located just inside the entry door. We waited while Adam was informed of our arrival, and after a few minutes, he walked in smiling, gave us all a hug, and thanked us for coming. Oddly, Andrew seemed familiar with Adam and the facility itself. Then I realized that Elaine must have already brought him here to visit Adam.

Dad and Bianca brought along several pairs of new shoes for Adam to try on and some hamburgers for him to dine on. So we talked a bit, while Adam tried on the shoes and happily consumed his lunch. It appeared that only one pair of the shoes fit, but instead of giving the shoes that didn't fit back to Dad, Adam called out to some guy passing by our table, "Hey, do you need a pair of shoes?"

"Sure," the guy said.

Adam then told the guy he would get with him later.

I was stunned that Adam didn't even consider that Dad may have wanted to return those shoes and get his money back. Nonetheless, it didn't seem to bother Dad, so perhaps Adam gave Dad the money to buy the shoes. Anyhow, I didn't question it any further as it was simply none of my business.

Once Adam was finished with the shoe business and his lunch, I told him I wanted to discuss Elaine with him. His face changed, and his words took on a defensive tone. "Elaine and Andrew have been visiting me here, and Elaine's come clean about everything." I looked at him incredulously. "Including her affair with Frank," he added.

I wasn't surprised that Elaine had been visiting Adam and taking Andrew to visit him, but I had to marvel at her swift success in charming her way back into his life, and I tried to consider how she pulled it off.

I was going over a few scenarios in my head when I looked up to see Adam glaring at me. He must have been reading my mind. "Whatever you think of Elaine, you have to think that of me too."

I started to express some concerns, but he stopped me and said that he wasn't going to discuss her with me any further. At that point, I realized I had no other choice but to acquiesce and reluctantly did so, and as a result, the uncertainty that Adam had the ability to make good choices for Andrew or himself was set in motion.

After Adam's time at the rehabilitation facility was complete, he was moved to the Williams Street Half Way House in Denver. Then in November of 2006, Adam, who was made to wear an electronic ankle monitor, moved in with Dad and Bianca under the intensive supervision program–inmate (ISP-I). He requested to live with Elaine, but his request was denied.

(ISP-I is a nonresidential community-based program that is an earned option for adult inmates transitioning from a community corrections residential program or CDOC (Colorado department of corrections) prison facility. ISP-I is the only nonresidential CDOC incarcerated program, which allows selected inmates to be monitored daily and closely supervised for up to six months while living on their own or an approved residence.)

CHAPTER 22

Sorrow comes in great waves...but rolls over us, and though it may almost smother us, it leaves us. And we know that if it is strong, we are stronger, inasmuch as it passes and we remain.

—Henry James

On October 5, 2006, I reluctantly called Elaine. At this point, my relationship with her was civil for Andrew's sake, but that was as far as it went. However, I needed to find out if Adam's employer provided insurance because his oldest son was having a lot of pain in one of his shoulders and needed to see a doctor. Adam was still in rehab at that time, but because he was on a work release program, I was hoping his employer provided insurance, and unfortunately Elaine was the quickest way to get to him.

During our discussion, the phone clicked, indicating she had another call. She asked me to hang on a moment; before I could respond, she clicked over to the call waiting. I was holding for a couple of minutes before she got back on line. Sounding frantic, she said that her daughter Becky was on the other line crying hysterically because her boyfriend just shot himself in the head. I gasped at first and then realized that this was surely one of Elaine's conjured-up stories. I mean what were the odds that such a situation could arise in such a timely fashion; just as we are on the phone together?

After her shocking statement, Elaine said she would call me right back and then hung up. She called back about thirty minutes later. Without preamble, and among sniffles, she asked, "Could you watch Andrew tomorrow so I can drive out to Pueblo to be with Becky?"

I wondered what she was up to. "Yes. I'll watch him."

"I'll drop him off in the morning on my way to Pueblo."

"That works for me," I said before hanging up. However, as anticipated, Elaine called back a little later to amend her original plan of dropping Andrew off in the morning.

"My friend is going to drive me to Pueblo because I don't think I'm in the right frame of mind to drive myself, so do you think you or Liam could come pick Andrew up tonight?" she said.

As always, I agreed to her request, and Liam drove by after work to pick up Andrew and as soon as he put Andrew in his car seat, Andrew declared with great enthusiasm, "My best friend Tim shot himself in the head, and now he's dead." Clearly upset, Liam gave Elaine a disconcerting look before leaving with Andrew.

Elaine called me later that evening, and in a feeble attempt to rationalize Andrew's earlier statement, she reasoned that Andrew was only repeating what he overheard her say during her earlier conversation with me. However, in our earlier conversation, we never spoke of a "best friend" nor was there any mentioning of anyone being dead. Even so, I didn't mention any of this to Elaine.

Surprisingly, Elaine called me the next day to give me her account of the events from the prior day. She basically conveyed that Becky's current boyfriend, Dion, beat the heck out of Becky's ex-boyfriend, who was visiting his and Becky's child at Becky's apartment. After the beating, Dion finally responded to Becky's screams and ran off. He ended up at a friend's apartment and called Becky relentlessly. Even so, and with good reason, Becky did not respond to his calls. Feeling slighted, Dion took his friend hostage, then called the police and demanded to see Becky. The police managed to locate and transport Becky to the standoff location. At that same time, the police forced their way into the apartment using flash grenades, and when they entered they found Dion and his hostage in the bathroom, both dead from gunshot wounds to the head.

Elaine told the story with such detail that I began to wonder if it was true. So I searched for the story over the Internet and was horrified to find that Dion's murder suicide was all over the news and that the Pueblo chieftain even captured a picture of Becky crying near the scene.

A week later, Elaine called to inform me that she and Andrew were on their way to Pueblo to attend Dion's funeral when her car broke down, and as a result, she needed to have it towed back to Denver. While the car was being towed, she was going to leave Andrew with Becky and then advised that she was actually leaving Andrew with Becky for the whole weekend because Becky was having a birthday party for her daughter, Andrew's niece, that same weekend and wanted Andrew to attend. Her nonchalant approach was really pissing me off.

"Since it seemed to slip your mind, we already made plans to take Andrew to see the *Lion King* this weekend, you know, during *my* parenting time," I said crossly.

"Oh, I'm sorry," Elaine said in a feigned concerned voice, "I forgot about that." I was so tired of her deceitful crap and her illusions of self-importance.

Still, I took a calming breath. "We already paid for the tickets, and after everything that happened last week, why would you even want to leave Andrew at Becky's? I'm sure she's not even up to it, and what if her ex decides to come back and seek revenge from Becky? I mean, wasn't it her boyfriend that beat the crap out of him?"

"Oh, I'm sure that won't happen, and Becky is fine with it."

"Well, I'm not fine with it," I retorted.

Even so, Andrew was already at Becky's and there wasn't a damn thing I could do about it. I had already filed so many motions with the court that it was almost laughable, and at this point, social services simply refused to listen, as did Adam.

Liam managed to exchange the *Lion King* tickets for the following Sunday matinee, and we spent the remainder of the weekend worrying about Andrew.

CHAPTER 23

~~~~~~

But whoso shall offend one of these little ones which believe in me, it were better for him that a millstone were hanged about his neck, and *that* he were drowned in the depth of the sea.

—Matthew 18:6, KJV

It was December 18, 2006 and, as usual, past Elaine's scheduled time to pick up Andrew, when Adam called. Since Adam had moved out of the halfway house and into Dad and Bianca's residence, Elaine cut off all contact with me, and as a result, Adam became the liaison between the two of us, even though she and Adam were no longer a couple. "Hi, Chris," Adam said.

"Hi, what's going on?"

"Elaine just called and said she can't pick up Andrew tonight because she needs to pick up a car in Pueblo."

"What does that mean?" I said uneasily.

"I guess she just bought a new car and had to go pick it up."

This news was alarming to me as I was well aware of Elaine's history with cars. "Would it be all right if Andrew stayed an extra night with you, and I'll find a way to pick him up in the morning before you guys leave for work?" Adam said.

"No problem. Andrew can stay an extra night, and I'm sure Liam won't mind dropping him off over there on his way to work in the morning." Adam seemed relieved and thanked me before hanging up.

After Liam dropped Andrew off that next morning, he called to let me know that Andrew was dropped off safe and sound. That same day, already reaching the afternoon hours, Elaine still had not picked Andrew up from Dad's house. So Dad called Adam, and Adam called Elaine. A little later, Elaine called Dad's house to say she was on her way and strangely asked that Andrew's two backpacks be emptied of all his clothes and toys as she wanted to pick them up empty.

Elaine arrived at Dad's house between 1:00 and 1:30 p.m., and according to Dad, she appeared haggard, was slouched like she had a bad hangover, and had big bags under her eyes. She was dressed in a jacket, knee high black boots, and probably a skirt. After getting Andrew and his backpacks together, she put them in the SUV and drove off.

Even with Elaine's odd behavior and haggard looks, Dad did not intervene or take any action to stop her from taking Andrew, of which I've struggled to understand.

Soon after Elaine and Andrew left Dad's house, Elaine made a stop somewhere and picked up Frank who had just recently gotten out of jail. They were all traveling westbound on US-36 toward Boulder. Elaine was in the right lane when she began to slow down and start to drift off the right side of the roadway. She struck the end of the guardrail, which caused the SUV to roll over into a ditch.

The SUV then rolled out of the ditch and continued to roll over, ejecting Elaine out of the window. The SUV landed on its passenger side on a paved area under a bridge. It then continued sliding under the bridge until the roof over the driver's compartment struck a concrete support, which caused the SUV to spin around counter clockwise and then come to rest on its passenger side underneath the Sheridan Boulevard bridge.

After the vehicle came to rest, Frank eventually crawled from the wreckage. He claimed that he was unable to pull Andrew out of the SUV due to his own injuries. So Andrew was made to remain in the most frightening of circumstances all alone until some bystanders arrived and managed to remove a bloodied and terrified Andrew from the wreckage and lift him over the meridian wall. The fire department soon arrived and began treating both Andrew and Frank.

A police officer discovered Elaine approximately seventy-five feet north of the crash site, lying on her right side next to a cement wall and a bridge pillar. She was unresponsive when the officer found her but began moaning at the sound of the officer's voice.

Both Elaine and Frank were taken to St. Anthony's Central Hospital for treatment. Soon thereafter, a police officer would arrive at the hospital and collect a felony blood draw and urine sample from Elaine as there was some drug paraphernalia found at the crash site.

Surrounded by unfamiliar people, Andrew was taken by the Westminster Fire Department and Rescue to Children's Hospital where he arrived and was admitted at 2:23 p.m. He was given a CT (Computed Tomography) scan to rule out any brain injuries, and several x-rays to check for bone fractures. Once his injuries were determined, a fractured right humerus (the long bone in the upper arm that runs from the shoulder to the elbow), a fractured right index finger and several head lacerations, he was placed in a drug-induced sedation so the doctors could work on his injuries.

His fractured right humerus was reset and splinted, his fractured right index finger was splinted, the lacerations at the top of his head were mended with four staples, and the lacerations on the upper part of his forehead were mended with twenty-two stitches.

That same evening, having no knowledge of the accident, I arrived home from work at around 5:00 p.m. I went into the kitchen to feed the dogs and noticed the light flashing on the answering machine. I hit the button and proceeded to rinse out the dog bowls. I had just turned off the water when I heard that the call was from Children's Hospital. A woman was speaking. "Andrew was involved in a car accident, could you please call me back?" I stood there confused for a couple of seconds, trying to understand what the woman had just said. When I got hold of myself, I listened to the message again, wrote down the number, and proceeded to punch in the number while asking God to please let Andrew be okay.

"Hello, this is Samantha Billings," a woman answered. In a very shaky voice, I took a moment to introduce myself, then immediately asked about Andrew. Ms. Billings advised that she was a social worker for the hospital. "Andrew's mother was severely injured in the car accident, and Andrew has been asking for his auntie. He couldn't give us your name, but eventually I found you through the mom's closed dependency and neglect case."

I thought to myself, *That's not what I asked*. "How is Andrew and how long has he been there?" I said in a trembling voice.

"Andrew's been here for a couple of hours, since around 2:30 p.m."

My heart sank. "How is he? What's happened to him? Is he going to be all right?"

"I'm sorry," she said, "I can't give you any information over the phone regarding Andrew's injuries."

"I don't think you understand, I need to know if he's all right!" I exclaimed.

Understanding my desperation, she graciously said, "It appears that his injuries are not fatal." I thanked her with all my heart and advised that I lived quite a distance from the hospital but would leave immediately. She asked if I could speak to one of the officers that was at the scene before hanging up.

"Yes, but briefly," I replied. I could hear her hand the phone to the officer, and when he got on the line, he asked me a few questions regarding Elaine and Frank as they were both in the car at the time of the accident. I answered as quickly as possible and hung up the phone.

I knew I was in no condition to drive, so I called my sister Anna, who lived a couple of blocks from me. I asked between sobs if she could drive me to the hospital.

"Andrew was taken to Children's Hospital downtown after a car accident."

She gasped, but before she could ask any questions, I said, "I'll tell you what I know when you get here."

Trying to mask her fear, she said as calmly as possible, "I'll be over in a couple of minutes."

While I waited for her to drive up, I called Liam and, in my current state, conveyed to him as precisely as possible what Ms. Billings conveyed. Though he was obviously distraught, he told me not worry. "I am heading out the door for the hospital this very moment," he said. I felt better knowing Liam would soon be there with Andrew as he worked fairly close to the hospital.

Anna arrived in record time, and amid my sobbing, I brought her up to speed as we both got in the car and headed for the hospital. While in the car, I called Dad to inform him of the accident and let him know that the social worker I spoke with said she left Adam a message. "In case Adam didn't get it, could you get a hold of him and let him know about the accident?" Dad said he would contact Adam, and that he, Bianca, and Adam would meet us at the hospital.

"Liam is already on his way," I said.

Liam later conveyed that when he arrived at the hospital, he informed the male receptionist that he was there to see his nephew Andrew Perez. The receptionist looked up the name and advised that an Andrew Perez was not a patient there. "How about Andy Perez?" Liam said.

"Sorry, no Andy Perez either."

Now totally overwrought, in an unmistakably desperate and loud voice Liam said, "Look, my nephew was in a car accident, and he's somewhere in here (referring to the emergency room)."

"A two- to three-year-old John Doe was brought in earlier from a car accident."

"That must be him, where is he?"

The receptionist swiftly walked Liam to the location of the John Doe. At the realization the child was Andrew, Liam shuddered and had to stifle the anguish he felt as Andrew looked up at him with a smile and simply said, "Uncle."

Anna and I got lost on the way to the hospital. Being suburb girls, we were not familiar with the city. Anna contacted Bianca, who had already arrived at the hospital and was able to direct us to the hospital's emergency room entrance. When we arrived, Anna dropped me off at the entrance. "I will be in as soon as I park the car." As I ran for the glass doors, I could see Bianca waiting for me.

Without speaking a word, I followed her, not knowing what to expect and terrified at what I might find. I felt as though everyone and everything was transformed into slow motion as I made my way to Andrew. The hospital bed came into sight, and I wondered if I was walking toward it or if it was somehow moving toward me. Breathing suddenly required great effort, and as I looked down at the little guy, absolute anguish flooded through me and seized my very core.

CHAPTER 24

~~~~~~~~~~~~~~~~~~~~~~~~~~~~~~~~~~~~~~

However long the night, the dawn will break.

—African proverb

*A*ndrew's eyes were closed, and he was breathing softly. An IV needle was protruding out of the back of his little hand, and some kind of monitor was linked to his chest. His right arm was splinted and bandaged, and a large V shape made up of dark sticky blood and numerous sutures now replaced his once smooth forehead. There was dirt embedded in the cuts on his hands, beneath his fingernails, and within the creases of his mouth. He was cocooned in white hospital blankets, and his skin was very pale. The contrast of his dark hair against his pale, delicate features and all that white, gave him a luminous appearance.

In my effort to comfort him, I repeated softly, "Andrew, Auntie's here. I'm so sorry I wasn't here earlier, but I'm here now." As if relenting to my somber mantra or perhaps in an effort to put an end to it, Andrew finally opened his eyes and looked up at me with a slight smile. "Auntie," he said softly. I smiled and gently kissed his plump little cheek, and as he began to fall back to sleep, I whispered, "I'm so sorry you're hurt. I love you so much." I watched as he gently drew breath, and I thanked God for saving him.

When he was back to sleep, I began thinking how those who claimed to care about his best interests and those who claimed to love him have so greatly let him down. The sadness, anger, and frustration I'd been feeling for so long had come to a head as I felt myself spiraling down into emotional wreckage. I yelled out to those around me, "Elaine did this, didn't she?" Surprised by my outburst, they all just stared at me, mouths agape, yet no one said anything. "Elaine did this! I know she did!" I yelled again.

To silence me, an unknown woman grabbed me by my arm and asked me to keep my voice down as "Andrew may hear." I pulled my arm away and turned to snap at her when she gently took my hand and introduced herself as Ms. Billings. When I managed to calm down, I asked her about the accident. "I only know that Andrew's mom was thrown from the car as it rolled down the highway embankment," she said gravely. I was trying to process her words when she advised that she needed to ask me some questions regarding Andrew. We spoke for some time as I informed her that Elaine and I both shared in the caretaking of Andrew and gave her a bit of history to help her better understand how and why our odd custody arrangement transpired.

As our conversation waned, I felt compelled to explain or even justify the emotional frustration engulfing me. "You know, I contacted social services in February regarding some alarming information I was given about Andrew's mom and her boyfriend. Yet they dismissed my complaint without an investigation, and when I challenged their resolve, the caseworker said she would not discuss it with me any further."

Ms. Billings seemed to be listening attentively. "Since social services refused to listen or take action, I had my attorney file a motion with the court along with a request that Elaine submit to a hair follicle test, but at the hearing, the magistrate informed me that he couldn't make Elaine take a hair follicle test." I looked directly at Ms. Billings and said with resignation, "They failed him. They failed to protect him from her."

After my emotional discussion with Ms. Billings came to an end, Liam and I met with Andrew's doctor. The doctor first mentioned the medication (morphine) that Andrew was given for the pain caused by his various injuries, which consisted of multiple lacerations at the front of his head, a couple of large lacerations toward the back of his head, a fractured right humerus, and a fractured right index finger, not to mention the many scrapes and bruises covering his little body. "Andrew needs to stay in the hospital overnight for observation," the doctor said. And to my relief he added, "Andrew's injuries will heal just fine."

I thanked the doctor, and as I walked over to check on Andrew, I noticed Adam was looking overwhelmed. When he saw me, he called and waved me over. I walked up to him, and sounding frantic, he said, "They're asking me all kinds of questions about Elaine, and that lady over there," he pointed to a woman standing behind a desk, "needs me to fill out some paperwork for Andrew. Could you complete the paperwork on Andrew since I don't know or have any of the information they need?"

"I'll fill out the paperwork," I said, "and if you need any information on Elaine, I'm sure I can help with that too." I completed Andrew's paperwork as agreed, and when I was done, I went back to see how Adam was doing.

He looked at me with unease. "Elaine is probably going to die tonight," he said.

"Elaine's not going to die," I said impetuously. "She's like a cockroach, and like a cockroach, she will still be here long after we are all gone."

At first we were both stunned by my words, but then we chuckled a bit. After a few moments, Adam's expression turned grave. "I don't want to be the one to make any life-or-death decisions for Elaine," he said with dismay.

"I'm sure it won't come to that," I said trying to sound convincing.

Several weeks later, Bianca would send me an e-mail stating, "Adam transferred power of attorney over to Becky, so he is out of the loop with Elaine." Even though Adam was married to Elaine, he didn't want to make any decisions regarding her health, nor did he want to end up being responsible for her hospital bills. So, in an effort to evade both, he transferred power of attorney over to Elaine's daughter, Becky.

As we waited for Andrew to be moved to his hospital room, Liam and I discussed which of us would stay with Andrew that night as someone had to go home to care for our dogs. However, we both knew that I was not about to leave Andrew, and Maria was not leaving either, so before Liam left for home, we held one another, and I told him that I would call him in the morning to let him know what time he should pick us up.

Anna left shortly after Liam. She asked me to be strong, and as we hugged good-bye I expressed my gratitude to her. "Thank you for being here for me. I am so lucky to have you for a sister. And thank you for not slapping me in the car for panicking when we got lost on our way here, no matter how much I'm sure I deserved it." She smiled at that.

As Andrew was being set up in his hospital room, Adam turned to me. "Could you stay here with Andrew tonight?" he said.

I looked at him for a moment, annoyed by the question. "No one could drag me away," I replied. "Aren't you staying?"

Adam shook his head to indicate he wasn't staying and made an effort to justify his decision with the pretext, "The most important thing for me to do right now is to work."

I tried to understand, but still felt that Andrew should be the most important thing to him, especially now.

Before Dad, Bianca, and Adam left the hospital, we talked quietly in Andrew's room while he struggled to sleep. Dad informed us on the terrible condition Elaine seemed to be in when she arrived at his house to pick up Andrew. He said she was wearing knee-high boots and a very short miniskirt, and she had bags under her eyes. "She looked like she was rode hard and put away wet," he joked.

The nurse entered the room to check on Andrew, and without warning, Bianca asked her, "Could we have a hair follicle test done on Andrew?"

"We only do those tests if a custody case is pending," the nurse replied.

Bianca said with certainty, "Then we definitely need a hair follicle test done." Adam and I nodded in agreement. The nurse advised that she would need to get approval from the doctor, and upon approval, she would administer the test. We all thanked her as she left the room.

Across the curtain, staying in the same room was a young boy who was preparing to go home. He was accompanied by a man who I assumed was his father. The man walked over to the curtain separating the room and asked if he could interrupt us for a moment. When we waved him in, he held out a brown teddy bear. "My son wants your little guy to have this," he said. The teddy bear was accepted on Andrew's behalf with much gratitude. Looking back, I wish I had taken a moment to meet with that young boy. At such a difficult time, his compassion and kindness was a much-needed distraction.

I was relieved when everyone finally went home that evening. Maria and I were then able to concentrate solely on Andrew's needs. As we were settling in, the nurse returned to administer the hair follicle test on Andrew. After the nurse left the room, Maria jumped up. "I have pajamas in the car that we could wear tonight." When I asked why she had pajamas in the car, she said, "I bought them for you for Christmas and haven't taken them out of the car yet." We both giggled.

Once we changed into pajamas, Maria and I took turns taking on the heart-wrenching task of trying to sooth Andrew's insurmountable physical and emotional pain, but our efforts were in vain. While he would manage to fall asleep, within an hour or so, he would wake from the sound of his own screams. Sadly, things continued like that throughout the night.

A brand new morning eventually replaced the unkind night, and we managed to face it with much gratitude.

The wind blew and the snow fell tirelessly throughout the morning, as we eagerly waited for the doctor to release Andrew. Jefferson County Department of Social Services had already notified the hospital and authorized Andrew to be released to me and my family. I know I should have been grateful for this, but how could I, knowing that they only use Liam and I as nothing more than Andrew's provisional safe haven. Counting on us to mend the broken pieces, they've allowed his *natural* parents to leave behind.

The snow increased as did my concerns about the road conditions by the time (11:30 a.m.) Andrew was finally discharged, and we were on our way home. Due to his broken arm, we were unable to strap him into his car seat, so I held him in my arms in the backseat of our SUV. He was in a lot of pain, but due to the hazardous road conditions, Liam had to drive slowly and cautiously, so it was taking a lot longer than usual to get home. When we finally managed to get on the highway, the snow was moving so fast that visibility must have been less than one hundred feet, and snow drifts were starting to build on the sides of the road. It seemed to take an eternity, but thankfully we arrived home safely.

Later, the local news channels would refer to that particular snowstorm as the 2006 holiday blizzard. The blizzard eventually crippled the region forcing the closures of three major interstate highways. Drifts in the Denver area reached up to five feet, and a statewide disaster was declared. Even so, the hurt and anguish resulting from Andrew's own senseless disaster remained indoors.

The pain in Andrew's broken arm was so severe, he remained bedridden for three days, which made applying the antibiotic ointment to his many sutures and staples, practically effortless. However, once he was out of bed, the once effortless task turned into quite a struggle. That is until I started using the dabbing of ointment and song technique, "Dab, dab, dab the scabs, gently as we can, sticky, yucky ointment, icky all over your head," which of course was sang to the tune of, "Row, Row, Row Your Boat." It made applying the ointment more of a game, and Andrew's resistance lessened more each time the ointment was applied.

As Andrew's physical suffering began to ease, his emotional and psychological anguish was escalating. The nightmares he experienced would cause him to wake screaming and sobbing in a state of total fear. On the worst nights, he would cry out, "I can't get out!" while his little hands would appear to be digging as if he was trying to escape the wreckage of the car accident all over again. Liam and I would try to rouse him, but it was hopeless as he was unable to hear or even recognize us. Then a sudden state of recognition would take hold, causing him to collapse into a bout of inconsolable tears. It was heart wrenching to witness, and it left Liam and I feeling completely helpless.

With the accident occurring just a week before Christmas, Liam and I could have easily refrained from celebrating, yet we understood that having Andrew safe and back within our care was a gift from God, so bringing some Christmas spirit into our home was essential. With that, we hosted our traditional holiday party, surrounding ourselves and Andrew with people we love and essentially bathing in the warmth and glory of Christ's birth.

The party came with an extra special gift from our friends, Rick and Mo, who were also our next-door neighbors. They gave us a special visit from Santa Clause, played by Rick himself.

I giggled like a little girl when Santa walked into our living room with a boisterous, "Ho ho ho." He sat next to our beaming little Andrew, giving him the priceless gift of a personal appearance as Santa had indeed deviated from his usual beaten path just to spend some time with our very special boy.

Soon after the holidays, Anna and I took Andrew back to Children's Hospital to have his sutures and staples removed. As the doctor began to remove the first suture from the front of Andrew's head, he let out a blood-curdling scream. It was so shocking, even the doctor took a step back. I moved in and tried to calm Andrew down, but he was having none of it. So I asked the doctor if he could administer something to relax the little guy, but the doctor apologetically shook his head no, then warned he was going to try again. He again attempted to remove another suture as a nurse made an effort to restrain Andrew. However, he broke loose and began screaming, hitting and kicking at anything within reach. His actions were so disruptive that nurses were appearing left and right inquiring with obvious concern, "Is everything all right?" or "Do you need me to assist?"

Ultimately, it took four adults to finally restrain Andrew long enough to allow the doctor to remove all the sutures and staples from his little head. Andrew's complete overreaction was both frightening and agonizing for all concerned.

CHAPTER 25

The wolf was sick, he vowed a monk to be / But when he got well, a wolf once more was he.

—Walter Bower

On December 31, 2006, I found myself peering into Elaine's room in the intensive care unit of St. Anthony's Central Hospital, overcome with shame as the purpose of my visit was to contentedly observe the much-deserved suffering Elaine, by her own hands, was made to endure. Even so, Elaine's alarming condition absolved all the hatred and vengeance that consumed me just moments before, and now only shame remained.

When the nurse left the room, I approached Elaine's hospital bed and noticed that her once pretty blond hair was now greasy and unkempt. Not yet recognizing me, her crazed eyes darted around the room as her arms flailed about. "Elaine, it's me, Crystal," I said. She looked up at me with crazed eyes, her lips cracked and colorless, and tried to say something, but the respirator wouldn't allow it. "I don't understand what you're trying to say."

She looked up at me again with the same crazed eyes and mouthed the words, "Take me home."

"Elaine, you need to stay here and get well before you can go home," I said somberly. She kept struggling to reposition herself as if she was trying to escape the unbearable pain that was now her reality, then looked up at me, her arms still flailing about, as her cracked lips formed the word "Please."

As the tears welled up in my eyes, I said, "I can't, I'm sorry." She began kicking the blanket off of her legs. Worried that she was having some kind of tantrum, I called the nurse. When the nurse arrived, I explained that Elaine was kicking her legs as if she was having a tantrum. The nurse, seeming unconcerned, advised that Elaine found that particular blanket to be itchy. "Then why put it on her?"

She smoothed out the sheets bunched up at Elaine's feet and re-covered her with a new blanket. " Elaine's dad was here earlier, and since he brought it for her, he keeps putting it on her," she replied.

I looked down at Elaine who had already fallen asleep. "Her dad?" I said incredulously.

"Yes," she said. Then she looked at the whiteboard apparently created for Elaine. "Gleeson is his name."

I said incredulously, "Ray Gleeson?" as I recalled the first time me and Mr. Gleeson met. It was after the motions hearing to restrict Elaine's parenting time. Anna and I left the Jefferson county courthouse and noticed Elaine and an older gentleman sitting on one of the benches just outside the courthouse lobby doors. I didn't wish to be rude and simply walk right past them, so I stopped, said hi to Elaine, offered the older gentleman my hand, and introduced myself. He shook my hand and pleasantly introduced himself as Ray Gleeson, Elaine's friend.

The nurse looked again at the whiteboard and said, "Yes, that's right."

Tired of the relentless lies, I said, "Just so you know, Ray Gleeson isn't Elaine's dad or even a relative for that matter."

She looked puzzled. "Well, that's odd."

"I'm sure he lied, so he would be allowed to visit her," I said. This seemed to upset her though she didn't comment. "Why does Elaine have pot holders on her hands?" I said.

"We had to put something on her hands because she keeps trying to remove her breathing tube."

"Yes, she's a stubborn one." She raised her eyebrows as if my comment was a complete understatement. "I'll be back to visit her next week," I said, looking over at Elaine.

"I'm sure she'll like that."

While my need for retribution toward Elaine had absolved, the anger remained as I observed Andrew's suffering. Due to the severity of the break in his upper arm, the healing process required several cast changes and continual monitoring, to rule out the need for surgery so his orthopedic appointments continued for a staggering six months.

As Andrew's physical injuries began to heal, his behavior grew more volatile to the point that even the smallest incident would send him into a heightened state of rage or inconsolable tears. He would barely eat, had developed a profound fear of the dark, and was overly concerned with death, and though he had been potty trained for over a year, he was frequently wetting the bed. In such unfamiliar territory, Liam and I recognized that Andrew needed professional help.

Because Andrew was a victim of a crime, I received some information from the Adams County Victim's Assistant Program and decided to contact them to inquire on child therapist's referrals. I was given several referrals and reviewed all of them, but only one stood out as she specialized in childhood trauma, and her therapy treatment included animal-assisted therapy. Knowing how much Andrew loved animals, I made an appointment to meet with her.

CHAPTER 26

Many people look forward to the new-year for a new start on old habits.

—author unknown

Having to get back to work even though Andrew was not yet physically ready to go back to daycare, though hesitant, I agreed to Andrew staying with Adam at Dad's house for the work week. Adam reasoned that with Dad being retired, he could care for Andrew while he was working. And honestly, Liam and I needed the rest.

Upon returning to work on January 2, 2007, I checked my messages to find that Dottie Macintyre had left a message asking me to return her call. I recalled the first time I met Dottie:

I had gone to the apartment Elaine leased after she was evicted from the condo to pick up Andrew and found that Elaine had company over for dinner. Dottie, along with a guy named Doug, was sitting at Elaine's dinner table, enjoying a bucket of chicken. Elaine introduced them as "friends from my church," which threw me for a loop. I mean, when did Elaine start going to church?

They waved hello, and I waved hello in return. I helped Andrew put on his coat as Elaine performed her customary over-the-top and boldly inappropriate send-off, covering Andrew in overwhelming kisses, all the while saying, "Yum, those are good kisses. I could just suck your lips off," as Andrew struggled to break free.

Keeping my revulsion in check, I told Elaine it was time for us to get going. She released Andrew, and he ran to open the door. I waved good-bye as we headed out. To my surprise, Doug followed us out to the car and introduced himself as Doug Nader. "Dottie and I are sort of mentors to Elaine."

"And you met Elaine at church?" I asked incredulously.

He smiled knowingly. and said, "Actually, Elaine and Andrew went to the Denver Rescue Mission when they were homeless, and the Denver Rescue Mission got them in touch with our church. Our church assisted in getting Elaine this apartment, and we have been checking in on her and Andrew from time to time ever since."

Recognizing that this was Elaine's newest scam, I sighed and rolled my eyes. "And when exactly was Elaine and Andrew supposedly homeless?" I said. "And when is it okay to give handouts to drug-abusing career criminals?" The dumbfounded look on Doug's face made me soften a bit. "Look, you seem like a nice person. I just want you and your church to be careful because Elaine can't be trusted. She will say or do anything to get what she wants."

After making the statement, I realized how much I'd come to sound like so many others who have been victimized, in one way or another, by Elaine.

Obviously uncomfortable, Doug cleared his throat. "I came out here to request your contact information in case an emergency arises with Elaine or Andrew."

I took out one of my cards from my wallet and handed it to him. "I see she's already convinced you that I'm the bad guy here." Without making eye contact, he took the card and headed toward the apartment. "Please let me know if at any time you suspect she's using drugs." He looked back at me for a moment. "For Andrew's sake," I added in earnest.

He waved at me without verbally responding and went back inside.

I returned Dottie's phone call. A woman answered, and I asked to speak to Dottie Macintyre. "This is Dottie."

"Hello Dottie, this is Crystal Sanchez returning your call." "Oh yes, thank you for returning my call. I was calling to inquire on Elaine. Since my church gave her a car, no one has heard from her. We've called her several times, but she has not responded."

"Your church gave Elaine a car?"

"Yes," she said. "Elaine really wanted to start working but didn't have any transportation, and since the church receives donated vehicles, one of those vehicles was given to her."

"Your church donated a vehicle to a known drug addict?" I said with reproach.

Dottie remained silent as I went for the throat. "Well, let's just pray that Elaine wasn't on drugs when she drove that donated vehicle off the highway and seriously injured Andrew."

"What!" Dottie exclaimed.

"Yeah, Elaine drove off the highway in that car your church gave her, with Andrew in it," I said with contempt.

She began to cry. "I am so sorry." Unable to say anything nice, I said nothing.

When Dottie managed to get herself together she disclosed, too late to be useful, that she has had concerns regarding Elaine. She said she discussed her concerns with Doug, but he felt they should give Elaine the benefit of the doubt.

"What kind of concerns?" I said.

Dottie explained that she had dropped by Elaine's apartment now and then, and on one occasion Andrew, who was only three years old at that time, answered the door. When Dottie asked to see his mom, "Mommy isn't talking," Andrew said. Dottie said she also called occasionally, and there were several times when Andrew said, "Mommy is sleeping."

"Why didn't you contact social service? Andrew could have been left alone for all you knew!" Dottie remained silent, and I added callously, "Oh yeah, you were giving Elaine the benefit of the doubt."

Dottie disregarded my words and conveyed that in November, she picked up Elaine and Andrew to take them to Andrew's doctor appointment. Andrew had a previous ear infection, and the appointment was to follow up on that. "Elaine was acting weird, and on the way to the doctor's office, she kept falling asleep in the car. She couldn't keep her head up, and it kept bobbing around while she continued to apologize for being very tired," she said.

"Didn't you think she was on drugs?"

"I really thought it could be something like that."

"Why didn't you ask her about it?"

"Well, when we arrived at the doctor's office, I spoke to the doctor about it and asked if someone could call social services. The doctor said she would take care of it. I just assumed she reported it."

"Did you follow up with the doctor later?"

"I called back the next day and left a message with one of the receptionists, who said she would get the information to the doctor, but I never heard anything after that." Dottie started crying again. "I'm really sorry," she said between sniffles. "Elaine said a lot of bad things about you, but when I finally met you in person, you were nothing like what she said, and I knew something wasn't right."

Tired of Dottie's useless information and useless regret, I told her where she could find Elaine and disconnected the call.

It was disconcerting to think that Dottie said something to Andrew's doctor about Elaine, and it went unreported. So I called the doctor's office to inquire on Dottie's claims. I spoke with a receptionist, and she had a nurse return my call. When the nurse called, she said that she herself spoke with Andrew's doctor about my inquiry, and the doctor advised that she never had a conversation with anyone about Andrew's mother.

CHAPTER 27

Everything is fine today, that is our illusion.

—Voltaire

During Andrew's stay with Adam at Dad's house, Dad and Bianca agreed to take him to his orthopedic doctor appointment. After the appointment took place, I called to see how it went. Bianca advised that everything went great. I called several more times throughout the week to check on Andrew to ensure he was sleeping and eating well, and every time, I received the same response, "Everything is great. Andrew is doing great."

I understood Bianca's vagueness, knowing she was displeased with me for not taking Andrew to visit Dad or her when he was solely in my custody. Then again, they were unaware that when Adam and Elaine were both incarcerated, Adam asked if I would care for Andrew and was adamant that he did not want Dad and Bianca to be Andrew's caretakers. They were also unaware that Elaine insisted that I do not allow Andrew to be with Dad and Bianca unsupervised at any time.

That Friday, wanting to keep my family informed on anything significant where Andrew was concerned, I requested a family meeting at my house to discuss obtaining a therapist for Andrew. Dad, who still thought of himself as a cool dude, strutted into the house snapping his fingers, with Bianca, Adam, and Andrew following behind. Andrew, glad to be home, asked if he was staying and gave me a big smile and a big hug when I nodded my head yes.

Dad, acting anxious and irritated, said, "Man, I'm missing the fight (referring to a boxing match being held on cable television)."

I ignored his statement. "Thanks for coming," I said.

Bianca went into the kitchen, and Dad sat on the couch acting annoyed and impatient. Andrew went up to Dad and tried to play with him, which seemed to increase his impatience. Unable to sense this, Andrew persisted, and Dad hauled off and smacked him on his cast. The pain must have been excruciating because it took a few seconds of silent, blue-lipped screams before sound finally came out of Andrew's mouth. I ran over and picked Andrew up and scolded Dad, who just smirked and said, "Hey, he started it."

I wanted to punch him in his face and throw him out of my house, but I managed to collect myself in spite of the ignorance I was dealing with. Instead, I began the meeting with a recap of Andrew's accident at which time Adam and Dad decided to start poking fun at one another. I stood in horror as Dad insisted that Adam was the one who called Elaine to pick up Andrew so he was at fault for what happened to Andrew. Then Adam insisted that Dad was the one that let Andrew go with Elaine even though she was "obviously high", so really, he was the one at fault for what happened to Andrew. I was appalled by their ability to be so insensitive, and in an effort to shut them up I looked at Dad. "Why did you let Elaine take Andrew when it was so obvious that she was on something?"

Dad shrugged his shoulders and answered as if the answer should have been obvious, "I didn't feel it was my place."

I looked at him with disgust as I stifled my need to scream and proceeded with my proposal. "Andrew has been through a very scary and confusing event. He's experiencing recurring nightmares. He goes from tears to outrage in a matter of seconds, and he seems to be in a constant state of anxiety."

Adam and Dad were looking at me with annoyance. and the moment I suggested we obtain a therapist for Andrew, Adam declared that he was totally against Andrew going to therapy. "Andrew didn't have any nightmares when he was staying with me," he insisted. "And I don't like people trying to get in my head and don't want anyone getting in Andrew's head either." Aware that Adam was kicked out of the therapeutic community program in prison, I wasn't surprised by his response.

I turned to Dad who was nodding in agreement. Dad looked up at me as if he was going to say something so I raised my eyebrows, but he remained silent and Adam seemed to think that was funny. I was tired of their juvenile behavior. I turned to Adam. "Andrew needs help, the kind of help we're not qualified to give him, so even if I have to get a court order, I am going to get Andrew some help."

"Why do you always have to go there? Why do you have to start threatening with court?" Adam whined.

I ignored his question and turned to Bianca. "I could take Andrew to some of the sessions," she said. I smiled at her and nodded in agreement.

Then Adam interjected, "I want to meet with the therapist before agreeing to Andrew going to therapy." So I informed him of the appointment I had scheduled for that next morning, and he agreed to meet me at the therapist's office.

I arrived at the therapist's office that next morning, and I was surprised and annoyed to find not only Adam but also Dad and Bianca sitting in the waiting room, all sipping coffee from their

Starbucks cups. Before I got the chance to speak with them, the therapist came out of her office, and because I was the only one standing, she smiled at me. "Are you Crystal?"

I offered her my hand. "Yes, and you must be Alice."

She nodded in confirmation.

I turned toward my family. "I didn't realize all three of you were coming." Alice, also surprised by everyone's presence, advised that she usually likes to meet with just the parents first, but since we were all there, she graciously invited us all into her office.

We took a seat, and Alice went over the services she provided and described the process of play therapy, which I felt would be ideal for Andrew. Adam revealed his concerns and fears regarding therapy, and Alice seemed to alleviate those concerns and fears with some factual information. By the end of the meeting, Adam was in agreement with the therapy sessions, so without delay, I scheduled an appointment for the therapist to meet with Andrew.

As the week before, I still didn't feel that Andrew was ready to go back to daycare, and since, according to Bianca, "Everything was great" that past week, I agreed to Andrew staying with Adam at Dad's house for one more work week. Consequently, on the evening of January 8, 2007, Dad and Bianca came by my home to pick up Andrew.

As soon as Andrew heard Dad and Bianca's voices, oddly he ran and hid in the closet. Liam and I thought he was just playing around, but when we opened the closet door, he was actually crying. As I went in to reach for him, he started screaming and kicking me away. We were dumbfounded. "What's wrong Boo?" I said. Boo being my pet name for him.

"I don't want to go." he cried. We waited for him to calm down a bit. "What's wrong Boo?" I repeated. "I don't want to go there," he said, softly this time.

He wouldn't allow me take him out of the closet, so Liam sat in the closet next to him while I went to talk to Dad and Bianca, who were talking quietly among each other in the living room. Not understanding Andrew's behavior myself, I tried to explain to them that he was experiencing a lot of uneasiness and anxiety since the accident, and he's probably tired on top of that. So we all agreed that on his way to work, Liam would drop Andrew off at Dad's that next morning.

As Dad and Bianca were on their way out of the house, I overheard them talking in a thoughtless and insensitive manner about Andrew's behavior, which I ignored, believing it was a result of their own embarrassment and insecurity as I was certain they felt snubbed by Andrew.

Once Andrew was sure they were gone, he came out of the closet, acting as if everything was fine. I asked him why he didn't want to go with Grandpa. "Grandpa Paul is mean to me."

I was taken aback by this. "Why do you think Grandpa is mean?" I said softly.

He just shrugged his little shoulders and said he didn't want to talk about it. Feeling that he had been through enough for one night, I didn't press him.

The next morning, Andrew seemed fine about going to stay with Adam. Even so, he still didn't want to talk about his Grandpa. So Liam drove him over to Dad and Bianca's and then called to let me know that he seemed fine at being dropped off. With that, I was able to convince myself that the weird episode the night before was due to the recent trauma Andrew had experienced.

CHAPTER 28

~~~~~~~~~~~~~~~~~~~~~~~~~~~~~~~~~~~~~

Hope for the best, but prepare for the worst.

—English proverb

On January 7, 2007, Maria and I went to visit Elaine, who was still on a respirator in the intensive care unit. Maria, who was unable to handle the foul smell and gurgling sound coming from Elaine's room, remained near the curtain while I walked over to her bedside. Being on strong pain medication, she was awake but hardly lucid. When she noticed me, she began to cry. Naively, I assumed she was crying for Andrew, so I showed her the picture of Andrew that I brought for her and said that he was safe with me. With her cracked dry lips, she mouthed something I was unable to interpret. Then just like that, she fell into a deep sleep. Before leaving, Maria and I took a moment to talk with the nurse about Elaine's recovery progress. The nurse advised that Elaine's quick progress was better than expected.

On our way home, Maria, who believed the accident was due to Elaine's drug use, said she didn't understand the compassion I expressed toward Elaine. I admitted that the first time I went to see Elaine, I felt only anger and hatred toward her, but when I observed her suffering and reminded myself that she is Andrew's mom, my anger turned to pity, and I decided that even though it's highly likely she was on drugs when the accident happened, until her blood test results are in and reveal that as fact, we should not jump to conclusions.

Once Elaine was off the respirator and moved out of the intensive care unit into rehabilitation, Sandra and I acknowledged that she was facing on-going extensive physical therapy and would be unable to care for Andrew for some time. So after we discussed this, Sandra generated a stipulation regarding modification of parenting time and decision-making responsibility, which would permit me to care for Andrew while Elaine was incapacitated and also enable me to obtain the necessary medical and psychological help that Andrew needed.

On January 11, 2007, Anna and I took the stipulation to the hospital for Elaine's approval. When we entered Elaine's room, we found that Ray was visiting. I introduced Anna to him as they had not yet met.

Ray was a heavyset man with a W. C. Fields' nose, and though he was Caucasian, his health issues gave his skin a bit of a brownish-green hue. He appeared to be in his mid to late sixties, was very intelligent, and always very cordial.

After the introduction, Anna and I spent some time talking with Elaine, who seemed to be recovering very well. I informed her on Andrew's injuries and discussed the medical attention he required. "Even though Andrew was released to me by Jefferson County Department of Social Services from the hospital, in order to obtain the medical care he requires, I need to obtain temporary custody of him." Elaine looked at me, unconvinced. "Unless you prefer that Adam and Angela care for him?" I added. At this, Elaine's eyes darted my way. "Oh, you didn't know, they were seeing each other again?"

She stared at me for a moment as if she was trying to find some hint of a lie, but I wasn't lying. Adam was seeing Angela again, and later, they would even purchase a home together.

The very mention of Angela infuriated Elaine. I wasn't sure why, as she was again seeing Frank, but she hated Angela and didn't want her anywhere near Adam or Andrew. And I too didn't want Angela anywhere near Adam or Andrew for many reasons, one of them being that during Adam's incarceration, I spoke to Angela over the phone and she confessed to assisting Adam in cooking meth. "Adam's eyesight was so bad that when he was cooking I had to stand behind him and read off the instructions." She also divulged, to my disgust, that she and Adam would cook and smoke meth in succession for days on end without even being aware if it was day or night.

When I recently discovered that Adam was again seeing Angela, I felt that he was going backward instead of forward in his recovery and told him as much, which only managed to put him on the defensive. He claimed that Angela was off the meth and advised that it wasn't any of my business who he was seeing anyway. To which I said, "That may be true, but I don't want Andrew around her, and that *is* my business."

Elaine put out her hand for me to give her the document. She looked it over and handed it to Ray. "If my Dad thinks it's all right, I'll sign it," she said. Elaine's nurse was in the room at that time and verified that Elaine was alert and clearheaded. I told Ray that he could take as much time as he needed to review it, but he said he was okay with it, and to my relief, Elaine signed and dated the stipulation.

Ray then asked if I could care for Cash, Elaine's pit bull, while Elaine was in the hospital. He said that Cash had been staying with him, but he couldn't keep him for much longer. I agreed to find a temporary home for Cash until Elaine was able to go home, so Ray gave me the information on where to pick Cash up and asked me to call him with a date and time.

That same day, I received an e-mail from Bianca, which stated, "I'm so sorry, I had Adam cancel today's appointment." She was referring to Andrew's therapy appointment, of which she and Adam agreed to take Andrew. After reading the e-mail I quickly called Alice to reschedule the missed appointment and to convey that because Adam didn't meet the twenty-four hour cancellation policy, I was aware that I was to pay for the missed session and planned on doing so at the next appointment. I was angry but not surprised by the canceled appointment and the belated e-mail notice.

The next day, I arrived at Dad's house to pick Andrew up from his work week visit with Adam. Andrew, anxious to go home, put his hand on my shoulder and said, "Let's go home, Auntie."

Adam looked at Andrew. "You are home, silly."

Andrew, ignoring him, turned back to me. "C'mon, let's go home, Auntie."

Suddenly feeling uneasy, I said, "Okay let's go."

When we got in the car, I asked him if he had fun. He shook his head. "I don't want to stay there anymore."

"Don't worry, next week you're going back to daycare." He smiled at that.

That same day, I contacted Detective Loya, who was the detective working on Elaine's case. I inquired on the progress of the case and Elaine's blood tests. He informed me that there was no new information on the case and the blood tests had not yet come back. "Have you met with Elaine?" I asked.

He explained that he didn't have a chance to speak with her this week but planned on seeing her next week. "I'm sure she will be in the hospital for a long time," he said.

Startled by this misconception, I informed him that Elaine is completely off the respirator and is not only talking but also walking and asking to be moved. Obviously taken aback by this, he said he would be visiting her soon. Then he asked me to call him at the end of the week, and hopefully by then he would have more information.

"Do you think there will be any charges filed against her?"

"Well, if anything, she will have issues with traffic," he said as vague as possible. I understood the detective couldn't give me any information at that time, but it was still very frustrating.

After agreeing to find a temporary home for Elaine's dog, Andrew and I met Ray at a nursing home where he claimed to be recovering after enduring a surgical procedure. Cash was housed in a very small bathroom located within Ray's room. When he heard Andrew's voice, he seemed to jump for joy, and Andrew was very happy to see his "Cashy" as well.

We stayed a while, so Andrew could visit with Ray for a bit, and so Cash and I could get reacquainted. As I watched from across the room, I could see that Andrew enjoyed Ray's company, and Ray seemed to be very fond of Andrew. When it was time to leave, Ray stuck a ten-dollar bill in Andrew's pocket and shook his little hand, then handed me Cash's leash. Then Andrew and I walked out into the hall to leave.

We must have looked ridiculous, Andrew and I walking as quickly as possible down the long white corridor in our meager attempt at discretion in spite of the big black dog walking beside us in an establishment where dogs weren't allowed.

Once we got Cash home, he stayed with us for that afternoon, so Andrew could spend some time with him. Later that evening, we drove him over to my friend Dolores's house with dog food, dog treats, a toy, and blanket in tow as she offered to care for him while Elaine was in the hospital. Cash, being a very sensitive dog, took some time getting comfortable in his new surroundings, but eventually he fit right in.

On January 16, 2007, Sandra submitted the stipulation, which Elaine and I both signed, regarding the modification of parenting time and decision-making responsibility to the court for approval.

Magistrate John Sanderson, who knew our case well, no longer worked for Jefferson County Courts, so Sandra worried that the stipulation would not be approved by the new magistrate as our case was so complex. However, to our relief, Magistrate Gonzales approved the stipulation and made it an order of the court.

Once the stipulation was approved, I applied for victim compensation on Andrew's behalf, which would help pay for his costly therapy sessions. After the Victim Compensation Board made the decision to guarantee Andrew's first three mental health therapy sessions, they ultimately approved an additional amount of twenty-one hundred dollars for thirty more therapy sessions, the maximum allowed for a primary victim.

I also submitted an authorization for disclosure of protected health information to the Children's Hospital Records Management Department, requesting copies of Andrew's medical records in regards to the accident along with the lab reports concerning the hair follicle test. I faxed the form to Samantha in the Records Department, and she informed me that she would call when the records were ready to be picked up. I prepared myself for a difficult wait.

A couple of weeks after Andrew's approval for victim compensation, Alice e-mailed me a letter she received from a law firm, requesting a copy of Andrew's therapy records. The letter included an authorization to release medical information and was approved by Adam. Confused, I contacted the law firm to make inquiries. I spoke to a Ms. Kennedy, and she advised that the information requested was needed so her firm could put together a claim they plan on filing with the insurance company. "If the claim you're referring to concerns Elaine Perez, she didn't have insurance at the time of the accident, and there were no other cars involved, so really, there is no claim to be made."

Ms. Kennedy seemed to understand, yet later, Alice would receive another request along with another authorization to release medical information approved by both Adam and Elaine.

I again contacted Ms. Kennedy, and this time I advised that I had temporary custody and decision-making authority for Andrew, and so without my consent, the law firm would need to refrain from sending out any further requests to Alice. Ms. Kennedy apologized and agreed that no other requests would be sent out.

I found it ludicrous that Adam would work so hard at trying to have Andrew's therapy records released in order to file a lawsuit for monetary gain, I assumed, but couldn't even manage to take Andrew to an actual therapy session given that he canceled another appointment just one week after he canceled the last appointment. When he informed me of this new cancellation, I was infuriated, not only because this was the second appointment he canceled, but also because he again did not give the required twenty-four hour notice so payment was still due.

Given that Adam was not taking Andrew's need for therapy seriously, after the second cancellation, Liam and I assumed all the responsibility of transporting Andrew to each therapy session, attending each family session, learning all we could about Andrew's posttraumatic stress disorder diagnosis and taking care of the fees associated with all.

In our effort to learn all we could about Andrew's behavior issues, Liam and I made arrangements to attend a six-week course that Alice was offering. The course, "Early Childhood Trauma," we were told, would offer us a better understanding of the trauma associated behaviors Andrew was experiencing and would offer us some insight on the posttraumatic stress disorder he was diagnosed with. At first, I was worried that at the rate we were already going, we would be too exhausted to gain anything from the evening classes, but I was wrong, as it proved to be a really great tool. After the full course, we more clearly understood Andrew's diagnosis and were more confident in our abilities to help him cope with what he was made to endure, such as his irrational fears, impulsive behaviors, volatile moods, and overreactions.

CHAPTER 29

~~~~~~~~~~~~~~~~~~~~~~~~~~~

One may outwit another, but not all the others.

—François de La Rochefoucauld

On January 20, 2007, Andrew and I went to the hospital to visit Elaine. The moment we walked into Elaine's room, she turned to Andrew. "Hi, my little love. Guess what, you're going to be in a wedding," she exclaimed.

Andrew looked at me blankly, so I asked, "Who's getting married?"

Elaine said, "I am," holding out her hand to show us an emerald-looking ring. "Yeah, Frank and me are getting married."

Her announcement was so absurd given that she was still married to Adam I had to stifle a chuckle. Andrew, however, looked terrified, so I smiled at him and said, "Wow! A wedding sounds like a lot of fun," which seemed to ease him.

Frank entered the room, and Andrew seemed happy to see him. While Frank and Andrew were catching up, I informed Elaine of the night Andrew hid in the closet from Dad and Bianca. "When Adam and Bianca last came to visit me here, they said that your dad had to spank Andrew," Elaine said.

"For what?" I demanded.

"Bianca said her phone is made to go straight to speaker phone, so when you called, Andrew heard your voice and just went crazy. He ran toward the bathroom with Bianca chasing after him. When he got to the bathroom door, he slammed it on Bianca's foot. Your dad got mad and spanked Andrew on the butt."

I could feel my cheeks go flush. "That stupid story doesn't even make sense. Why would Andrew start running around for no reason other than hearing my voice? And with a broken arm, how was he able to slam the door so hard it hurt Bianca's foot? There's a lot of gaps in that story, don't you think?"

Elaine, who was sitting up in her hospital bed, seemed uninterested and even bored with my argument. "Hasn't Andrew been through enough?" I said. Elaine, wanting to move past the discussion, quickly agreed, then swiftly changed the subject matter back to her supposed engagement. Unable to swallow her lack of empathy and latest pipe dream, I told her that I was going to wait out in the hall for a bit so they could all discuss the upcoming wedding among themselves. Elaine nodded, and I left the room.

I returned about twenty minutes later, and Andrew immediately ran over to me and said with eager anticipation, "Is it time to go, Auntie?"

Seeing that he was good and ready to go I took his hand. "Yes, we have lots to do today."

Elaine, as usual, overwhelmed Andrew with her excessive and overstated kisses as we said our good-byes.

When Andrew and I got in the elevator, he said, "I don't want to visit her again."

His words surprised me. "Why don't we talk about it later, okay?" I said, thinking he would probably change his mind.

Liam was waiting for us in the lobby, and Andrew jumped into his arms. As we walked to the car, I told Liam about Elaine and Frank's engagement. He just rolled his eyes, and we both giggled a bit. Then on the drive home, I quietly reiterated to Liam what Elaine conveyed to me regarding Dad spanking Andrew. We were both taken aback when Andrew interjected. "No. Grandpa Paul pulled my hair and hit my head and spanked me for being a bad boy, and I cried."

Liam and I looked at each other, and I turned back to look at Andrew. "Well, that doesn't sound like a nice thing to do to a little boy."

Andrew shook his head. "It hurt," he said glumly. He fell asleep soon after his declaration, and Liam and I remained quiet for the rest of the drive home.

The thought of Dad and Bianca bullying Andrew when he was already suffering from the physical injuries and psychological trauma brought on by the accident was both infuriating and heartbreaking, and I knew I needed to calm down and think about how I should handle it.

Two weeks after Andrew's last stay at Dad's house, Adam called to inquire on when he could have him over again. I took a deep breath and reiterated what Andrew told both Liam and I about Dad and Bianca hurting him. Without consideration, Adam disputed Andrew's claims and said wryly, "He's conning you."

I struggled to maintain my composure. "I'm pretty sure three-year-olds don't con like that. Something had to happen over there, otherwise why would Andrew be so adamant about not wanting to go over there anymore?" Adam scoffed, but before he could say anything further, I informed him on how Andrew reacted the last time Dad and Bianca came to pick him up.

"Yeah, something did happen here, but not what you think."

"You're right," I said. It's not what I think, but what Andrew told me."

Ignoring my comment, he repeated Dad and Bianca's version of the story, which was the same as what Elaine conveyed to me in the hospital.

"Well, at least you all have your stories straight," I said sarcastically.

Adam didn't comment, and we both remained silent for a moment. Taking another approach, I said, "You weren't there when it happened, right?"

"No, I wasn't there."

"And neither was I, but Andrew was, so shouldn't we go by what he said happened? Because I'm pretty sure a three-year-old doesn't have the ability to make something up like that."

Unmoved, Adam again advised that Andrew was conning me. I was tired of his denial and seemingly lack of concern for his son. "I have no intention on sending Andrew back over there if he so adamantly doesn't want to go."

"That's crap! You can't keep my son from me."

"I'm not keeping your son from you," I said wearily. "I'm keeping him from the two bullies you live with. You can come here to see him, but I'm not making him stay over there."

"I'll just go to your house with the cops and take my son," he threatened.

"Well, you'd better have some legitimate custody papers in hand when you do."

"You're going to get hurt real bad, and I'm sorry for that because you're my sister," he said before hanging up on me. I shuttered at his cold words and his even colder tone.

Just days before Andrew's fourth birthday, Elaine called to ask if I could take him to the hospital to see her on his birthday. I informed her that we already had a party planned for him but I could take him to see her the weekend after his birthday. She was furious. She didn't like anyone saying no to her. Even so, Andrew deserved to have a birthday party. So, in spite of her angry words and threats of retribution, I was going to give him one.

The weekend after Andrew's birthday, Elaine was still angry with me. So Maria took him to visit her. They arrived at Elaine's room and were surprised to find that Adam was waiting to see Andrew too. Unfortunately, Adam made the visit very difficult. Instead of making it a positive and cheery experience for Andrew, he chose to use the time to make underhanded comments about me and Liam, which of course made Maria and Andrew very uncomfortable.

I couldn't comprehend Adam's obvious anger at my decision to keep Andrew away from Dad and Bianca since it was a contradiction of sorts as it was he who wanted to keep Andrew from being cared for by Dad and Bianca in the first place. I also couldn't grasp why Adam wouldn't even make an effort to understand what was going on with his son, that Andrew's sense of security was shattered as a result of the accident and that he needed more than anything to feel safe.

That because Dad and Bianca chose to discount this and foolishly punish him for behaving like the scared, traumatized child he was with broken bones and a broken heart was disturbing at best. And it really didn't matter what they did to him, whether it was simply a swat on the butt or something worse, because in Andrew's already fragile state, to him it was a scary and hurtful experience.

CHAPTER 30

Deceit is in haste, but honesty can wait a fair leisure.

—proverb

As Detective Loya requested, I contacted him a week after our last phone call and inquired on the case. He advised that Elaine's blood test results were back, but he could not release that information to me. However, he did say that criminal charges have been filed against her.

On January 29, 2007, a social worker from Adams County stopped by for a follow-up visit with Andrew. Liam was home with Andrew as he was every Monday and called me at work to let me know about the visit. I immediately left work and because my place of employment was about a five-minute drive from home, I arrived in no time. The caseworker introduced herself as Diane Waters and asked to spend some time with Andrew alone. She then introduced herself to Andrew, who asked if she wanted to see his room. She agreed and followed the little guy to his room, which is where the assessment took place.

DIVISION OF CHILD WELFARE ASSESSMENT SUMMARY, JEFFERSON COUNTY:

The Adams County Case Worker (CW) met with the child (Andrew Perez) outside the presence of the alleged perpetrator of the abuse and/or neglect (referring to Elaine). The CW met with the child at the home of his paternal aunt, Crystal Sanchez. Andrew has a broken arm and scarring around the head from the accident. His aunt reported that she takes him to Children's Hospital for his follow-up care for his injuries related to the accident. Other than his injuries from the accident Andrew appeared healthy and well cared for. He was clean and appropriately dressed. He appeared to be comfortable in his environment and appeared to be very bonded to his aunt and uncle. He showed the CW his room. The room was nicely furnished and had many toys. The CW played with Andrew and attempted to question him about the accident. He stated that he was in the car with his mother and her boyfriend Frank. He stated that his mother was driving. He stated that his mother and Frank were talking and looking at each other and then they hit a bridge. He stated that he was then upside down in the car. He reported that he was very scared. The CW asked him if it hurt and he said yes. He said he was bleeding and that his arm hurt. The CW asked Andrew what happens when he gets into trouble at his mother's home and he did not give the CW an answer. He was very distracted and had trouble focusing on the CW's questions. The CW asked who lives with him and he states that he lives with his aunt and uncle. The CW asked him who lives with him at his mother's home and he stated, "Just me and my mom." The CW asked him if he feels safe at his mother's home and he said yes. The CW asked him if he likes living with his aunt and uncle and he said yes. He reported feeling safe there. The CW asked him what happens when he gets into trouble at his aunt's home and he said nothing. The CW asked Andrew if he knew what drugs were and he said no. He did not appear to have any knowledge of drugs. The CW attempted to talk with Andrew about any possible domestic violence in the home but he was not focusing on the CW's questions and did not answer. The CW attempted to talk with the child about any incidents of sexual abuse, but he was not focusing on the questions and did not answer. Due to Andrew's age and the fact that he was no longer answering the questions the CW was asking the interview was ended.

After Diane spoke with Andrew, she briefly met with both Liam and me. During our discussion, I asked if she knew whether or not Elaine was on drugs at the time of the accident as the detective only advised that charges were going to be filed against her but wouldn't advise on the blood tests. Diane looked at me gravely. "Elaine's blood tests came back positive for methamphetamine among other things." Even though I suspected as much, her confirming words were still so difficult to hear.

After Diane's visit, I called Sandra to inform her on what the detective informed me on and also what the caseworker conveyed regarding Elaine's blood tests. Sandra immediately filed a motion to restrict Elaine's parenting time, requesting that any parenting time exercised by Elaine with Andrew be professionally supervised. After review of the motion, the court requested a hearing to be set within seven days.

Later that day, the caseworker, Diane, who met with Andrew earlier, called to inform me that she recently had an interview with Elaine, and during the interview, Elaine stated that since she was facing jail time, she was going to leave the hospital against her doctor's wishes and go to your home and kill you.

"Did she seem serious?"

Diane's stated that she was uncertain. "I contacted Detective Loya," she said, "and informed him of the same."

I was somewhat concerned by Diane's information because Claudia phoned me several days earlier to warn me that Elaine had announced to her family, which I assumed was Becky and Becky's dad, that she was going to kill me and my whole family. But figuring it was more than likely one of Elaine's attention-seeking tactics, I didn't concern myself with the information; however, Claudia seemed to be very concerned.

In light of the new information I received from Diane, I decided to call the hospital to find out if Elaine had checked herself out and was relieved to find that she was, for the time being, a patient of the hospital.

Regardless that the day had taken its toll, the evening was not showing any improvement. The doorbell rang, and in my vigilant state, I peeked out the window and saw that a police car was parked out front. I figured the police had stopped by as a result of Elaine's threat.

When I opened the door, I found two police officers standing on my porch, and without preamble, the first officer asked, "Do you know Adam Perez?"

"Yes, he's my brother."

"Adam asked that we assist him in removing his child from the premises so he can take the child home."

I looked at both of them, obviously confused; then the second officer said more cordially than the first, "Look, I don't know what's going on here, but Adam claims that you have his son and won't give him back."

"Yes, I have his son, who is my nephew, because I have custody of him." At that time, Liam and Andrew came upstairs to see what was going on. The officers talked with them about nothing in particular as I went to get the court order. When I returned to the living room, I asked Liam to take Andrew back downstairs. When they left, I handed the officers the court order. "Adam is currently under the jurisdiction of the department of corrections and is being monitored through an ankle bracelet." They both looked up from the document with obvious curiosity. "He was in prison for three years on drug-related charges."

When they finished reviewing the court order, they apologized for the interruption, and as they headed for the door, the first police officer asked if I knew who the woman accompanying Adam was. I looked out the window. "Where are they?"

The same officer said that they were in the black SUV parked across the street. So I looked to the SUV, but its windows were too dark to see in.

"The woman appears to be Hispanic and has long black hair," the officer added.

"Oh," I said, "that's probably Angela Knight, Adam's girlfriend."

Again, they apologized and went on their way.

Peering outside, I could see the officers talking with Adam, and after a few minutes, the first officer headed back toward my front door. I opened the door. "Ma'am," he said, "a police car will be patrolling your area for the rest of the evening in case Adam returns." He then advised that I call 911 should Adam decide to cause any trouble. I wondered what Adam said to them as it obviously was cause for concern.

That next afternoon, I again called the hospital to see if Elaine had checked herself out; unfortunately, this time I was informed that Elaine was discharged that morning. I asked the lady on the phone to transfer me to the nurse's station where Elaine had currently been staying. The lady transferred me, and a nurse answered.

I introduced myself to the nurse as Elaine's sister-in-law, and she immediately acknowledged that she remembered me. I inquired on Elaine's early departure from the hospital to which she said with concern, "Elaine left the hospital against the doctor's wishes." I affirmed Elaine's foolishness, and knowing she couldn't offer any further information, I thanked her for her time before hanging up.

A bit shaken, I contacted Detective Loya and told him that Elaine actually left the hospital against her doctor's wishes.

"Are you sure?" he said incredulously.

I reiterated the conversation I had with the nurse. Afterward, he said he would notify the Northglenn Police Department, and advised that I contact them too.

As advised, I contacted the Northglenn Police Department, and the officer I spoke with recommended that I take Andrew and leave the house until that next day. "I will send an officer out to patrol the area," he said. So I packed a bag for me and Andrew, and we went to stay at Dolores's house for the night while Liam and our grownup nephew Jason stayed at the house to ensure our dogs remained safe.

Fortunately, Elaine was a no-show. Evidently she just wanted to scare me, and I have to say, she did a good job of it. Even so, I vowed that would be the last time.

I later discovered that on the day Elaine left the hospital, January 30, 2007, she filed a motion with the court to terminate all my rights where Andrew was concerned. And also requested the issuance of a temporary restraining order and an order of relief for placement, which if approved, Andrew would be made to return to Elaine, and I would be prohibited from having any contact with him while the motion to terminate my rights was pending.

Three days after Elaine checked herself out of the hospital, Children's Hospital called to inform me that Andrew's medical records were ready to be picked up. I was filled with anxiety on the long drive to the hospital. When I arrived, I went immediately to the records department and requested the documents, paid for them, and hurried back to my car.

I took a deep breath, exhaled, and then opened the manila folder. I began to shuffle through the sixty-eight pages and stopped at a page that read, "Miscellaneous Laboratory Test Information." As I made it to the next page, which listed all the test results relating to Andrew's hair follicle test, I was horror-struck when I found that the first result, which was for methamphetamine, revealed that Andrew tested positive. I felt ill. How was Andrew exposed? Was Elaine giving Andrew meth? Could he test positive just for being in close proximity as she smoked meth? Were she and Frank cooking meth? I didn't know, and that scared me.

CHAPTER 31

When my father and my mother forsake me, then the LORD will take me up.

—Psalms 27:10, KJV

*O*n February 7, 2007, a day prior to the hearing regarding the motion to restrict Elaine's parenting time, Adam and Elaine filed a joint motion requesting that Adam be allocated temporary parental responsibilities and primary care and decision making for Andrew.

Consequently, Sandra filed a response to Adam and Elaine's joint motion and added a request for paternity testing to confirm that Adam is Andrew's biological father now that he was going to be an actual party to the case, rather than in name only. Both Sandra and I felt that the paternity test was a reasonable request since Adam and Elaine were not married at the time she had become pregnant. They weren't married until after Adam was incarcerated.

However, because Adam was named as the father on Andrew's birth certificate and swore in court that he was Andrew's biological father, the court denied our request for a paternity test and ordered that the motion be set for hearing to be first preceded by a status conference. Both proceedings were to be set upon notice. The notice to set the status conference was to be filed by Elaine within the next twenty days.

Along with their joint motion, Elaine filed a motion to revoke the stipulation that she signed in the hospital that previous month. Within the motion, she claimed:

> At the time I signed said stipulation, I had just recently come out of a drug-induced coma and was not cognizant of the document, which I had signed. I further was not cognizant or aware of events that had taken place during my coma. I was compelled to sign the stipulation by Crystal Sanchez, who misrepresented the contents of the stipulation as well as the facts and circumstances that had taken place during the time I was in a coma. I was placed under very intense pressure by Crystal Sanchez to sign the stipulation against my will and was not given time to review it.

Ultimately, the court denied the revocation.

The next day, Maria, Sandra, and I sat waiting for the hearing on my motion to restrict Elaine's parenting time to commence. Court was to begin at 10:00 a.m., but it was already 10:10 a.m. when Elaine and her entourage entered the courtroom. Elaine was in one of the courthouse's wheelchairs and was dressed in black with her long blond hair looking great, but everything else looking not so great. Her entourage consisted of her friend Rita, Rita's boyfriend, Adam, Adam's new attorney, and my mom and dad. I was prepared to see my dad, but I was caught completely off guard when I saw my mom.

As I sat waiting for the hearing to commence, I looked over at Mom and suddenly became very conscious of the fact that her love for me has always been conditional.

I was the first and only person to testify at the hearing. Alone, I sat on the witness chair and spoke of the accident, Andrew and

Elaine testing positive for methamphetamine, and the fact that felony charges were pending against Elaine.

Throughout the whole ordeal, Elaine sat across from me, continually mouthing the words, "You're going to die." Her tactlessness was both ludicrous and disturbing. However, in the end, her parenting time was restricted to supervised parenting time, and Adam's efforts to crash the hearing and request parenting time proved to be ineffective as his request was denied.

The magistrate advised that Adam was a party to the case in name only as he never objected to the permanency placement plan and refused to take advantage of the writs that were issued to him in the dependency and neglect case. However, because his parental rights were not terminated, the magistrate advised that he had the right to petition for allocation of parental rights and parenting time. When the hearing concluded, Adam declared that he was going to do whatever was necessary to gain full custody of Andrew.

Maria and I were leaving the courtroom when I noticed Mom actually kissing Elaine's forehead in an effort to console her. At that, something in me snapped. Infuriated, I turned to her and said with reproach, "Mom, she was on meth when she drove off the highway. She hurt herself, she hurt little Andrew and exposed him to meth. He had meth in his system the night of the accident. Weren't you listening? The test results are proof of that, but go ahead, Mom, keep kissing her."

She looked at me with distaste, but before she could say anything, I added harshly, "You have to be the worst mother ever."

She scoffed. "Are you talking about yourself?" Before another unkind word could be said, Maria pushed me out the courtroom doors. As we started down the hall, Elaine, who was now positioned just outside the courtroom, yelled out with all the superiority she could manage, "Look, your whole family is behind me, they all hate you."

I recoiled and told myself, *Ignore her. Just keep walking. Whatever you do, don't turn around.* Yet I did turn around to find my mom, dad, and brother all literally standing behind Elaine. With the pretense of indifference, I shrugged. "Yes, I can see that." Then I turned away to continue down the hall. As we approached the elevator doors, a crushing flood of sorrow took hold of me, and my shoulders began to shake. Maria put her arm around me, and the pain that was all twisted up inside found its release through inconsolable tears.

Because I advised the court during our last hearing that Elaine was on meth at the time of the accident, Sandra advised that we needed to obtain proof before the next anticipated hearing regarding the joint motion filed by Adam and Elaine. So I phoned Detective Loya to see if there was any way he could release the positive drug test to my attorney so it could be used in court.

Detective Loya advised that he could not release the records because charges have not yet been filed. "Your attorney," he advised, "would need to subpoena the records, and the DA's office would have to approve the subpoena since the case has not yet been processed." He paused for a moment and then asked me to hang on. When he returned to the phone, he said, "Let me call you back." He called me back a little later on, but because I was unavailable to answer the phone, he left me a voice message. In the voice message, he informed me that he called the DA's office, and they authorized the release of information by subpoena, so I needed to have my attorney subpoena him for the information.

I conveyed the message to Sandra who immediately sent a process server to serve Detective Loya a subpoena, and a little over a week after serving the subpoena, Sandra received Elaine's toxicology report revealing that she did have methamphetamine in her system at the time of the accident.

Two months after Detective Loya submitted Elaine's case to the DA's office, I called the intake department to check on the status. I gave the woman on the other end Elaine's name. She tapped a few keys and said she couldn't find any information on the case. "It has to be there, the detective that worked on the case said he submitted it to your office on January 17."

The woman tried again. and said, "I'm sorry, there is no case under that name."

After hanging up, I called the DA's office directly. There I spoke to a woman who was able to find the case. She advised that Elaine was now using a hyphen in her last name, which meant she was now using her ex-husband's last name and Adam's last name, an addition to her many aliases. I thanked the woman for her assistance. And with the new information, I again called the intake department. The woman was able to find Elaine's case but advised that it had not been put into the system as of yet. I asked her what that meant, and she said her department was two weeks from adding the case to their computer system.

Suddenly exhausted from all the madness, I began to cry. After a moment, the woman on the other end asked me if I was all right. I spoke softly as I explained to her my dilemma. I told her that I needed proof when I go back to court that there are felony charges pending against Elaine. I explained my fears of Elaine getting Andrew back while I'm waiting for the information to be inputted into the computer system. After listening to me ramble on, she excused herself for a moment, and when she returned to the phone, she assured me that she would be adding the case to their computer system that day. Extremely grateful, I thanked her several times before hanging up.

CHAPTER 32

~~~~~~

Strong and bitter words indicate a weak cause.

—Victor Hugo

*I*n late February, I received a long letter from Mom, which in part stated:

Crystal,

When I watched you in court I knew I could never hate you. What I hate is your attitude. The only reason Adam and Elaine gave you permission to care for Andrew is because you promised to give him back when they were out of jail. You never said until they pass your perfect parent test. Adam still has the letter you mailed him saying that you will care for Andrew until he can do it himself. You made Adam a promise and if you don't keep that promise then you will never be trust-worthy again. How are you going to live with this on your conscience?

God's greatest gift to mankind is a child. You got yours and Adam got his. God also gave mankind free will. What you chose to do with your child was up to you, and what

Adam chose to do with his children was up to him. In the end we will all stand before the Lord and be judged.

Adam deserves a second chance. If he fails then let it be his failure not because he was set-up to fail. Don't set him up to fail like you did Elaine. Elaine had no family, Adam does. I understand how you feel and respect your right to fight for Andrew, but Adam is my son and he has the right to fight for his son too. It's his son not yours. Adam is angry at me because I asked him to be considerate of your feelings and then you decide he can't see his own son. What were you thinking? I thought you were smarter than that. I never thought you could be so hateful to your brother. Why couldn't you have worked things out with Adam instead of destroying your entire family? He may have decided he wasn't up to the task of raising Andrew, and wanted you to keep him, but we'll never know now. Now his feelings have been hurt and he's mad as hell for trusting you and me.

The letter also included several reproachful and inaccurate statements about Liam, but aside from her accusing me of setting up Elaine, the most disturbing part of her letter was how concerned she was that Adam's feelings had been hurt, yet the fact that Andrew's body, mind, and spirit had all been seriously injured didn't come up once. I balled the letter up in my hands and threw it in the trash only to dig it out again. I read it several more times and thought about responding with my own letter, but I was too angry at that point to put anything reasonable into words. So I waited a couple of weeks then responded with the following letter.

March 5, 2007

Dear Mom,

I read the letter you sent me. As one of the few adults that Andrew has come to trust, I will continue to do what is in his best interest, not what would make me popular or loved by my family. There are a lot of circumstances dictating the decisions I have made, circumstances that you are not aware of. Things are not always what they seem, and in situations like this, having faith is crucial.

I realize your anger and pain as you have expressed that in your letter. I want you to know one thing, you couldn't be further from the truth with the remarks you made about Liam, and deep down in your heart, I know you are already aware of this. Liam has held my family, you especially, in the highest esteem. He is a man of integrity and honor and has provided me and my family with his constant and dedicated love and has asked for nothing in return. Sadly, by honoring my wishes, he has become a target of my family's scorn and this is what I regret.

I will always honor you as my mother, but please try to remember that you were chosen by our creator to take care of the child I once was. Since I've become an adult, I don't expect anything more from you. Therefore, please don't overestimate your place in my life by thinking your potential hatred for me will drop me to my knees or influence my judgment in any way. Your love is not what I need to thrive or survive, though if you chose to give it freely, without conditions, I would cherish it.

I am a child of God, created in his own image. I have lived my life with this in mind. I serve only him, and answer only to him. I have continually prayed about Andrew and know in my heart that it would not please God to place Andrew in yet another potentially risky situation only because it is the easiest choice.

I will stand by my decision to do my best to keep Andrew safe. If you feel my decision is setting up Adam for failure, which I assume you mean Adam may start using again, then maybe you also think I alone am responsible for his choice to try meth the first time, and continue meth, and cook meth and sell meth, and expose his child in the womb to meth, and have a baby with a meth addict who again exposed their son to meth, and ruined a family who bought the house where the meth lab took place, and on and on. C'mon life is all about free will, if Adam does fail, he will fail by his own choices, not by mine.

As I already told both Adam and you, my only objective is to keep Andrew safe. It is what it is. It holds no evil, thievery, lies or premeditated conspiracy. If your interpretation of this is misconstrued, it is not up to me to convince you or anyone else otherwise.

Sincerely,

Crystal

I read the letter several times before sending it to Mom. After receiving the letter, she never spoke to me again, but I believe she was already on that path. Even so, already coming from a place of total disenchantment I accepted the outcome as I no longer wished to cling to unreciprocated love.

Even though the court previously denied my request for Adam to undergo a paternity test, through his attorney and for whatever reason, Adam agreed to being tested. I made the appropriate arrangements with Colorado DNA Services, Inc. in Lakewood, Colorado, and paid the close to four-hundred-dollar fee. The plan was for Andrew to be tested first and Adam a week later. So on March 3, 2007, Maria and I took Andrew for testing. The person administering the test only needed to swab Andrew's mouth. Andrew was all right with the swabbing as long as I promised he wasn't going to get a shot. We were in and out in a matter of minutes. Adam went in to be tested a week later.

Due to loss of concentration and the constant stomach aches I was enduring waiting for the paternity test results, I found myself struggling through my work days. I knew nothing could change the love Liam or I had for Andrew. He has been a part of us since just before he turned five months old. We were there for his first solid foods, the first time he sat up, his first tooth, the first time he tried to crawl, his first words, his first steps, the developing of his character. Hell, we've had long discussions regarding the color of his bowel movements, the kind of cough that required a doctor visit, and always watching for any negative signs of his exposure from his parents' drug use. Our love was solid. For us, the test would either substantiate Adam's paternity and our painful process will continue, or Adam is not the father and a new and possibly less painful process will commence.

On March 19, 2007, an employee from Colorado DNA Services called to let me know that the paternity test results were in, and he would be sending them out in today's mail. I thanked him and asked, "Could you give me the results now, or do I have to wait for the mail?"

He said, "The probability of Adam being Andrew's father is greater than 99.999 percent." My heart sank. I thanked him again and immediately called Sandra to give her the results.

CHAPTER 33

Common sense is not so common.

—Voltaire

On April 15, 2007, Elaine left a message on my voice mail stating that she was unable to get a hold of my attorney and asked me to pass on some information to her. "A status conference is scheduled for April 16 at 4:00 p.m. at the Jefferson County Courthouse in Division 10 with Judge Jackson."

Being that April 16 was that next day, I called Sandra immediately. Sandra, or I for that matter, was not happy about the short notice or that we didn't know what the status conference was regarding. Nonetheless, we agreed to meet at our usual spot in the courthouse that next day.

My sister Anna went with me to the courthouse. We arrived a little before 4:00 p.m. and met Sandra at our usual spot. Sandra advised that the status meeting was concerning the joint motion Adam and Elaine filed on February 8, 2007. She also advised that she checked with the clerk earlier and was told that the conference was to be held in courtroom 1C with Magistrate Gonzales. She wasn't sure why Elaine said we were to meet with Judge Jackson.

When we reached courtroom 1C, no one was to be found. Sandra went to the clerk's office to check in. When she returned, she said that we needed to meet in Magistrate Gonzales's chambers. As we were gathering our things to go, Ray Gleeson entered the courtroom in a wheelchair with his nursing assistant pushing him from behind. He looked at me and said, "Hi."

"Ray, is that you? I didn't recognize you because you're so skinny."

"I'm dying," he said wryly.

"I thought since your surgery, you were getting better."

He shrugged. "Well, I am I guess."

Anna came over to where Ray and I were chatting. "Let's get going," she said.

I informed Ray that we were told we needed to meet in Magistrate Gonzales's chambers, so like a herd of confused cattle, we all followed Sandra to our destination. Adam's new attorney, John Samuels, was already present when the clerk asked us to wait. There was no place to sit, so we all just stood there looking at one another, waiting for Elaine and Adam to show.

After a few minutes, Elaine entered the room, also in a wheelchair, with Adam pushing from behind. In the quietness, Ray, who introduced himself as "Elaine's dad," yelled over to Adam's attorney, "Hey, come over here." He was wheeling himself toward a far corner of the room while indicating with a head movement that's where he wanted to meet.

Adam's attorney seemed embarrassed by the outburst and said harshly, "I don't represent you, I represent Adam."

Ray turned to Adam and asked, "Can your attorney talk to me?"

Adam, also looking a little embarrassed, shrugged. "If he wants to."

Adam's attorney seemed annoyed with the two of them and turned to Ray. "I'm really not interested in keeping secrets from any of the involved parties," he said. At this, Ray mumbled something under his breath and wheeled himself out the door. I had to bite my lip to keep from laughing. The whole scenario was nothing less than comical.

We all continued to wait, and about fifteen minutes later, the clerk came in the room and informed us that we would be meeting Magistrate Gonzales back in courtroom 1C. I was irritated but figured that due to the two wheelchairs, more room was required. So we all headed back up to courtroom 1C.

The magistrate was already present when we arrived. Both attorneys started off by informing Magistrate Gonzales of my and Adam's current position in the case as did Elaine, who was representing herself. Sandra then presented and distributed to the magistrate and the other parties the documents from the district attorney's office disclosing Elaine's first court appearance in her new criminal case and the charges filed against her along with a copy of her toxicology report confirming that she had methamphetamine in her system at the time of the accident and also Andrew's toxicology report revealing he tested positive for methamphetamine the day of the accident. With that, the drama commenced.

As I sat quietly, Elaine and Adam verbally attacked every aspect of my being. In the midst of all the verbal abuse, Magistrate Gonzales stunned us all by telling Elaine to "Shut up." Even so, Elaine continued her tirade. Growing more impatient, Magistrate Gonzales threatened to place her in contempt of court. Playing the "I'm in pain" card Elaine said, "I would go to the hospital."

"No, you will go to county jail," Magistrate Gonzales retorted.

"No, I'm on too much medication and would have to go to the hospital."

Finally to everyone's relief, Elaine did shut up. Then Adam, acknowledging an opportunity in the new stillness, in his best attempt at sincerity, said, "Your honor, I just want to see my son."

At that, Magistrate Gonzales softened and suggested that Adam file a motion for parenting time (visitation), then he turned to me. "Although I won't authorize any parenting time today, I would not intervene if you two (referring to me and Adam) wanted to work something out between the two of you."

When the status conference came to an end with all previous orders remaining status quo, Sandra asked if I wanted her to consult with Adam's attorney on the supervised parenting time. I wanted to say no; however, noticing my hesitation, Sandra advised that eventually Adam is going to obtain parenting time, and at that realization, I reluctantly acquiesced.

Magistrate Gonzales left the courtroom while the rest of us remained to negotiate Adam's parenting time. After some discussion, I agreed to the proposed parenting time, which was to take place at my home every Sunday for two hours. If these visits were found to be successful, the schedule would be amended accordingly. However, Adam argued against the supervised visits and insisted that he should be able to take his *own* son out for a couple of hours without supervision.

"It's not going to happen that way." I said. Adam glared at me as Sandra suggested that we move on. Adam, with obvious irritation, turned to Sandra. "Do you think this is funny?" Sandra looked at him with obvious confusion. "You kept snickering during the court proceeding like something's funny. How would you feel if your child was stolen from you? How would that make you feel?"

Sandra held her ground. "Well, if I smoked meth and ran my child off the road—"

"I don't want to hear about that. That's over and has nothing to do with this," Adam interrupted.

Worried that Adam may strike Sandra, I told him to back off while Anna advised that we needed to move forward, not backward.

At that point, Adam's attorney moved in, and in an effort to diffuse the nasty situation, he looked at Adam and said as gently as possible, "Why don't we start visitation with baby steps." After a brief discussion between Adam and his attorney, Adam reluctantly agreed to the proposed supervised visits.

Does Adam really think that Elaine's offense has nothing to do with us being in court today? Does he really think that Andrew's victimization is simply over? I thought. Adam's distortion of the truth made me want to scream.

On April 29, 2007, Adam's supervised parenting time with Andrew commenced. Just before 10:00 a.m., the doorbell rang, and I opened the door to find Adam ready for his visit. I hadn't told Andrew about the visit because I didn't want him to be disappointed if Adam didn't come, so he was very surprised to see his dad. They played first in Andrew's room and then out in the backyard on the swing set. After the visit was over, I walked Adam to his car, and we talked for a while. With all the trust issues between us, nothing was ever resolved when we talked, but we were warm to one another, and it felt good.

After a couple more supervised visits, I agreed to Adam taking Andrew to the park around the block from my home, and because those visits went well, I agreed to Adam having four-hour unsupervised visits with Andrew under the condition that they spend the time between just the two of them as this was a time for bonding. Also, and more specifically, Dad, Bianca, and Angela were to have no contact with Andrew whatsoever.

When Andrew came home from that first four-hour unsupervised visit with Adam, he said he didn't want to go with his dad anymore. I asked him why, but he only shrugged. I called

Adam to inquire on the visit, and all he said was that he took Andrew to Lakeside, an amusement park in Denver, and they had a great time. Even so, I could tell he was holding something back. I reiterated what Andrew said about not wanting to visit him anymore. "Why do you think he would feel that way if you both had a great time?" I asked.

"Well, we never wanted to visit Dad either, but we still had to go." I argued that he was missing the point, but because he didn't like what I was saying, he simply stopped listening. His lack of concern was bothersome as was Andrew's statement, yet without good reason, it wouldn't be fair to just suspend the visits. So I agreed to another four-hour unsupervised visit that next week.

Four hours into the visit, Adam called to say he was going to keep Andrew for a while longer to see a movie. I reminded him that we agreed on a four-hour time frame. "I know, but Andrew really wanted to come see a movie, and we're already here," Adam said. He then went on to say that he didn't realize it was so late and would have Andrew back right after the movie. Recognizing his manipulation but still not wanting to disappoint Andrew I acquiesced. "Just have him home right after the movie."

The next morning, Andrew and I were out back on the patio swing when out of the blue, he said in a soft voice, so soft it was barely audible, "Grandpa Paul went with me to Lakeside."

I kept swinging, trying to appear unruffled. "Oh, so you and your dad and Grandpa Paul all went to Lakeside together?"

"Yes," he said. Then after a moment he added, "Bianca too." I remained quiet for a moment as I considered his words "Are you mad?" he asked.

"No," I lied.

Andrew seemed to ease at that.

"Angela went with us to the movies."

"That must have been fun," I said.

He shrugged. "Can I have a cookie?"

Knowing Adam my whole life as he is my brother, I am well aware of his difficulties with following the rules, his knack for overstepping boundaries, and his ability to manipulate others. Still I allowed myself to believe that he was being responsible with Andrew. However, by allowing my dad and Bianca to join them on their outing to Lakeside, he placed Andrew in an unexpected and disquieting situation, which resulted in Andrew no longer wanting to visit with Adam.

In view of this, I became incredibly aware that the visits shouldn't continue without a written down and detailed, court-approved parenting time (visitation) schedule. I believed that the threat of legal consequences may be the only thing that would deter Adam from any precluded deviations.

Sandra, who was unable to contact Adam's attorney, left a message at the attorney's office advising that because Adam was not adhering to the conditions of our verbal agreement regarding visitation, the visits will no longer take place without a court order.

A week later, I was in Sacramento, California, attending a work-related class. Knowing that Sandra had not yet received a response from Adam's attorney regarding the terminated visits, I was worried the message wasn't passed on to him, and consequently, he would be expecting to pick up Andrew for a visit that coming Sunday. So that evening, I took a deep breath and phoned Adam.

I was sick to my stomach by the time the call ended. It was standard for my and Adam's conversations to begin and end with everything being my fault. And for the most part, I usually tolerated his tirades, but not this time. This time, I lowered myself to his level and said a mouth full. I can even say I went a little overboard. No, I went way overboard. The worst part was that it wasn't worth the guilt and shame that consumed me as soon as the conversation ended. While everything I said that evening was the truth, some truths are best left unsaid.

CHAPTER 34

Trickery and treachery are the practices of fools that have not the wits enough to be honest.

—Benjamin Franklin

On May 16, 2007, I left work early to attend Elaine's preliminary hearing for her criminal case. Anna and I drove to the Jefferson County Courthouse together. The hearing was to commence at 1:30 p.m.; however, the DA's office asked if we could arrive an hour early to meet with the prosecutor, as a month or so earlier I called to inform the DA's office that I wanted to be involved in all aspects of Elaine's case on Andrew's behalf.

When Anna and I arrived at the courthouse, we found ourselves waiting in the victim/witness holding room as requested by the woman at the desk. When the prosecutor arrived, he and two women, the assistants on the case, led us to a conference room and we all took a seat. Maria arrived shortly after. The prosecutor introduced himself as Braden Diaz. He was very tall, with dark hair and olive skin.

After I conveyed what I knew about the accident, he informed us on how the court system works in this kind of criminal case. In my effort to be as proactive as possible, I brought along a certified copy of Andrew's medical records so the DA's office would not have to go through the process of obtaining them. I also brought along some pictures of Andrew.

Braden advised that he understood that this case was a very emotional thing for us but wanted to make it clear that he could not work the case with any effort to benefit my on-going custody case. I nodded to show my understanding.

After our discussion, Anna, Maria, and I went to the courtroom to attend the hearing. Elaine was already present, sitting in the aisle in her wheelchair two rows down from the defendant's table. We took a seat in the back row on the prosecution's side. We watched as Elaine frantically scratched at something on the left arm of her wheelchair. When the judge called her case, she and Braden approached the front of the courtroom.

The judge was already upset at the fact that Elaine had just turned in her paperwork for a public defender the day before, which didn't give the public defender any time to review Elaine's case. The judge was also upset because there were a couple of officers present to appear as witnesses, and their time had been wasted. Even so, the judge granted Elaine a continuance until that next month, June 13, 2007, and informed her that she would give her this one chance as she was wasting the court's and witnesses' time.

Elaine, whose new deception was to speak with the disposition and verbal communication of a mentally challenged individual, explained that she had been in the hospital with a brain injury and didn't understand the rules about getting a public defender. Anna, Maria, and I were totally taken aback by this. I myself figured Elaine would play "the poor victim" card. But I never expected her to act as though she was mentally challenged from an alleged brain injury.

Unless you can catch a brain injury like you can catch a cold, Elaine was totally misrepresenting herself since just four weeks prior to this hearing, she had the ability to represent herself at the status conference concerning our custody case without displaying even the smallest hint of a brain injury. I scolded myself for being so surprised by the brain injury bit, knowing Elaine as I did, and vowed to be prepared for anything from that time forward.

While Elaine was being wheeled out of the courtroom, she actually raised her frail looking arm and said in her best feeble-minded voice, "Good-bye. Have a good day." Maria, Anna, and I just sat there bewildered, mouths agape trying to understand what just happened.

After the hearing, Braden requested that we wait in the courtroom's conference room so he could speak with us for a moment. As we sat in the conference room waiting for Braden, we discussed Elaine's bizarre behavior and tried to keep from surrendering to the giggles as this was a very serious matter. When Braden entered the room, he thanked us for waiting and then conveyed that he was worried about the case as his office was unable to locate Frank. Apparently, Frank was on the run from three outstanding warrants.

Braden explained that his office needed to speak with Frank so he could corroborate that Elaine was driving the vehicle at the time of the accident. Without his corroboration, Elaine could claim that Frank was driving the vehicle at the time of the accident. Braden's words were disconcerting as it hadn't even occurred to me that Elaine could say she wasn't driving. I assumed that the witnesses' testimonies at the time of the accident would be enough to prove that Elaine indeed was the driver. Yet I would find out later that not any of the witnesses actually saw who was driving the vehicle. "For what it's worth," I said to Braden, "I'll find out which counties Frank has been issued a warrant and contact those jails on a daily basis to inquire if he's been incarcerated."

As luck would have it, a week later, I learned that Frank was arrested two days earlier and was being held in the Jefferson County Jail. I immediately called Kathy, Braden's assistant on the case, to inform her of Frank's arrest and where he was being held so that the DA's office could send out an investigator to speak to him.

Almost a month after Elaine's preliminary hearing was continued, on June 13, 2007, the rescheduled hearing would take place. Anna and I arrived at the courthouse a half hour early, and as I checked in at victims/witnesses, Anna agreed to stay in the hall near the window to keep an eye out for Elaine as we were curious if she was able to walk since as of late, she was using a wheelchair.

The woman at the front desk asked me to have a seat in the waiting room and told me that someone would be in to talk with me. I waited for about ten minutes, then went out to the hall to check on Anna. When she saw me, she waved me over. "Elaine just got here, and she's walking." She hesitated a moment, then said, "Adam drove her in and then parked over there." She pointed in the direction of Adam's car. "I think he's coming in with her."

I walked quickly over to the metal detectors and looked into the lobby but didn't see either of them. When I turned to walk back to where Anna was standing, I heard the exit door open, and I turned back around. Without noticing me, Adam grabbed the handles of a wheelchair that was apparently put aside for Elaine, then turned to leave. "Adam," I called out in a calm but loud voice.

He looked up at me, and his face lost all color. I looked at him with disgust as he mumbled, "I had to give her a ride." Without comment, I turned on my heels and walked back down the hall. I returned to the victims/witnesses waiting room and found Anna waiting for me. We both just sat there stewing over Adam's lack of sensitivity toward Elaine's victim, Andrew. Kathy, Braden's assistant, walked into the room, and we made the customary greetings. Then she turned to me and said, "The prosecutor doesn't want you to sit through the preliminary hearing because you may be called in later as a witness."

"How can I be a witness if I didn't witness the accident?" I asked with obvious confusion.

"Since you're Andrew's primary custodian and took care of him after the accident, you can be called as a character witness."

"If I can't sit through today's hearing, I would like my sister and daughter to attend."

Acknowledging my determination, she smiled. "Let me talk to Braden about that, and I'll come back here and let you know what his advisements are."

I nodded, and Kathy walked out of the room. Moments later, Maria arrived, and Anna filled her in on the conversation I had with Kathy and then told her about Adam driving Elaine to the courthouse.

"No!" Maria said incredulously.

Anna and I both nodded our heads and in unison said, "Yes!"

Court was to begin at 1:00 p.m. I looked at my watch and it was already 1:07 p.m. I asked Anna and Maria to wait where they were. "I'll be right back."

I walked up to the front desk and requested to speak with Kathy, and as I began to explain my situation, Kathy walked into the room, apologized for the wait, and escorted me back to the waiting room, where she informed us that Elaine's attorney waived the preliminary hearing.

"This is actually good news for the prosecution," she said smiling, "because now our office doesn't have to take on the task of proving Elaine was driving the car the day it drove off the highway." We looked at each other with relief. Then Kathy asked if we would mind waiting a couple more minutes to speak to Braden. We agreed to wait and a few minutes later, Braden entered the room, "The next court date, Elaine's arraignment, is scheduled for July 23, 2007," he said without preamble. I began adding it to my calendar. "I offered Elaine's attorney a plea bargain," Braden advised.

Surprised, I looked up at him. "I thought Elaine was going to take this to trial."

"I've advised Elaine's attorney that if she chooses to take this to trial, she will be tried as a habitual."

"Last time we spoke, you said Elaine didn't have enough on her record to be tried as a habitual."

"Well, after we spoke, I reviewed the file again along with the information you provided and took it back to the assistant district attorney, and she established that Elaine met the criteria to be tried as a habitual. So if Elaine ends up going to trial and loses, she could end up receiving a prison sentence of forty-nine years." We all looked at one another, mouths agape. "However, if Elaine takes the plea, she could end up with a six to thirteen year sentence," Braden added.

"I don't care if she takes the plea and ends up only getting six years. I just want her to be convicted of the crime she committed."

Braden looked at me inquisitively. "Child abuse," I said.

CHAPTER 35

You may juggle human laws, you may fool with human courts, but there is a judgment to come, and from it there is no appeal.

—Orin Philip Gifford

On September 10, 2007, I called Braden to inquire on Elaine's upcoming motions hearing. The phone only rang twice when he answered, "Braden Diaz." Expecting his voice mail, his voice caught me off guard, and I fumbled through my introduction. He said considerately, "I remember who you are."

"I'm calling to see if anything's been filed for tomorrow's motions hearing."

"The hearing is being held next month, October 11."

Now feeling stupid, "Oh, for some reason I thought it was tomorrow," I confessed.

Ignoring my comment, Braden changed gears. "I received your phone call last month, but after I spoke to Kathy, she informed me that she spoke to you on what to expect from the motions hearing."

"Yes, I did talk to Kathy, and she did inform me on the motions hearing, but my reason for calling initially was to find out if Elaine is in fact going to stand trial as a habitual."

"Well, so far I have the information on the things she's done in Colorado, but I haven't received anything on Nevada or any of the FBI information. Hopefully, I will receive that information prior to the deadline. I know that she has been in prison before, but I've been unable to locate the information required to file the motion."

"What kind of information do you need?"

"I need case numbers and disposition dates, that kind of thing."

"I know the name of the detective that was looking for her in Nevada, would that help?"

"Do you have case numbers or her DOC number?"

"No, but the detective might know where those things can be located. I'm referring to the detective who was on her *Unsolved Mysteries* episode."

"She was on *Unsolved Mysteries*?" Braden said incredulously.

"Yes, that's how the feds found her. Someone turned her in after an episode aired. The episode portrayed her as a woman using fraudulent cashier's checks to purchase high-priced items in Las Vegas."

With obvious surprise, he said, "This is news to me."

"Yeah, at that time, Elaine was using the name Beth McGuire, one of her many aliases. Then when she was caught and the US Marshals flew her out of North Carolina, she was already using a new alias.

"All those names will come up under her fingerprints," Braden advised.

"I sure hope you're right."

"Well, I'm waiting on some information, but I will let you know if I can use your help," he said.

I thanked him for his time, then we said our good-byes and hung up.

Later that evening, I started reviewing the paperwork I had on Elaine's background and found a case relating to the fraudulent cashier's check in Nevada and another relating to her fugitive status in North Carolina. I scanned the documents and e-mailed them to Braden along with the link to the update of Elaine's *Unsolved Mysteries* episode. In the e-mail, I stated, "At the end of the episode it's mentioned that Elaine has also been in trouble in Oregon, which I was unaware of and felt it may be helpful to the case."

Elaine's criminal, pretrial conference and motions hearing were to commence October 11, 2007, at 8:00 a.m. Due to an important meeting at work, I was unable to attend. However, Kathy advised that she would call me once the hearing concluded to inform me on what transpired. Kathy called earlier than expected. "The defense attorney asked for a continuance."

"On what grounds?" I sighed.

"He claimed that, Elaine takes a lot of medication in the morning, and therefore is not clear minded enough that early (8:00 a.m.) to attend a hearing. So, he requested that the hearing be rescheduled for a time later in the day."

"Well, I guess I'll just continue to wait."

"It's better to do as they ask so they can't come back later and use it for an appeal," Kathy advised. And I reluctantly agreed even though I found it to be absolutely absurd. I mean, why wait until the last minute to request a continuance if the morning medication problem was really an issue. Two weeks after Elaine's motion hearing was continued, I received an envelope in the mail from Sandra. Enclosed was a notice to set the hearing for temporary orders by telephone. It stated, "Please take notice petitioner will contact the courtroom clerk, located at 100 Jefferson County Parkway, Golden, Colorado 80401, by telephone on Friday, October 26, 2007, at 11 a.m. for the purpose of setting a hearing for temporary orders in this matter. You may be present at that time. If you are not, you will be contacted by telephone shortly thereafter." The notice was signed and submitted by Ned Berkshire, attorney-at-law. I had no idea what the incredibly vague notice meant or who Ned Berkshire was, and I didn't have a clue on what kind of temporary orders he was proposing. Regardless, I was afraid that it may have to do with the custody case I was now caught up in with Adam. The same custody case I hoped he had dropped since I hadn't heard from him in four months. I phoned Sandra to inquire on the notice only to learn that she was going to be out of town for the next two days.

I didn't sleep at all that night. When I arrived at work that next morning, I called the clerk of the court first thing to see if someone could shed some light on the notice I received. However, the woman I spoke with could only convey what I already knew; absolutely nothing.

In an effort to at the very least be well equipped enough to identify any fabrications that may arise during any upcoming court hearings with Adam, that next day, I contacted the Department of Corrections to get the status of his parole. The man that answered the phone gave me the name and number of Adam's case worker, Joel Campbell. Joel didn't answer the phone, so I left him a message inquiring on Adam's inmate or parole status.

Joel returned my call within a half hour. He introduced himself and then asked, "Why do you need to know Adam's correctional status?"

This immediately made me angry. "Isn't it public information?" Thinking again, I said, "My name is Crystal Sanchez, and Adam is my brother. He and I have a hearing coming up (I lied) as he is trying to gain custody of his four-year-old son, whom I've had custody of for the past year. When I attend the court hearing, I would like to have the facts on Adam's status within the Department of Corrections."

"What do you need to know?" he said, to my surprise.

"Has Adam been paroled?"

"No, he has not been paroled he is on ISP-I, intensive supervision program- inmate," he said.

"I thought he was eligible for parole in June of 2006."

"He was, but he has not been paroled."

"How many times has he been up for parole?"

"He's been up for parole twice."

"So does that mean he's been turned down for parole twice?"

"Yes."

"Is Adam still wearing an ankle monitor (electronic monitoring device)?"

"Yes."

I thought about this for a moment. "How is it possible that Adam can take me to court to try and gain custody of a child when a parole board doesn't even feel that he should be released into the community without an ankle monitor?" I said, thinking out loud.

"That's up to the courts to decide, not the Department of Corrections," he advised with a tone of annoyance. I apologized, and explained that I was merely thinking out loud and not really looking for an answer.

"Anything else?" he said impatiently.

"No, nothing else," I said. Then I thanked him for his time before hanging up.

On November 1, 2007, Sandra returned my call regarding the notice of hearing. After our short greeting, she said, "I haven't talked to Adam's attorney yet, but the court dates he mentioned won't work for me."

"What is this all about? What does temporary orders mean?" I asked impatiently.

"I'm sure Adam didn't tell this new attorney everything that was going on, so he probably filed the wrong paperwork. I'll try to get a hold of him to discuss it."

"Would it be possible to hold him off from going to court for whatever this is until after the holidays?"

"I'll see what I can do," she said.

I called Sandra the next day to see if she heard from Mr. Berkshire. She wasn't available, so I left her a voice mail. A while later, she returned my call, and informed me that after speaking to Mr. Berkshire, she was certain the wrong paperwork was filed, so she didn't really know what to expect from the hearing. "Unfortunately, I was not able to hold off Mr. Berkshire until after the holidays, so the hearing date is scheduled for December 10, 2007, which was the latest date he would agree to, or rather the latest date Adam would agree to." In preparation for the temporary orders hearing, Sandra spoke to Alice to get her thoughts on Adam obtaining parenting time (visitation). Alice was not in agreement with Adam having parenting time because she believed Andrew required continued stability, so going from one household to another would not benefit his recovery process. At Sandra's request, Alice agreed to testify to the same at the December 10 hearing. Consequently, I forwarded Alice's information to Sandra, and she sent out the subpoena.

The temporary orders hearing commenced on December 10, 2007 as scheduled. During the hearing, Magistrate Gonzales ordered therapeutic supervised parenting time for Adam (visitation with a therapist supervising) and ordered me to pay half the cost. "What?" I said confused as Sandra signaled for me to be quiet.

The magistrate then ordered Adam and I to agree on a CFI (child and family investigator) and advised that the cost of the CFI would be split between the two of us. *You've got to be kidding*, I thought. I had no idea how Liam and I were going to pay for these additional expenses. Even though victim's services paid for the first seven and a half months of Andrew's therapy, Liam and I had been paying from then on. With the therapy cost, the cost of Andrew's daycare, court stuff, and Andrew's normal expenses,

Liam and I had already gone through all our savings and even refinanced our home to pay off some outstanding bills and were now simply living paycheck to paycheck.

Adam must have read my mind because after the hearing, he confronted me with a smirk. "I'm going to take you for every penny you have." Adam, who never helped with any of Andrew's expenses, or even reimbursed any of the money I sent to him while he was in prison, was indeed taking me for every penny I have. I expressed my concerns to Sandra about having to pay half of Adam's supervised visits, which I felt was ridiculously unfair. Sandra advised that we had to play the game and jump through all the hoops.

After the hearing, I began researching CFIs. I managed to narrow down my search to five potential and affordable candidates and e-mailed each one requesting their information regarding their CFI experience. I also ran a search on visitation centers that offered therapeutic supervised parenting time since I was to pay half the cost, then I created a list of both and e-mailed them to Sandra so she could forward them to Adam's attorney. Even so, Adam wasn't interested in any of my findings and instead proposed we use Dr. Rob Reed as the CFI in our case, and although I found Dr. Reed's fees to be too high and he was located sixteen miles from my home, in my effort to "play the game" I agreed to him being appointed as the CFI in our case.

Adam's attorney filed the motion to appoint Dr. Reed as the child and family investigator in our case and also filed a motion for modification of parenting time.

CHAPTER 36

Men become accustomed to poison by degrees.

—Victor Hugo

On February 26, 2008, I received an e-mail from Sandra asking me to contact Dr. Reed's office because he needed my contact information. As instructed, I made the call, and one of his assistants asked if it would be possible for me to meet with Dr. Reed that next day at 11:30 a.m. I agreed to the appointment, though reluctantly due to the short notice, and that next day drove the sixteen mile distance to Dr. Reed's office. When I arrived, I was requested to complete a medical form. I completed the form and returned it to the front desk. I sat down on a long green couch and assessed the room.

The room didn't yell out "well-paid psychologist." A coffee table was located directly in front of the long green couch and held a big bowl filled with penny store candy such as Tootsie Rolls, Dots, and Dum Dums. The furniture in the room consisted of not only the long green couch and the coffee table but also a blue wing chair that was positioned caddy corner from the coffee table and a book case that was situated on one side of the entry way. The décor was nothing more than a pink-and-yellow flower pot containing an ill-looking plant and a candle holder containing a leaning candle stick. Other than that, there were two matching prints hanging on a wall and looked as if they would be better housed in a low-budget motel and a few calendars were tacked on the walls here and there. Oddly, the lack of harmony in the room increased my feeling of unease.

Dr. Reed waved me into one of the three offices. When I entered, I asked where he would like me to sit. There was a cushy black leather recliner, a couch, and a chair. Dr. Reed pointed to the black leather recliner and said, "That's my chair, so you could sit anywhere else." I chose to sit on the not-so-comfortable couch. We made the necessary introductions, and he went over the process of the upcoming investigation, which consisted of individual interviews between me and Dr. Reed; a joint interview between Adam and I; an interview with Dr. Reed and Liam; a home visit at my home, at which time Andrew, Liam and I shall all be present; a home visit with Adam, at which time Andrew shall be present; a parent child interaction, one with me and Andrew and one with Adam and Andrew; personal references, either in person or in writing; and professional references, either in person or in writing.

After explaining the process, Dr. Reed informed me that one of the assistants at the front desk would get me started on my evaluations, which turned out to be a ninety-eight question psychological evaluation and several pages of written questions relating to my social and economical history. I grew frustrated over the written questions as they kept repeating themselves, but I answered every question as directed. When I was finished, I gave the evaluations to one of Dr. Reed's assistant, paid my half, fifteen hundred dollars, of the costly retainer, made an appointment for the next week, and then began my sixteen-mile drive home.

On the drive home, I thought about all that was yet to come and made the decision to write down and summarize everything

I felt should be mentioned to Dr. Reed during our next interview with the hope that one costly session would be sufficient for his report. However, my efforts were for none because with all of Dr. Reed's questions, writing, and more questions, I would end up having eight costly individual sessions before they would finally come to an end.

In early March of 2008, because Liam and I were growing more concerned with all our new financial responsibilities, I went to the Adams County Department of Social Services to see about obtaining TANF (Temporary Assistance to Needy Families), knowing that Adam would be made to reimburse any money I would receive. (TANF is a federal public welfare program that provides temporary cash assistance to relatives for children under their care.)

I met with a TANF worker, and once we began talking, she informed me that since Adam had a job, it would be better for me financially if I went through the child support enforcement office to obtain child support from him. "Why hasn't the magistrate in your ongoing court case issued a child support order?" she asked.

"Well, I guess because I never requested or filed for one." I laughed. "But then I never requested Adam to have supervised parenting time either, and yet the magistrate ordered me to pay half the cost." She gasped. "Yeah, that's how I feel," I said.

On March 14, 2008, I filed for child support through Adams County Child Support Enforcement (CSE). Consequently, a negotiation conference was scheduled for April 24, 2008, only to be rescheduled by Adam's attorney for April 29, 2008.

In preparation for the upcoming negotiation conference, I contacted a CSE worker to inquire on the paperwork I was to complete. "Where do I add the daycare fees?" I asked. The worker advised that her office doesn't negotiate daycare expenses. "That would be something for a judge to decide." Consequently, the April 29 negotiation conference was canceled, and a court hearing was scheduled in its place for July 2, 2008.

It was April 22, 2008, when I gave the house a good cleaning in anticipation of Dr. Reed's home visit that next morning. He was to arrive at 8:00 a.m. So I woke early, took a long shower, and got dressed. Liam must have awakened Andrew because I could hear giggling from his room as I brushed my teeth. I put Andrew in clean pajamas because it was pajama-and-movie day at his preschool, and Liam made him breakfast. As Andrew ate his breakfast, I went out back to water the flowers. Liam came out a few minutes later to inform me that Dr. Reed called to say he was just getting ready to leave even though it was already ten minutes till 8:00 a.m.

Dr. Reed finally rang the bell at 8:45 a.m. I answered the door and said lightheartedly, "You're late." He made the comment that traffic was awful as I led him to the kitchen where Andrew and Liam were.

"This is what is going to happen," he said straightforwardly, "first, I need a tour of the house. Then I will let Andrew show me his room, and then we will meet back here in the kitchen so I can ask all of you some questions." As requested, we gave Dr. Reed a tour of our unpretentious home and backyard. Andrew then showed him his room while Liam and I waited in the living room. Afterward, we all met at the kitchen table as Dr. Reed proceeded with his questions. The first question was directed at Andrew. "What kind of things do you get in trouble for?"

To my horror, Andrew blurted out, "I drink too much." I began to explain Andrew's meaning, but Dr. Reed hushed me and continued on with his questions. When the visit came to an end, I walked Dr. Reed to the door and explained that just that morning while Andrew was drinking his milk, Liam told him to put it down and eat some of his breakfast before he gets too full. Dr. Reed assured me that he suspected it was something like that and thanked me for letting him into our home. The whole process was harmless enough, and I felt, or hoped, the visit went well.

Six days after our home visit with Dr. Reed, Adam's home visit was to commence. At that time, Adam was renting a house that Dad owned while it was up for sale, which was fortunate for him since due to his criminal record, it would have been next to impossible for him to rent anything on his own. Because the home visit was to include Andrew, I agreed to transport him to Adam's for the visit. As usual traffic was terrible that morning and we ended up arriving fifteen minutes late. I honked, but no one looked or came out of the house, so I parked behind Dr. Reed's van and walked Andrew to the front door. His mood was subdued while I was anxious.

Adam answered the door. "I'll be waiting in the car," I said to both he and Andrew. I got back in the car and put on my earphones and began listening to a book on my iPod. I kept my eye on the window to search for movement in the curtains and at the door. A couple of minutes went by when Adam came out and approached the car with a steaming cup of coffee. When he got to the car door, I rolled down my window a bit, and he asked if I wanted some coffee. "I already have some," I said pointing at my coffee cup. He looked disappointed, and for a moment, I felt a little sorry for this and said, "Thank you anyway." When the visit was over, I asked Andrew how it went, and being a child of few words, he said, "Good, Auntie."

Two days after Adam's home visit took place, Andrew and I were scheduled to have our parent-and-child interaction session at Dr. Reed's office. As I approached Dr. Reed's office building, I saw Sandra smoking a cigarette out front. As I parked the car, I waved and smiled at her. She stubbed out her cigarette, and as she came over to the car, she said, "Hi, Crystal, I just finished meeting with Dr. Reed, and he said you two were his next appointment, so I waited to see you guys." I removed Andrew from his car seat, and we chatted as we all rushed into the building.

When we walked in the front door, Dr. Reed pointed at me, and I'm sure unintentionally, called me "Mom." "Mom," he said, "you need to follow me, and Andrew needs to stay here for a moment."

Noticing my concern, "I'll keep an eye on him until you get back," Sandra said.

I smiled at her and followed Dr. Reed as he led me into a room that was furnished with mismatched toys. He placed two chairs directly across from one another. "This is how I would like these chairs to stay."

"Okay," I said with uncertainty.

Then he led me into his office and handed me a card that had a list of directions typed on it. He hurried through the list. "I will call you on the phone when I want you switch to the next item."

"Okay," I repeated.

He then pointed to a picture on the wall. "This opens into a two-way mirror, and I will be viewing your interaction with Andrew from here. When you first go into the toy room, you can play freely until I call, at which point you will need to play something of your choice."

"Okay," I said for the third time.

I began experiencing pretest panic as I followed Dr. Reed back to the toy room. I smiled when I saw that Sandra and Andrew were both on the ground playing. That is until Dr. Reed said hastily, "Sandra, you have to leave."

I was embarrassed by his rudeness, but Sandra didn't appear to be offended. "All right," she said. Then she waved to Andrew and disappeared out the door.

Andrew and I looked around the toy room as Dr. Reed left the room and closed the door behind him. Already forgetting about the "play freely" part, I grabbed two figurines, a small lion, and a large lion. "Let's play baby lion and daddy lion," I said to Andrew.

"I want to be the baby," he yelled. So I handed him the baby, and we played follow the leader. Only a couple of minutes into our play, the phone beeped.

I picked up the phone. "It's time for you to choose something to play," Dr. Reed said.

"Okay," I said feeling a bit confused since I thought that's what we were already doing. Then I remembered that we were suppose to start out playing freely.

I looked over at the toys and picked up a bag of blocks. "It's Auntie's turn, so how about we play with blocks."

I took the baby lion from his hand and placed it back on the shelf next to the daddy lion and started to pull blocks out of the bag that held them. I could only find four blocks that were the same. I looked down and saw a bag full of cars and planes. I pulled three cars and an airplane out of the bag. I stacked the blocks, and very naturally Andrew and I began to jump the blocks with the cars and airplane as if we were stunt men. After a couple of minutes, the phone beeped. "It's now time for you to teach Andrew something," Dr. Reed advised when I answered the phone.

"Okay." I put the cars and blocks away when the phone beeped again.

"Leave the toys out. If you keep putting them away there won't be any left for Andrew to pick up when it's clean up time."

"Oh, okay."

I grabbed a book that was sitting in front of us. I pointed to a word and instructed Andrew to spell out the word and then sound it out, then tell me what it is.

Andrew was excited when he spelled, "R-a-b-b-i-t."

I asked him to sound it out. He began, "Rrr" and yelled out "Rabbit."

I beamed. "You're even smarter than I thought!" Once I remembered we were being watched, we continued with a couple of other words and then started working on addition when the phone beeped.

"Now I want you to talk with Andrew about something distressing. I don't want him holding anything because I want him to focus on the conversation. The discussion could be about anything, but I want you to start with his dad." Not being very happy about this part of our session, I nodded my head and hung up the phone.

I sat Andrew down in front of me. "Now we're going to talk for a little while."

He disputed this and said he wanted to play with the toys.

"Now we are going to talk for a little while," I repeated softly.

He looked up at me and acknowledged my resolve. "Okay, Auntie."

"How did you feel when you went to visit your dad yesterday?"

"Good."

"What kind of emotions were you feeling?" I asked, knowing he's been learning about emotions in therapy.

"Good."

"Tell me what some emotions are."

"Happy and sad."

"Do you feel your dad is a safe person?"

"No. 'Cause he was in the accident." Then he thought for a moment. "You mean Adam, not Frank?" I nodded. "Yeah, Adam is a safe person." Andrew often had Adam and Frank mixed up not only because Elaine had him calling both men "dad," but because they looked so much alike.

"How would you feel if you were to spend the night at Adam's house?"

"No no no," he cried. "Adam would sleep at our house with me, Uncle, and Auntie."

"How about we talk about your mom," I said, shifting gears.

He looked at me puzzled. "You are my mom." I was both stunned and thrilled by his statement. He had called me mom several times before but never declared that I was his mom.

"I mean Elaine, your mom who was in the accident with you and Frank."

"I don't want to talk about her."

I pressed him to talk about Elaine a bit further but only managed to bring him to tears. His sad little face made my heart ache. "I don't want to talk anymore either."

"Auntie!" he exclaimed, "call Dr. Reed and tell him that we don't want to talk anymore and tell him that I even cried."

"How did you know Dr. Reed is the person I've been talking to on the phone?" I laughed.

"I just know. Call him, Auntie."

Then the phone beeped. "All right, it's time to clean up," Dr. Reed said.

As we were leaving, Dr. Reed smiled at me. "You did good," he said. I was surprised by his comment because I had not received any kind of feedback from him before.

CHAPTER 37

If time be of all things the most precious, wasting time must be the greatest prodigality.

—Benjamin Franklin

On May 13, 2008, the first joint session with Adam at Dr. Reed's office was to commence. I wasn't sure what to expect but felt nothing good could possibly come from it. I went to work that morning but should have stayed home since concentrating was impossible with the butterflies wreaking havoc on my insides. I left work early enough to stop by my house to feed the dogs on the way to Dr. Reed's office. The highway route I took was a slow one, so to divert my thoughts, I turned up the radio. While my appointment time grew nearer, I began to worry that I may be late, which would not be a good way to start off an already unsettling situation. Fortunately when I finally arrived at the office, I was on time.

When I walked into the waiting room, Dr. Reed greeted me and said that Adam was held up in traffic and asked me to take a seat in the waiting room. Adam arrived about fifteen minutes later, and I was surprised when he sat next to me on the couch. He looked over at me and asked, "Was traffic bad for you?" But before I could reply, Dr. Reed appeared and asked us into his office.

We sat in two chairs placed in front of his desk while Dr. Reed explained the process. I had to interrupt him when he advised that we would be having these joint interviews until they were no longer necessary. "Do you mean I'm going to have to come back again?"

"You will need to come back again and again."

This confused me because during our first meeting he said there would be a joint interview with Adam. He didn't say there would be several joint interviews with Adam. Dr. Reed then advised that we would all be meeting one more time after the joint sessions are complete to discuss a parenting plan.

Again, I interrupted, "Isn't that what you're here for, to make recommendations to the court regarding parenting time?" He agreed that it was his job to make recommendations, but it was part of his process to have Adam and I give input on the parenting plan. It was obvious that my interruptions were beginning to annoy him, so I refrained from asking anything further but clearly realized that his fees could quickly get out of hand.

Dr. Reed explained that the joint sessions would be taped, and those tapes would be erased once his report was complete. He also advised that he didn't want me or Adam taking notes as he wanted us to focus on the topics at hand, and that during the sessions we were to look at one another rather than at him. He then went over the rules, which included, "There will be no interrogating or physical fighting." I wondered how many physical fights took place in this office before that became a rule. Annoyingly, several times during his instructions, Dr. Reed stated, "I know you hate each other."

Having heard it enough, I finally said, "I don't understand why you keep saying we hate each other. I don't hate him." I looked over at Adam. "He's my brother. I love him. As children we were very close."

Dr. Reed looked over at Adam. "Well, I know he hates you. He's told me on several occasions." I looked at Adam in disbelief, but he didn't deny it. "So you don't hate him, and he hates you. Let's continue, shall we?" Dr. Reed said smugly. I wanted to give his fat, smug face my middle finger, but I came to my senses and refrained.

Moving on to the actual session, Dr. Reed asked what topics we wished to discuss. Adam threw out a couple of topics, and although I was prepared with various questions, not actual topics, I did the same. Dr. Reed turned on the recorder. "Who wants to start first?"

Adam turned to me. "You go first."

I nodded my head in agreement. "Why do you want custody of Andrew?" I said with uncertainty.

You would have thought that I spit in his face by the way he glared at me. "Why do I want to parent my son? He's my son. He has my hands." I looked at him, wondering if that was his full answer and what it meant.

"Why do you want to keep my son from me?"

"That's not the case."

"Then why did you stop my visits with him?"

"After your second visit with Andrew, he told me that he didn't want to visit with you again. Remember? I called and told you this."

"You never called me."

"I did call you, and you said, 'When we were little, we didn't want to stay with our dad either, but we had to'."

He smiled knowingly. "You never called me." He lied.

"I did call you, and you know it," I retorted.

Realizing this argument was going nowhere, I took a moment to calm myself and take a different approach. "After Andrew told me about what Dad and Bianca did to him and the fear he showed towards them, I felt it would be best if they no longer had contact with him. But on your first unsupervised visit the first thing you did was allow them to have contact with him, and because of that he no longer wanted to visit you."

No matter how I tried to explain the reasoning behind my decisions, he just continued accusing me of keeping his son from him. Then he asked several questions all at once, which in essence were not questions at all, but rather accusations and implications. "Why didn't you take Andrew to see me in prison? Why did you turn my other two sons against me? Why did you and Liam take such an interest in my kids? Don't you think that's weird?"

What is he trying to imply? I thought to myself. But I didn't ask, because I didn't want to hate him. Adam smirked at my unmistakable pain as I tried to gather my thoughts. But before that was possible, he bombarded me with several more unsettling so-called questions along with some blatant accusations, including that I previously used cocaine with him. Things were getting so out of hand, at one point I looked up at Dr. Reed, wondering why he hasn't put an end to Adam's unquestionably pointless badgering, but could see by the obvious intrigued look on his face, he had no intention of doing so.

Eventually, Adam's trumped-up accusations and empty questions hurled me into fight mode. I eagerly argued and disputed all his claims until my head started buzzing and I could feel heavy anxiety coming on. My eyes welled up with tears, and I rose from the chair, "I'm sorry, but I can't do this," I said to Dr. Reed. I looked down at Adam and said softly, "Liam and I took care of your kids because you were absent, and it was the right thing to do. If you would have chosen them over meth, none of this would be necessary."

As I headed for the door, Dr. Reed yelled out, "If you walk out that door, you're taking your power with you."

I again said I was sorry and walked out the door. "Please don't schedule any more appointments for me," I said as I passed by the receptionist. I then hurried to my car, but before I left the parking lot, I took some time to completely crumble.

I drove home fuzzy headed and nauseated, after regaining a bit of composure. I called Liam on the phone when I finally pulled into the garage. When he answered, "I walked out on the session," I said without preamble.

"I know. Sandra called me. She wants you to call her."

"I think I really blew it," I cried.

"No, honey, you didn't," he said softly.

"Well, I better call Sandra."

"I love you, honey."

"I love you too."

Sandra was angry that I walked out of the session. She reminded me that this was for Andrew, not about me, and recommended that I call Dr. Reed and request another appointment. I was fuming after we hung up, but as I sat there in the car for a couple of minutes feeling sorry for myself, I knew she was right. I needed to continue to jump through hoops and play the game for Andrew's sake.

I settled overnight and then called Dr. Reed's office the next morning. I apologized and requested another appointment. He agreed to let me make another appointment, and for this I was both grateful and uneasy.

Just shy of a month after that first brutal joint session with Adam, I was sitting on the long green couch, waiting for our second joint session to commence. Adam walked in, glared at me, then sat on the wing chair across from me. I looked down and fiddled with my phone. I could feel his eyes on me and began to feel very uncomfortable.

"You've gotten fat," he said spitefully. Even though I was not fat, his harsh words still hurt. I looked up to find him grinning, obviously pleased with himself. "Not everyone is on a meth diet." I retorted. He glared at me, and to my relief, Dr. Reed came out to greet us. We followed him to his office and sat in our usual seats.

Dr. Reed started the meeting with a recap of our last session, including the last part, when I refuted Adam's accusations then walked out. Dr. Reed then turned on the recorder, and Adam began the conversation by saying with obvious enjoyment, "You did use cocaine with me." Without flinching, I refuted his claim. Not getting the response he wanted, he tried a different approach. "We can't do this if you're going to just sit there and lie," he said.

"You know I'm not lying," I calmly countered.

Acknowledging that I was no longer taking the bait, Adam began challenging Dr. Reed's decision to allow me to return to the sessions after I walked out on the last one. "This session shouldn't even be taking place since you walked out on the last one." He was annoyed that I didn't have to face any consequences.

"I called Dr. Reed's office and apologized for walking out and requested another appointment, if Dr. Reed would allow it. My apology was accepted and I was told that I could make another appointment, and I did."

"You talk about following the rules made by social services and the court system, but then you just get up and walk out even though Dr. Reed told you that if you walk out the door you would be taking your power with you. But you didn't lose any power or have to face any consequences, did you?"

"What kind of consequences would you like me to face—prison?"

"If I would have been the one to just get up and walk out, this whole thing would be over, but since it was you, no consequences," he said bitterly.

I restated that I called Dr. Reed's office and rescheduled upon his approval, but Adam would not listen and continued on with his unrelenting, time-sucking, pity party until I finally looked directly at Dr. Reed and said, "Can we just move on please?" Dr. Reed nodded in agreement.

Adam glared at me and said with disdain, "You think you're better than me, don't you? It's all a control thing with you, isn't it? You need to have all the say, don't you?"

Trying to appear unmoved by his outburst, I switched gears by reminding him that during our last session, one of the questions he asked was, "Why did you and Liam take such an interest in my kids?" From a folder sitting on my lap, I pulled some copies of the letters he sent me while he was in prison and handed them to him. "If you read those letters, you will see that you asked me to be a part of Andrew's life." He looked down at the letters. "In every one of those letters you request something of me for not only Andrew, but also your other two boys, so why did *you* want me to care for Andrew? Because you knew you could count on me and Liam to do what's best for him under any circumstances as we did and still do for your other two boys?" He tried to interrupt, but I continued, "I'm sorry, but I had to put my foot down when it came to Andrew. I couldn't let you hurt him like you hurt your other two boys."

He just looked at me as if I was crazy. Even so, I held my ground. "In that first letter, you asked me to be an aunt to Andrew. You said I would fall in love with him and that he needed me. I told you that I couldn't get involved with another one of your situations, but you and Mom convinced me to visit him." Adam seemed to be searching his memory, so I added, " He was two weeks old at the time." Adam nodded with uncertainty. "Yeah, Elaine was crying because she said you left her and Andrew in that hotel room with no money for diapers, formula, or rent. So Maria and I went to the store and bought everything she would need and even paid her rent."

"I didn't know about that," he said incredulously.

"How could you, you left them."

He shook his head. "Elaine conned you."

"Is that always your response when you have no response?"

Adam didn't comment, Instead he changed the subject. "You set Elaine up."

"What are you talking about?" I said totally baffled.

"The night of Andrew's accident, you were the one that wanted a hair follicle test done on him."

"Bianca is the one that asked for it at first, and then we all agreed it was a good idea," I said.

"No, you asked for it, and you seemed to want it real bad."

"We all agreed one should be done. Anyway, what does it matter who asked for it? It needed to be done. So what are you getting at?"

"I've been thinking about this for some time. You were at the hospital alone with Andrew for a long time."

"Maria and I both stayed with Andrew at the hospital, and remember, you even asked me to stay because you weren't going to. Why didn't you stay?" I asked.

"I couldn't stay because of my ankle monitor."

I looked into his eyes. "Which was a consequence of your choices."

"You were the one who gave the meth to Andrew," he said with reproach.

"What? That's just crazy talk, even for you."

Disregarding my comment, he said with certainty, "When you were at the hospital with Andrew, you gave him the meth to set Elaine up."

I was stunned into silence.

"I was one hundred percent behind you before all of this, but after everything you've done to me, I do believe you gave Andrew the meth in order to get what you want. You must have put it in his shampoo or sprinkled it in his hair."

His unfeasible and outlandish accusation sent shivers up my spine. *Was he serious?*

"You can't believe that. It's not even possible. To test positive for meth through a hair follicle test, the meth would have to be in your blood system, not sprinkled onto your hair." Adam just stared at me, grim-faced. "And how is that setting up Elaine?

She's in trouble because *she* was under the influence of meth when she drove her car off the highway and seriously injured Andrew."

"You and Liam are evil, evil, people and cannot be trusted. I was wrong to ever trust you guys. The car accident was not Elaine's fault, and all the charges are going to be dropped, and I'm going to take Andrew from you, and you will never see him again," he threatened.

"You are in complete denial," was all I could manage to say. He scoffed and then mumbled something about me giving Andrew attachment issues by keeping him away from Elaine and him.

"Andrew's attachment issues started the day you were incarcerated and carried on when his mom was taken off in handcuffs and he was made to live in foster care. If you recall, after that he lived and bonded with Liam and I for a year and a half, then was returned to his mom, and you know what happened there. So now that he's happily and safely back with Liam and me and in spite of everything he's already been through, you want him to be uprooted again and be placed with you?"

"Yes," he said without consideration.

Irritated by his hasty answer, I said, "Children don't work that way, Adam. You can't just pass them around like they're some kind of object." I tried to reason with him, but he was having none of it. Instead, he changed gears again and started talking about the quickly approaching Father's Day holiday.

"Are you having a big party on Father's Day for Liam so you can all pretend that Andrew is his son? Are you guys planning something big?" He said coldly.

"Are you really worried about what our plans are for Father's Day when you haven't bothered to send Andrew a card or call him on any given holiday, including his birthday?"

"I've tried to call him, but you changed your phone number."

"Really," I said incredulously, "because we've had the same phone number for the past twelve years. It's never been changed."

"Well, I've called several times, and no one answered, and then some strange guy would come on your answering machine," he said dimly.

"That voice came with our voice mail," I said, trying not to laugh.

He looked at me quizzically, but I made no effort to explain and instead said, "Well, since I have no record of your phone calls, your phone number must be blocked or shown as a private caller. We usually refrain from answering these types of calls since most are from solicitors. Why haven't you offered me your phone number? If there's an emergency with Andrew, wouldn't you want me to be able to contact you?"

Adam didn't reply. At that time, to my relief, Dr. Reed held up two fingers indicating that we only had two minutes left. After the session ended, Dr. Reed advised that we needed to make another appointment with his assistant.

"I've said all I need to say. I don't think we need another appointment," I said adamantly. However, Adam advised that he had plenty more to say and thought we did need another appointment, and I had no choice but to acquiesce.

Dr. Reed left us alone in his office while he went to speak with his assistant. "So are you going to let me have Andrew for Father's Day?" Adam said with a smirk.

I looked at him in disbelief. "No," I said with resolve.

He got up out of his chair, and with stone-cold hatred in his eyes, he cursed at me and walked out of the office.

I took a seat in the waiting room, and when I was sure Adam had gone, I went to Dr. Reed's office and asked if he had a minute. He waved me in, and as I tried to maintain some level of calmness, "He's going to kill me," I said.

"No, this may be hard for you, but I assure you it's not going to kill you."

"No I mean it literally, Adam is going to kill me. The longer we continue with these sessions, the angrier he gets. These sessions are placing me in a dangerous position." Dr. Reed tried to reassure me, but really, it wasn't his life on the line.

CHAPTER 38

Men use thoughts only to justify their wrongdoings and
words only to conceal their thoughts.

—Voltaire

After managing to maneuver numerous continuances, nineteen months after her alleged crime, Elaine's jury trial would finally take place. The trial was scheduled for three days. Anna, Maria, and I were present for its entirety. Liam was unable to attend as he had to work and be available to pick up Andrew from daycare. No other family member attended any part of the trial to support Andrew, the victim, with the exception of Dad, who was subpoenaed to testify and stayed just long enough to do so.

PEOPLE VERSUS ELAINE BARELA-PEREZ JURY TRIAL DAY ONE, JULY 8, 2008

Court convened at 8:04 a.m., and the judge said, "Good morning, people versus Elaine Barela-Perez."

"Braden Diaz and Tim Wright on behalf of the people," Braden said.

"Ned Berkshire appearing on behalf of Elaine Perez," Mr. Berkshire said.

After all parties made themselves known and present, the judge was handed a motion for continuance of trial, which was apparently filed by Mr. Berkshire five days earlier. There was a discussion held regarding Mr. Berkshire's inability to produce Elaine's medical records for the prosecution's review, thus the filing for a continuance. Fortunately, the parties came to an agreement, and the court denied the motion for a continuance of trial.

Preliminary matters were then discussed such as the timing of opening statements and jury seating. The judge then asked if there were any other preliminary matters to discuss of which there were several, one of them being Mr. Berkshire's objection to the introduction of any evidence revealing that methamphetamine was found in Andrew's system at the time of the accident.

"I understand a hair follicle test was taken that showed a slight amount of methamphetamine in the child's system," he said callously. He went on to argue that he didn't believe such information was relevant, and the prejudicial affect would greatly outweigh the probative value. "Plus the evidence is that Ms. Perez had picked the child up perhaps twenty minutes before the accident in this case, so obviously she's not responsible if there's any methamphetamine in the child's system."

Mr. Berkshire using the word *slight* while explaining the amount of meth found in Andrew's system was nothing less than shameful. Has the world really come to a place when there is actually a tolerable quantity of meth to be found in a child's system?

Ultimately, Braden conceded, indicating that the methamphetamine found in Andrew's system was not relevant to the charges. "On the child abuse charge, as we've alleged, it is essentially based on the driving conduct and the injuries sustained there, so we did not intend to go into that information."

The jury was brought in, and the judge read them the complaint in the case, "Count one, child abuse resulting in serious bodily injury. On December 19, 2006, Elaine Perez, unlawfully, knowingly, or recklessly caused an injury to or permitted to be unreasonably placed in a situation that posed a threat of injury to the life or health of a child, namely Andrew Perez, that resulted in serious bodily injury to the child in violation of section 18 -6-401 (1) (a), (7) (a) (III), Colorado Revised Statues. Count two, vehicular assault. On December 19, 2006, Elaine Perez, unlawfully operated or drove a motor vehicle while under the influence of alcohol, one or more drugs, or a combination of both alcohol and one or more drugs, and the conduct was the proximate cause of serious bodily injury to Andrew Perez in violation of section 18-3-205 (1) (b), Colorado Revised Statutes. Count three, vehicular assault. On December 19, 2006, Elaine Perez, unlawfully operated or drove a motor vehicle while under the influence of alcohol, one or more drugs, or a combination of both alcohol and one or more drugs, and the conduct was the proximate cause of serious bodily injury to Frank Hernandez in violation of section 18-3-205 (1) (b), Colorado Revised Statutes. Count four, driving under the influence. On December 19, 2006, Elaine Perez, unlawfully drove or operated a motor vehicle while under the influence of Alcohol or drugs or both, in violation of section 42-4-1301 (1) (a), Colorado Revised Statutes. The charges against the defendant are not evidence. By pleading not guilty to the complaint the defendant says she did not commit the crimes. The defendant is presumed to be innocent. The prosecution has the burden of proving the charges beyond a reasonable doubt. Reasonable doubt means a doubt based upon reason and common sense which arises from a fair and rational consideration of all of the evidence or lack of evidence in the case. It is a doubt which is not a vague, speculative or imaginary doubt, but such a doubt as would cause reasonable people to hesitate to act in matters of importance to themselves. The jury will decide whether the prosecution has proven beyond a reasonable doubt that the defendant has done the things contained in the complaint. Twelve jurors will be chosen to try this case. They will consider all of the evidence produced during the trial. It will be the sole responsibility of the jurors chosen to try this case to determine the facts from all the evidence received during the trial. This will require your close attention, absolute honesty, impartiality and sound judgment."

The lengthy jury selection process followed the complaint; then the jury instructions were read by the judge along with the rules governing jury trials.

Before the opening statements could take place, Mr. Berkshire requested to approach the bench, which the judge approved. Mr. Berkshire approached the bench and requested a bathroom break for Elaine. The judge was not pleased and, outside the hearing of the jury, said, "From now on, everyone needs to understand that we're going to go an hour and a half to two hours between breaks and need to plan accordingly." She then turned to the jury and said, "We're going to take a recess as quickly as possible."

After the short recess, opening statements were read. Then the lunch recess was taken at 12:15 p.m.

Court reconvened at 1:20 p.m. with the judge asking if there were any preliminary issues on behalf of the people or the defendant.

Braden advised that he had a few preliminary issues. "One of them deals with Mr. Frank Hernandez, who is actually sitting in the box right now. We anticipate him to testify third in this case. I believe there were some issues that he wanted to address to the court, and I figured it was appropriate to do so outside the presence of the jury." The judge agreed, then turned to Frank and asked him what he wished to address.

"Your Honor, I've asked the district attorneys on numerous occasions, every time I've talked to them, to not subpoena me on this case for the very fact that you know I am doing eight years in prison right now, and you know I don't think I'd be a good witness in this case. I mean, my safety would be a concern. The defendant and I know a lot of the same people." Frank went on to plead with the judge to not make him testify, but his efforts were futile as the judge advised that she doesn't get to decide which witnesses do or do not testify.

"If the people subpoenaed you, they have the right to put you on. I have no authority about whether or not you would be a good witness. Zero. It's not up to me, it's not a choice that I have or that I can make."

Some more issues were discussed and when the discussion came to an end, Frank was escorted out of the courtroom, and the judge asked that the jury be brought in. After welcoming the jurors back, the judge said, "We're now going to have the first witness for the people."

The first witness for the people was Paul Perez. Paul, who is my and Adam's dad, spoke to Elaine when she picked up Andrew minutes before the accident. He was called to the stand and sworn in. Braden asked him the required preliminary questions such as what does he do for a living, where does he currently reside, where he resided in December of 2006, and so on. "And, sir, do you have any type of relationship with an individual known to you as Elaine Barela-Perez?"

"Yes."

"And what was that relationship?"

"She was married to my son."

"Okay, how many children do you have?"

"I have five."

"Five?"

"Yes."

What? I was baffled. I thought perhaps he just got mixed up since Dad only has four children, only four that I'm aware of anyhow.

"Okay, and she was married to which son?"

"She was married to my son Adam Perez."

Dad was then asked to recall the events that took place on the day of the accident. Amongst other things, Dad conveyed that Elaine was late picking up Andrew, so his son, Adam, called Elaine to inquire on why she was late. Elaine mentioned car trouble and said she was on her way. When questioned on what Elaine was wearing at the time, Dad was unable to recall but did say she appeared to be very tired, like she had a rough night.

Actually, Dad was unable to recall a lot of things during not only the direct examination, but also the cross-examination, redirect examination, and recross-examination, perhaps at Adam's request. Nonetheless, when he was finally asked to step down, I was immersed in disappointment. Disappointment for his lack of recollection or his lack of integrity, I couldn't be certain.

The next witness for the people was Mike Graham. Mike was a student at the University of Colorado. Just prior to the accident, he had picked up his brother from Denver International Airport, and as they were headed back to Boulder on Highway 36, he noticed Elaine's vehicle had gradually started moving toward the right as if it was going to take the upcoming exit. However, it missed the exit by several yards and instead, struck a guardrail, then flipped several times.

Mike explained to Braden and the jury that he pulled over to the side of the road as fast as possible, and he and his brother ran under the overpass when they noticed a man (Frank) crawling out of the windshield area looking discombobulated. As they approached the wreckage, Mike's brother asked Frank if there was anyone else in the vehicle, and Frank said that there was a child in the back seat. Mike and his brother looked in the car and saw Andrew lying on his side.

"What was the child's demeanor?"

"It was just crying."

It? I thought. *Why is he referring to Andrew as "it"?*

"Okay. Where in the car was the child located?"

Mike could not recall.

"Okay. In other words, was the child in the car seat, do you recall?"

"No, it was not."

"Okay. At that time, did you or your brother do anything with the child?"

"No, we did not."

"Was there a reason why you didn't?"

"My brother's a lawyer, and he knows the liabilities."

"Oh, okay. You didn't want to move the child. And after you observed the child in the car, what did you do?"

"That's when I jumped back over the guardrail and went up to the top to recuperate."

"What do you mean when you say recuperate?"

"Well, I've never seen anything like that before in my entire life so I had to chill out and especially after seeing the child in the back."

My eyes welled up with tears, and I wanted to scream out, *How could you just leave Andrew in the car like that? He was terrified and needed someone right away!*

Mike then explained that his brother followed him up over the guardrail, and as he was speaking to him, they looked down and saw a mannequin-like woman next to the very last part of the pillar. They approached the mannequin-like woman and discovered it was not a mannequin but a real person. Mike's brother started screaming, "Ma'am! Ma'am! Ma'am!" They soon discovered the woman was Elaine.

"During the course of that afternoon prior to the vehicle hitting the guardrail, was there anything that you saw on the road, whether it be a person, an animal, another car, anything that you saw that would cause that vehicle to go off the road?" Braden asked.

"No, not at all."

"Anything with regards to the weather on the streets that day?"

"No, I especially remember how nice it was because it was a couple of days before that big blizzard hit us."

Mr. Berkshire did a cross-examination, and then Mr. Graham was asked to step down.

The next witness for the people was Frank Hernandez.

"Good afternoon, sir," Braden said.

Frank said, "Good afternoon."

"We obviously see that you're in an orange jumpsuit today, can you describe the circumstances of that?"

"I'm incarcerated right now at Fort Lyons on a special offender case. I'm actually doing five felonies right now. I have five priors," Frank said proudly.

"Okay. We're going to talk about those in just a moment, okay? Before we do, sir, do you want to be here today?"

"No."

"Okay. And we actually subpoenaed you to require you to be here, is that correct?"

"Yes."

"If you had your way, would you be sitting in that witness stand right now?"

Frank tossed his hair and said, "No, if I had my way, I'd be back in prison right now."

"Okay. Sir, do you know an Elaine Barela-Perez?"

"Yes, I do."

"And how do you know her?"

Frank, tossed his hair. "About a year and a half ago, she gave me a job at this night warehouse where she was a manager."

Then Frank went on to say that he just needed the paper so he could prove to somebody that he had a job, but he didn't actually go to the job because it paid a mere seven bucks an hour. "I just wasn't going to do that," he said with self-importance.

"When did you and Elaine start dating?"

Frank professed that he and Elaine never really dated because she was married but that they became romantically involved about six months after they met. He then maintained with much arrogance that he had a lot of girlfriends and they all had a specific task; however, Elaine's task was not revealed.

"Okay. Let's talk about December 19, 2006. On that particular day, you were involved in a car accident, weren't you?"

"Yes."

"I want to talk to you about the circumstances leading up to that car accident, okay?"

"Okay."

"Had you hung out with Ms. Perez the few days prior to that motor vehicle accident?

"The morning before, I took over breakfast, McDonald's, because it was around Christmas time. I had some gifts and stuff."

"At that time, did you have any means of transportation?"

"Yeah, I had like three or four different cars around town," Frank said smiling at the jurors as though they were his personal audience.

"Do you recall in that timeframe the vehicle that Ms. Perez was driving?"

"Yeah, I think it was a Rodeo that the church had given to her."

"Was that the one you were in during the course of the accident?"

"Yeah, I believe so."

"Do you know how long she had it prior to the accident?"

"Maybe two days, three days, something like that."

"Had you driven it before the accident?"

"The day before and the day of the accident."

"Can you tell us when was it that you met with Ms. Perez with her vehicle the morning of the accident?"

Frank was uncertain of the time.

"At some point, was it just you and Ms. Perez at her apartment or residence?"

"Yes."

"Okay. Did you guys leave from there together?"

"Yes."

"Who drove?"

"I did."

"Okay. Where did you go?"

"We went, I believe, up Kipling to Interstate Seventy over to my friend's house at Fifty-Second. My friend owed me some money for a haircut or something, and I asked Elaine to drop me off there and after she picked up her son, she could come back and pick me up."

"Is there any reason why you didn't go with her to pick up her son?"

"Well, yeah. Because for one, I needed to pick up this money, and two, I didn't want to cause any problems for her by me showing up at her husband's house."

"How long was Ms. Perez gone?"

"If my memory serves me right, maybe fifteen minutes, twenty minutes maybe."

"When she came back was she alone?"

"No."

"Was she still in her Isuzu?"

"Yes."

"Okay. And you mentioned a while ago that you guys had a plan that afternoon, what were you guys going to do?"

"Well, I had like some gift certificates and some money. When I picked her up that morning, I asked if it would be okay if she drove me to Boulder and I could buy the baby some presents and stuff like that."

"Did you ever head toward Boulder?"

"Yeah."

"Could you describe for us when Ms. Perez came back to your friend's house?"

"Well she called me on my phone and asked if I could meet her outside. So I walked up to the corner, and she pulled up."

"And did you get in?"

"Yes."

"What side of the car did you get in?"

"The passenger side."

"Okay. And you were in the passenger seat?"

"Yeah."

Frank explained that he was writing a song in his journal, and Elaine was talking to Andrew. Andrew was telling her about what he had done with his auntie and uncle (referring to me and Liam). Frank claimed that he saw a flash of red. They were in the second lane over, and he looked up and saw a bridge; then the vehicle rolled several times.

"During the course of those rolls, did you see what happened to Ms. Perez or the baby (referring to Andrew)?"

"Well, we hit, and I seen Elaine for a second, and then she just disappeared. We continued to roll. I thought the accident lasted at least two minutes, but after looking at the paperwork, it was a couple of seconds. All I know is when the car stopped, I was in the back, the very back, and I had to crawl all the way to the front. I had a broken right shoulder and a broken left wrist, and I couldn't hear anything. My hearing was gone. I could see the baby like upside down, and he had these two straps over him that strapped him in. And you know with a broken shoulder and with a broken arm, I couldn't get that thing open. I tried to get him out. I tried to pull him through, but he was just in there too good."

"You mentioned that you ended up in the back of the vehicle?"

"Uh-huh."

"Are you aware of how you got out?"

"No. I have five different theories, but no. All I know is that I passed the baby on the way out."

Hadn't it even occurred to Frank that he should at least stay there with Andrew until help showed up? Andrew needed someone to comfort him and tell him that everything would be all right, not someone to pass him on the way out of the wreckage.

After discussing the accident, Braden said, "Okay, let's go ahead and talk a little bit about your history."

"Oh, all right."

"You have eight felony convictions, right?"

Frank looked towards the jury, tossed his hair, and with a smile he said, "I have ten."

"Oh, you have ten. Let's see, your first one dates back to 1995?"

Frank concurred. As they discussed in detail Frank's extensive criminal history, Frank identified and counted each conviction on his fingers. It was apparent that he was very proud of his career criminal status.

Next, Braden and Frank went over Frank's injuries resulting from the accident, and among other things, Braden questioned him on some photos taken at the scene.

Throughout his entire direct examination, cross-examination, redirection examination, and recross-examination Frank smiled, tossed his hair, and seemed to not have a care in the world, though his orange jumpsuit indicated otherwise.

The next witness for the people was Dr. Abby Jewell. Dr. Jewell was qualified as an expert in the field of emergency medicine and emergency pediatric medicine. She was the emergency room physician at Children's Hospital who examined Andrew after the accident and testified to the fact that Andrew suffered serious bodily injuries as a result of the car accident that took place on December 19, 2006.

The next witness for the people was Stan Dole. Stan Dole, a detective with the City of Westminster Police Department, testified that he responded to St. Anthony Hospital to assist an investigation into a vehicular accident with injuries. At the hospital, he oversaw the blood and urine withdrawal taken from Elaine Barela-Perez and explained how the collections took place.

On cross-examination of Detective Stan Dole Mr. Berkshire asked, "Did you know that Ms. Perez had a blood transfusion?"

"I did not know that, sir."

"Judge, may we approach?" Braden interrupted.

"No further questions," Mr. Berkshire said.

"No, I want to approach," Tim then interrupted.

"You may approach. Ladies and gentlemen, if you'd like to stand up and stretch, go ahead," the judge advised.

Outside the hearing of the jury, Tim said, "Judge, we've had previous instances where we litigated this issue concerning the blood transfusion. Mr. Berkshire admitted on the record that the blood transfusion on Ms. Barela-Perez took place after these draws happened. He asked the question in bad faith."

"I don't know if it was in bad faith. I'm asking what he knows about—"

"What he knows about the medical records that we still don't have," Braden interrupted.

"What are you requesting? Do you want to move to strike?" the judge said.

"I would move to strike the question," Tim said.

"Do you want to say anything about that?" the judge asked Mr. Berkshire.

"I'm sorry?" Mr. Berkshire said.

"Do you want to say anything about that? I'm granting the motion to strike," the judge repeated.

"Was he going to withdraw the question or what?" Mr. Berkshire said.

"There's a motion to strike the answer," the judge said.

"Well, he answered he didn't know, and I said, 'No further questions.' If you want to strike, I don't know."

"That's fine," Tim said.

"Please be seated. Ladies and gentlemen, I am going to advise you that there's been a motion to strike the answer of the witness, and I'm granting the motion to strike. I'm ordering you not to consider the answer of the witness in any way."

With Tim not wanting to redirect, the judge asked the detective to step down. The evening recess was announced, and the jury was dismissed.

"Anything further on the record on behalf of the people?" the judge asked.

"Judge, I'd like to make a record with regards to the last bench conference. I have a number of concerns here with regards to how we've proceeded. You know in the last week or so, we've litigated this issue concerning the defendant's medical records, and when Mr. Berkshire first got on this case, he presented the potential issue of this blood transfusion as a matter of the hypothesis that somehow the blood that Ms. Perez received in the hospital was part of a transfusion that could somehow be tainted with methamphetamine, and we effectively litigated it. So his last question to Detective Dole, one, I don't understand the relevance of it, but obviously it's extremely prejudicial. It seems to put that issue into play when he knew in fact it can't possibly be in play.

"Now I understand that the court already sustained our objection, and that's as much as we can do. But we keep broaching this issue over and over again, sort of painting the edges of Ms. Barela-Perez's medical condition. And to accommodate this trial, which has gone on for a year and a half, we've basically gone forward and permitted certain stipulations as a condition to take place in the absence of those medical records.

"But it seems like through the testimony, Mr. Berkshire is trying to traipse on the edge of this and make her mental and physical condition at the time an issue. And I object and request some sort of order from the court or an extended motion in limine barring him from what I would call sort of these peripheral questions that places that as an issue to insinuate some sort of doubt."

"Mr. Berkshire?" the judge said.

"Your honor, I think somebody charged with a crime has a right in cross-examination to challenge evidence presented by the government. We have medical reports. I looked at the medical reports. As best I can tell, they indicated that the blood transfusions occurred after the blood draw, but I think I have a right to ask if a person is aware of when the blood transfusions were taken and that was the extent of it. Detective Dole said he didn't know or didn't know anything about them. I don't understand what the objection is really about."

"Well, I do, and I'm going to order you from now on, Mr. Berkshire, if you're going to ask any questions regarding the mental or physical or any condition of Ms. Perez, that you ask to approach the bench first. This is an issue that was litigated pretrial. I don't believe there was a good faith basis for it. You've still never provided the medical records, but you're trying to put these matters in issue, and I ruled pretrial that you could not do so without specific limitations and without providing the medical records. So if you wish to ask any questions regarding the mental or physical condition of the defendant, I want you to approach the bench first. Court will be in recess until 8:00 a.m. tomorrow morning. Ms. Perez, your bond is continued until that time."

At 5:12 p.m., court was concluded.

The agitation on Braden and Tim's face concerning Mr. Berkshire's obvious unwillingness to play fair, left me with a feeling of unease. That, along with the exhaustion I felt from being on pins and needles all day was pure agony. When I got home to my wonderful family, I gave Andrew a big hug and just like that, the day was washed away.

CHAPTER 39

Truth never dies but lives a wretched life.

—Yiddish proverb

PEOPLE VERSUS ELAINE BARELA-PEREZ JURY TRIAL DAY TWO, JULY 9, 2008

*C*ourt convened at 8:02 a.m. After the preliminary issues were discussed, the judge asked that the jurors be brought in.

The next witness for the people was Joe Barela (no relation to Elaine Barela-Perez).

Joe Barela, a police officer for the City of Westminster, testified to being dispatched to a serious rollover accident westbound at Thirty-Sixth and Sheridan and reported that he arrived from the east traveling westbound and observed a blue Isuzu underneath the overpass.

After some discussion regarding the accident scene and those parties involved, Braden said, "Okay. After you completed your on-scene investigation, what was the next responsibility you had?"

"Typically with these large accidents, officers are all on scene and we have different tasks. My task that day was to respond to the hospital to check injuries of the parties involved. See which level of case we have."

"And in an investigation like that, once you find out injuries during the course of an investigation, what do you do?"

Mr. Barela explained that he speaks to the doctors involved, and once they have determined what injuries are involved, if it rises to the level of serious bodily injury, he has the doctor complete a form.

"And did you collect forms in this case?"

"I did."

"Who did you collect forms for on this case?"

"I collected forms on the child, Mr. Hernandez, and Ms. Barela-Perez."

At some point in the redirect examination, Braden asked Mr. Barela, "As one of the first responding officers in this case, was it your responsibility to ask who was driving?"

"Correct."

"Did you do that on scene?"

"Correct."

"Who was driving?"

"He (referring to Frank) indicated that Elaine was driving."

Next witness for the people was Matthew Shaw. Matthew Shaw, a traffic investigator for the Westminster Police Department, testified as an expert witness in the field of accident investigation and reconstruction. Mr. Shaw said that accident reconstruction is basically explaining how the accident occurred from the physical evidence on the roadway to the damage on the vehicles. He then explained that he was dispatched to an accident scene on December 19, 2006. He responded to the westbound lanes of

Highway US 36 and east of Sheridan Boulevard. Once he arrived, he evaluated the scene.

"Now, Investigator Shaw," Tim said, "when you arrive on scene, you contact other officers to get information."

"That's correct."

"And do you also evaluate the physical scene?"

"Yes, I do."

"Now, did you end up basically getting accounts from the officers as to what other witnesses had said happened?"

"Yes, and they told me where there were two witnesses sitting."

"With regards to utilizing information from witnesses, is that the only thing that you utilize in determining the cause of an accident?"

"No."

"What sort of things do you utilize?"

"Physical evidence from the roadway and from the vehicle and statements from drivers."

Tim then turned Mr. Shaw's attention to some photographs taken at the scene of the accident. With each photograph, Mr. Shaw explained what they were looking at, what it indicated, and whether it was significant.

"Now, Investigator Shaw, to effectively summarize, what weren't you able to determine here?" Tim said.

"I wasn't able to determine the actual speed of the vehicle as it left the roadway, and I wasn't able to determine who was driving the vehicle."

"Now what were you able to determine?"

"I determined that the vehicle just drifted off the roadway, it wasn't forced off. It didn't skid off or swerve off. It drifted off. It struck the guardrail with its left side, which caused it to roll over two and a quarter times."

"Now with respect to the ejection of the defendant, was there anything about the dynamics of the spin or momentum of the crash that would give you any information or indication as to where she was inside the cab?"

"Well, the fact that she was ejected leads me to believe that she was the driver of the vehicle. As the vehicle rotated, the occupant is going to have a tendency to continue straight until somebody strikes them to alter their movement. So as the vehicle rotated up, the occupants moved probably toward the left side of the vehicle and remained there.

"As it hit upside down, I'm not sure. It's more consistent as it came back out, it was rolling pretty rapidly that the occupant was most likely ejected out the driver's window, and since she flew so far, it indicates that there's still some high velocity involved at that point, which there would be in this type of crash."

"And did you observe where the front windshield was?"

"It was broken out, and it was lying right in front of the vehicle."

"Right, so was there any indication that the driver could have gone out the front window?"

"There's no indication."

"Investigator Shaw, on the day this accident occurred, was that the only time that you basically took a look at the Isuzu Rodeo?"

"Yes."

"Okay, and as part of your investigation, do you also look for the condition of the car to indicate whether there was any sort of malfunction or any defects in the car that may have triggered this?"

"Correct."

"You do that?"

"Occasionally yes. On this one, I looked to see if there was any broken tie rods. I didn't push on the brake pedal to determine if there was a good brake pedal firmness. The steering wheel appeared to be okay. I didn't go in and actually steer the vehicle since it was on its side. All the components seemed to be okay."

"Was there anything about the undercarriage that seemed to be out of place?"

"No, I could see where it struck the guardrail there was some scratching on the driver's side."

"So as part of your investigation with that, did you reach any conclusion at that point that there were any defects or anything in the car that could have triggered this?"

"No, it appeared to be okay, and there was no physical evidence on the roadway to indicate that either."

The next witness for the people was Lorenzo Vilanova. Mr. Vilanova testified as a fleet mechanic for O'Reilly Towing.

"Now, sir," Braden said, "I'd like to talk to you about this specific inspection that you conducted back in…I believe it was the early part of 2008, if I recall correctly. Do you recall the date?"

After reviewing a document in front of him, Mr. Vilanova said, "I think December 28 at 3:00 p.m. in the afternoon."

"Okay. And when you say December 28, that was 2006 actually, is that correct?"

"Right."

"I think I accidentally said 2008 earlier. Now with respect to this inspection where did it take place?"

"At O'Reilly Towing in our service garage."

"Okay, and were there a lot of other automobiles in the garage at that time?"

"There was just one other vehicle in there. We moved it out of the way."

"Okay, and we've been mentioning this car, what was the vehicle that you were inspecting on that day?"

Mr. Vilanova explained that the vehicle was a 1992 Isuzu Rodeo.

"Now I want you to talk with us about what goes into your inspections. Do you have a systematic approach to it?"

"Yes, sir."

"And could you describe that approach?"

Mr. Vilanova explained that Westminster police supplied him with a step-by-step, two-sheet sequence that they wanted carried out, and it covered all the basic moving parts of the vehicle and an officer or multiple officers stood by as he took the wheels off or checked any electrical items, and they noted on the sheet what he found.

"Usually an officer will come in and photograph all sides of the vehicle before anything is removed and before we have to take any wheels off. And then I'll check the brake pedal first to make sure that it has adequate pedal travel, and then we'll move on to the pedal travel on the gas pedal, note any steering bindage.

"And then check the tires, tread depths, and any damages to the tire, and then we'll check the brakes and the axles and ABS systems if equipped. And that also covers going underneath and checking the transmission to see if anything has damaged the transmission to stick it into a certain gear, any exhaust system damage, the length of the exhaust pipe itself in the case somebody's modified it to make sure it's correct. And then I also call the dealership that the car's involved with, and you know if it's a Chevy, I call Chevy, or in this case I called Isuzu. I call for any outstanding recalls, and I get a complete history of the vehicles to note if any vehicles have been done or are still outstanding."

After Mr. Vilanova went over the extensive details of the inspection he performed on the vehicle in question, Braden asked, "Mr. Vilanova, in your expert opinion, in your field of expertise, was there anything that you found that would lead you to believe there were mechanical problems with this vehicle?"

"No, sir, it looked like it was pretty well kept up for its mileage. You know, it had 147,000 miles on it, and I've seen quite a few of these Isuzu Rodeos, you know, 250,000 or 300,000 miles on them with no problem. And the people that owned this vehicle looked like they were taking care of it. There wasn't a lot of damage on the seats or on the dash. You know, it looked like they were trying to take care of their vehicle."

The next witness for the people was Dr. Scott Foster. Dr. Scott Foster was qualified as an expert in the field of emergency medicine. He was the emergency room physician at St. Anthony's who examined Frank after the accident. Dr. Foster testified to the fact that Frank suffered serious bodily injures as a result of the car accident on December 19, 2006, and that during the examination, Frank did not exhibit any signs nor did Dr. Foster receive any indication that Frank was under the influence of any intoxicants.

The next witness for the people was Detective Mike Loya. Detective Mike Loya, a detective with the Westminster Police Department, was the lead investigator on the case.

"And what does that mean to be a lead investigator or lead detective, I should say?" Braden said.

"You collect all the reports from all the offices, the accident investigators, and so forth. You compile all the information, you interview the suspect or suspects in the case, and then you compile everything. And if criminal charges are present, if there are going to be criminal charges filed, then you file the case with the district attorney's office."

"Okay. How...aside from being the lead investigator, what responsibilities did you kind of take over with respect to this case?"

"Basically, what I did on this case is I compiled paperwork, but I also interviewed Ms. Barela-Perez."

"Where did that interview take place?"

"It took place at St. Anthony Central Hospital."

"When did it take place?

"It took place on January 16, 2007."

"Is there a reason it took place on January 16, 2007?"

"Ms. Barela-Perez, as she was ejected from the vehicle, suffered quite a few injuries. I initially got the report on December 19 approaching the holidays, so I called the day after Christmas on December 26 to see if I could interview her because obviously it was stated that she was the driver, so I wanted to interview her. And I called the hospital, and they said she was on a ventilator so I wouldn't be able to speak with her, so I had to wait until she was able to communicate."

"Did you keep checking back?"

"No, because it was over the holidays and so forth, and I have other cases I'm working, and I knew when I called and they said no she's on a ventilator, it's going to be a while."

"And that was on December 26. How did we get to January 16?"

"January 16, I called, and they said yes, she's here, obviously, and I said could I go talk to her. I usually call the nurse's station, and they said, 'Yeah, you can come in and talk to her.' So I grabbed another detective, and we went down there."

"Who did you grab?"

"Detective Dominick Buccini."

"Aside from accompanying you for this interview, did Detective Buccini have any other responsibilities in this case?"

"None whatsoever."

"Why did you grab a second detective?"

"We usually go out in pairs. In our line of work, a lot of people will allege something, and if you don't have a witness with you, so to speak, then it's harder to explain or to counter that allegation. Not to mention we take another detective with us for officer safety reasons."

"Okay. Now this interview took place at St. Anthony Hospital. Was it in a hospital room or a conference room?"

"It was in a hospital room."

"And physically what was the state of Ms. Perez at the time?"

"She was in the hospital bed."

"And with respect to how the interview took place, was there anybody else in the hospital room at that time?"

"Just Detective Buccini and I."

Detective Loya then explained that he knocked on the door and waved at Elaine and introduced himself and Detective Buccini. He informed Elaine on who he was and the reason he was there. He asked her if he could speak with her about the accident and said she didn't have to talk to him, but he was investigating the case and he would really like to speak with her. Elaine agreed to speak with him. He told Elaine that normally he records his interviews so he doesn't have to try to commit everything to memory or take lots of notes and he can pay greater attention to the person he is talking to. He showed her the rollaway tray table next to the bed and said he would like to record the interview and he'd like to set the recorder on the rollaway table, to which Elaine said it was fine.

"I want to talk to you about Mr. Hernandez. You actually never spoke with him yourself, is that correct?" Braden said.

"No, sir, I did not speak with him."

"But as the lead detective in this case and also the individual responsible for preparing the filing with the district attorney's office, were you looking at potential other suspects through the course of this investigation?"

"No, sir."

"Okay, and why was that?"

"Ms. Barela-Perez was identified as the driver. When I spoke with her, I addressed her as the driver, and she told me she was driving this vehicle and so forth, so I had no other suspect in the case."

"And you've obviously been sitting through the last day and a half of trial, you are familiar with the questioning of Mr. Hernandez, are you not?"

"Yes, sir."

"And you recall Mr. Berkshire asking some questions about criminal acts in this case?"

"Yes, sir."

"And, sir, during the course of your investigation, had it revealed that Mr. Hernandez was driving, what types of charges were you looking at?"

"He would have been facing careless driving resulting in serious bodily injury, and he would have been facing driving under revocation."

"And with respect to those charges, are those things you can go to prison for?"

"You could go to jail, but they're traffic misdemeanor charges. I mean, they're not even criminal misdemeanor charges. They're traffic misdemeanor charges."

"Okay, so when I said *prison*, you said *jail*, is there a difference between prison and jail?"

"Yes, there is."

"Okay, jail is across the street, is it not?"

"That's correct."

"All right. Now there were some questions by Mr. Berkshire on some of the other witnesses including Officer Barela this morning with respect to collecting labs for Mr. Hernandez, would that have been significant during the course of your investigation?"

"Collecting labs, you mean blood from him?"

"Yes."

"From Mr. Hernandez, no."

"Why not?"

"Because he wasn't the driver."

"Again, had you identified Mr. Hernandez as the driver, would you have been able to get labs?"

"No, you have to have probable cause to do a felony blood draw. A lot of people are under the misconception that if you have felony charges, you can automatically draw blood from someone. You can't. You have to have probable cause to believe they were intoxicated or under the influence of some type of drug. You can't just draw the blood because you want to draw it."

"As the lead detective in this case, the individual responsible for getting all the reports, all of the information, preparing it for filing for the district attorney's office, was there anything during the course of your investigation that you found with regard to Mr. Hernandez, any indicia of intoxication?"

"No sir."

Braden told the judge that he had nothing further.

Mr. Berkshire conducted a lengthy cross-examination on Detective Loya, and at one point in the cross-examination, Mr. Berkshire inquired on Elaine's condition in the hospital. "You said that Ms. Perez looked in a tough condition when you were in the hospital?

"I don't recall saying a tough condition."

"Rough, bad condition?"

"She was—I mean she looked like she should for having been in the accident she was in."

"Now you called the hospital right after Christmas, and they said she's on a ventilator, what does that mean to you?"

"A machine that helps her breathe."

"And she had a trach in her throat, did you know that?"

"I don't recall."

"Did they tell you she was in a coma?"

"When I called?"

"Uh-huh."

"When I called December 26, they said she was still in ICU and on a ventilator."

"Does that mean to you she's in a coma?"

"No."

"How many people have you interviewed with head injuries?"

"Objection relevance," Braden said.

"Let me withdraw that. I'll go this way, Your Honor. During the tape that's been played, Ms. Perez said many, many times, 'I don't remember.' From your experience as a detective and working traffic, you have encountered people with severe head injuries, haven't you?" Mr. Berkshire said.

"Yes, sir."

"And as happens from time to time, maybe more than not, that people with head injuries do not remember the incident where they—"

"Your Honor, may we approach?" Braden said.

"You may," the judge said.

"Judge, same objection as before in terms of this line of questioning," Braden said.

"Well, not remembering. She says she can't remember on the tape. I'm going into that," Mr. Berkshire said.

"The problem is you haven't provided the medical records so I'm sustaining the objection," the judge said.

"That's part of the tape. That's part of what they played. I'm just going to ask him generally," Mr. Berkshire said.

"What are you going to ask?" the judge said.

"I'm going to ask him if he's experienced that before in his investigation, people with closed head injuries cannot remember the incident that caused it."

"Then there's no relevance, so the objection is sustained."

Mr. Berkshire's lengthy cross-examination was followed by a lengthy redirect examination by Braden. The judge then presented some jury questions to be answered by Detective Loya, followed by a brief redirect examination and a brief recross-examination before Detective Loya was asked to step down.

The lunch recess was announced, and the jurors were excused from the courtroom. "Anything further?" The judge asked.

"Your Honor, one thing the defendant mentioned last night is that in the afternoon she starts feeling a lot of pain. Could she put her feet up on another chair? I mean, sit in the wheelchair where she is and put her feet on another chair? That would alleviate the pain," Mr. Berkshire said.

"Why don't you try to put a chair under the table and show me what it would look like and then I can make a principled decision. Or show me how it works, obviously the less noticeable the better."

After some consideration, I'm not certain, but I think it was a large briefcase that was used to elevate Elaine's legs. Was it her way to gain sympathy from the jurors or was she really in pain? I did not know, but I had my suspicions.

Following the lunch recess the next witness was called.

The next witness for the people was Sam Goode. Mr. Goode testified as an expert witness in the field of blood alcohol analysis. Mr. Goode who was employed as a chemist for the Colorado Department of Public Health and Environment in the toxicology lab. He received a request form the Westminster Police to analyze blood in the case. Mr. Goode analyzed Elaine's blood taken the day of the accident for the presence of alcohol and testified to the fact that there was no alcohol in Elaine's blood.

The next witness for the people was Janie Rodgers. Ms. Rodgers was qualified as an expert in the fields of the analysis of urine for the presence of drugs as well as the analysis of blood for drugs. Ms. Rodgers, who testified as a lab tech for the Department of Health toxicology lab, analyzed Elaine's blood and urine taken the day of the accident for the presence of drugs and received two results. With regards to the results of the blood screens, Ms. Rodgers testified to the fact that amphetamine and methamphetamine was present in Elaine's blood. The amphetamine was 83 nanograms per milliliter, and the methamphetamine was 805 nanograms per milliliter. With regards to the results to the urine screens, Ms. Rodgers found the amphetamine screen was presumptive positive and the benzodiazepine screen was presumptive positive.

The next witness for the people was Kate Stevens. Ms. Stevens testified as an expert in the field of forensic toxicology. Ms. Stevens, a program manager and forensic toxicologist for the State of Colorado in the state toxicology lab, explained that a forensic toxicologist is a person that analyzes poisons in the body via laboratory instrumentation.

"Now just to clarify here, in terms of the spectrum of forensic toxicology, does that also include the expertise to explain how specific drugs and/or alcohol may impact the human body?" Tim said.

"It does."

"And does that also include the ability to describe those effects in terms of what may be the effects on anatomy and physiology?"

"It does, sir."

"Cognitive effects?"

"Yes."

"And motor skills?"

"Yes."

"Now with regards to the drug methamphetamine, can you describe what methamphetamine is?"

"Methamphetamine is a central nervous system stimulant."

"Within methamphetamine, are there what science has determined stages of the high?"

Ms. Stevens explained that through published literature based on epidemiology and control studies, three phases of a high were established. She defined the epidemiology studies as studies that were gathered by scientists from accidents in the field and then correlated to a blood content and control studies. "Not done in the United States but in other countries, these are studies where people were actually dosed then put on the road with things that would normally occur in traffic such as somebody changing lanes and somebody having to stop suddenly, and based on those studies we know there's three phases with the first phase being called the rush."

"Can you describe what the rush phase is?"

"The rush is about a five-minute phase. It's when you ingest or inhale the methamphetamine and you release dopamine. You have intense euphoria. The next phase is called the run, and that lasts anywhere from when the rush ends to two to four hours. And that's a stage where you have dilated pupils, you become excited, you have psychomotor problems, you have risk-taking problems, critical judgment problems, degradation of motor skills, psychomotor, and cognitive skills. Cognitive is thinking, judging, and reasoning. Psychomotor skills is your ability to keep your motor vehicle on the roadway and to scan traffic for dangers and be able to stop in time in an event of an emergency.

"The last phase is called the crash phase and comes about twelve to twenty-four hours. It's similar to being under the influence of a CNS depressant, you become drowsy. They call it tweaking, which means you become irritated and also have problems driving because that's the phase in which you're most likely to fall asleep at the wheel."

At some point during the direct examination, Tim said, "Based on your review of the information and based on the results from the numerical values from the blood test, does this give you any frame of time as to when Ms. Barela-Perez would have ingested the methamphetamine?"

"The amount in the blood report is methamphetamine at 805. So it told me that methamphetamine had to be ingested near the time of driving or in the car."

"Now within the analysis, it appeared that there was also a positive for classification of benzodiazepine?"

"Yes, a central nervous system depressant."

"Does the presence of that have any significance to you?"

"Scientifically, it does. There was none detected, so it means it was below our detectible limit. When you're using a central nervous system stimulant, a central nervous system depressant is used to take what they call the side effects away from the stimulant. It's to take the edge off as you're coming down and also take some of the edge off of the increased heart rate, the increased blood pressure, the increased temperature, and the sweating. It's very common for methamphetamine users to use a central nervous system depressant to combat those side effects."

"And the presence of it—would that contribute or detract from the side effects of the methamphetamine in terms of how it might affect cognitive or psychomotor skills?"

"In this case the methamphetamine was so pronounced on board in the blood that I don't believe the central nervous system depressant had much effect because methamphetamine didn't potentiate (increase) the effects."

"Now with regards to the number that we have in terms of the methamphetamine, the 805 ng/ml (nanograms per milliliter), in terms of evaluating that number, can you say in your career how many times you've had the occasion to observe blood methamphetamine levels?"

"We've had a few in the lab, and until most recently, this was the highest. I had somebody that I just reviewed lately that had a higher numerical value than this. It was in the thousands, but this was the highest until recently."

"And does that number suggest to you anything about the dosage when the person took it?"

"It suggests to me that there was a lot of methamphetamine ingested. It's a very high number." Ms. Stevens went on to explain that when you compare the average number found in epidemiology studies, 200 ng/ml, and compare that to the 805 ng/ml number, the 805 ng/ml "is a very, very big amount of methamphetamine in the blood."

"Ms. Stevens, do you have any opinion as to what sort of cognitive or psychomotor effects a person with that level of methamphetamine in their system would be going through?"

"The cognitive effect on someone with that level of methamphetamine in their system would be increased risk taking. During that euphoria feeling, you will have rapid speech, and as that occurs, you will have problems with divided attention, and that crosses over in to psychomotor skills, which is brakes, steering, staying in one's lane, maintaining lateral travel, maintaining headway between cars, peripheral vision, depth perception, diminished hearing, diminished visual acuity, diminished reaction time and the inability to keep a motor vehicle in control." Ms. Stevens then explained that studies show there was a high increase of off-the-road accidents and non-collision accidents (vehicles crashed into something or were rolled) with methamphetamine use, due to the increase of failing to pay attention to posted speed limits or exceeding the posted speed limits.

"Based on that, would a person at this level have difficulty safely operating a motor vehicle?" Tim asked.

"In my opinion, absolutely."

"And on top of that, would their ability to safely drive a motor vehicle in your professional opinion be substantially impaired?"

"They would be."

With Ms. Stevens being the last witness for the people, the afternoon recess was announced, and the jurors were excused. "Are the people going to rest?" the judge said.

"Judge, the people are going to rest." Braden advised.

The judge and Mr. Berkshire then agreed that the Curtis Advisement would be given to Elaine at the end of the recess.

After the short recess, and outside the presence of the jury, the judge asked Elaine to direct her attention to her for the Curtis

Advisement. "I want to advise you that you have the right to testify. If you wish to testify, then no one can prevent you from doing so. You may take the witness stand even if it's contrary to the advice of your attorney. If you do testify, the people will be allowed to cross-examine you. If you have a felony conviction, the prosecutor will be entitled to ask you about that conviction or convictions and thereby disclose them to the jury. Does the defendant have prior felony convictions?"

"Yes," Tim said.

"Can you put them on the record please?" The judge turned back to Elaine. "While they're looking for that, I'll keep advising you." Elaine nodded. "If the felony conviction is disclosed to the jury, the jury will be instructed to consider that conviction or convictions only as they bear upon your credibility. You also have the right not to testify. The jury can be instructed about that right and that no inference of guilt can be drawn from the fact that you did not testify. The decision of whether or not to testify is a decision to be made by you." After the judge completed the Curtis Advisement, she turned to Braden. "Do you have those convictions, Mr. Diaz?"

"Judge, for the record, they're contained in the habitual offender counts that were added in counts five through nine."

"I just prefer that you put them on the record, but I guess I'll do it," the judge advised.

Braden nodded, and the judge started naming Elaine's convictions, "A conviction out of Nevada in 1992 for theft and burglary, a conviction in El Paso County in 1993 for possession of a controlled substance, a conviction in El Paso County in 1993 for violation of bail bond condition, a conviction out of North Carolina in 1998 for violation of parole."

"It's supposed to be 1990. It's a typo, but I know what they're talking about," Elaine interrupted.

"Well, there's not a date of conviction, there's a date of violation of parole apparently. Do you understand which conviction that is?"

"Yes."

The judge continued, "And an Adams County case from 2003 for controlled substance possession, schedule II. You also have a misdemeanor conviction of false information that the people could inquire about based upon the nature of the offense. Do you understand, Ms. Perez, that the people could ask you about those convictions?"

"Yes."

"Have you made a decision of whether or not you wish to testify?"

"Yes."

"How do you wish to proceed?"

"Not to testify," Elaine said.

"Has anyone forced you or coerced you to make that decision?"

"No, I can't remember anything about the accident, so there's no sense in me testifying."

You can't remember anything about the accident, but you can remember something from 1990, I thought to myself.

At that time, Mr. Berkshire moved for a judgment of acquittal based on the grounds, "There has been no evidence, credible evidence by the government, that Ms. Perez was driving the car. And I think that is an element in three of the offenses." Mr. Berkshire added that he didn't think there was sufficient evidence to support a verdict of guilty.

The judge thanked Mr. Berkshire and ruled that the motion for acquittal was denied. "When viewing the evidence in the light most favorable to the prosecution, I believe there's substantial and sufficient evidence to support a conclusion by a reasonable mind that the defendant is guilty of each count one, count two, count three, and count four beyond a reasonable doubt," the judge said. She then asked that the jurors be brought in.

"Please be seated. Ladies and gentlemen, we're now ready to continue with the trial," the judge said to the jurors. She then turned to Braden and Tim. "The next witness on behalf of the people?" She inquired.

"Your Honor, the people rest at this time," Braden advised.

"Thank you, Mr. Diaz. And the first witness for the defendant, Mr. Berkshire?"

"Your Honor, we would ask to read the deposition of Ray Gleeson," Mr. Berkshire said.

"Ladies and gentlemen, we're now going to have the deposition of Ray Gleeson read into the record as testimony. We have someone who has volunteered to stand in as Mr. Gleeson. This deposition was taken last week because Mr. Gleeson was unable to be here for trial. So Mr. Berkshire will ask this stand-in witness questions just as they were asked at the deposition as will Mr. Diaz, and he will answer them by reading from the deposition as Ray Gleeson. Go ahead, Mr. Berkshire."

After Mr. Berkshire asked the preliminary questions, he said, "I notice you are in a wheelchair, are you able to walk very far?"

"No, I'm not. I'm in the life-ending stages of liver disease and heart disease, and they have let me go from the hospital to be at home to be comfortable to die."

"I'm going to ask you if you know Elaine Perez."

"Yes I do."

"How long have you known her?"

"Twenty five years."

"Would you give us just a brief description of the relationship?"

"We have always held ourselves out as father and daughter."

"You are not the biological father?"

"I am not her biological father, no."

"Would you be able to describe that as a good friendship?"

"It's a very good friendship."

"Do you know a man named Frank Hernandez?"

"Yes, I do."

"How long have you known him?"

"I've known him for almost one year."

"Let me back up a bit. You, in fact, are staying now at Ms. Perez's residence, are you not?"

"I am."

"You have known Mr. Hernandez for a year, did you say?"

"Yes."

"How did you come to know him?"

"He was intimately related with Elaine Perez."

Did you see him many times?"

"All the time."

"I'm going to direct your attention to December. It will be December 20, 2006. Where were you residing at the time?"

"In a rest home in Lakewood."

"How long have you been in the rest home?"

"Approximately three months."

"For what problem at that time?"

"I had been on a ventilator for a long period of time. I was there for rehabilitation to recover."

"Did you learn that Elaine Perez was in the hospital on December 20, 2006?"

"Yes, I did."

"How did you learn that?"

"Frank Hernandez called me and told me there had been an accident. They were both at the hospital. That he was injured, she was injured."

"What did you do in response to the telephone call?"

"I immediately hired a cab and got in my wheelchair and had the cab come and take me to the hospital."

"What did you do at the hospital?"

"The first thing I did was go where Mr. Hernandez told me he was at. I don't remember what floor it was on. I remember it was a room over in the corner. He told me that there had been an accident. That he was signing out against medical advice. That Elaine was probably dead. That being he was out on so many bonds, he was going to sign out against medical advice. That he was the driver of the automobile and Elaine would never be able to say anything because she was probably dead already."

"How long did you visit with Mr. Hernandez that day?"

"Just long enough to learn that information and where Elaine was."

"What did you do after you talked with him?"

"I went to the intensive care unit where Elaine was."

"Do you recall how long Elaine was in the hospital?"

"She was in intensive care for about twenty days. And then she was in other areas of the hospital for about another twenty days."

"Were you at the hospital more than that one day?"

"I used to come every day and stay all day with Elaine at her bedside. I would take a cab, either a yellow or a checker, one that could handle my electric wheelchair. They would come and pick me up, and they would take me down there in the morning, and they would pick me up in the evening."

"I'm going to ask you if at any time while you were visiting Elaine at the hospital did you see a police officer at the hospital."

"Yes."

"Do you remember the date?"

"I don't remember the date, but I remember that we were not in the intensive care unit. I remember that they were apparently in her room when I got there."

"Was there more than one?"

"There seemed to be two police officers there."

"Did you see them both?

"I didn't see the second one until they left. They had her bed draped, and I went down to get a cup of coffee. When I came back, the nurse told me that they were undergoing a medical procedure in the room and that I couldn't resume my visit until a later time."

"Was that the nurse that told you that or was it a police officer?"

"The nurse told me that."

"When you say her bed was draped, does that mean the curtain that hangs around the ceiling from the bed?"

"That's what I mean, yes."

"Did you talk with the officer?"

"No."

"Did you ask if you could be admitted while the officers were there with Elaine Perez?"

"Yes, I asked the medical staff. They said no. 'This is a medical procedure going on and you are not allowed in the room.'"

"Did you learn later on whether or not there was a medical procedure."

"Yes."

"Had there been a medical procedure?"

"No."

"I want to go further into your relationship with Ms. Perez. Who took care of Elaine when she left the hospital, do you know that?"

"Some girl name Julie. A Mexican girl took care of her, her home companion or home nurse or whatever."

"I want to ask you this: was Mr. Hernandez involved in that also?"

"Mr. Hernandez used to come around, I think. While he was visiting Elaine, I was visiting Elaine one day, and he was crying about how much the cabs cost. I told him, 'Why don't we go buy a car. I'll take you down there, and we'll go buy a car, and then you will have transportation so you can come and see Elaine,' and we did that."

"You bought a car for him?"

"The three of us bought a car together—me, Julie, and him."

"And that was for what purpose?"

"For transportation of him and Julie to the hospital to see Elaine."

"Who provided the funds for that car?"

"I provided some of them, she provided some, and Frank even gave some up."

"Did you see Elaine after she was released from the hospital?"

"No."

"Not at all?"

"No, never."

"Did you go elsewhere after that?"

"Yes. I was in federal custody after that."

"How many times had you seen Mr. Hernandez after December 20, before you left the area."

"Maybe ten."

"Did he indicate that he had been driving the car that day?"

"Yes, he did."

"Okay. Did he ever change his statement that he had been driving the car?"

"I don't think we ever spoke of it again."

After some very confusing statements on Mr. Gleeson's part, Mr. Berkshire had no more questions, and it was Braden's turn to cross-examine.

During Braden's cross-examination, Mr. Gleeson's extensive criminal history was reviewed.

"Okay. We indicated that your criminal history dates back to 1960. You actually have, I believe, a dozen felony convictions, isn't that right?" Braden said.

"I don't know if it's that many, I have never counted them."

Mr. Gleeson's convictions included interstate transportation of forged checks, uttering and delivering fraudulent checks, interstate transportation of forged securities, uttering fraudulent checks, theft of rental property, theft of property and services, forty-six counts of fraud by check, false swearing and conspiracy to defraud the IRS. The states where his crimes took place included Texas, Montana, Missouri, California, Wyoming, Wisconsin, North Dakota, and Colorado.

I was shocked hearing about Ray's criminal history. He just seemed to be a nice old man to me. Still I should have known better.

At one point during Braden's cross-examination, he asked Mr. Gleeson, "You indicated on direct examination that Mr. Hernandez told you he was driving. When did he indicate that?"

"When they had the accident, he was driving that evening. They were going to Boulder to get drugs."

At that, I turned to Maria. "What? Did he just say that?" She looked at me with uncertainty. Neither one of us was sure of what we heard. I looked up at the jury, and they too seemed unsure of what they heard. However, later in Mr. Berkshire's redirect examination, he asked Mr. Gleeson if Frank informed him on why he and Elaine were driving to Boulder that day of the accident. To which Mr. Gleeson stated, "Yes, to purchase Christmas gifts and drugs."

"It was December of 2006 when he indicated that to you?"

"Whenever the accident took place. Yes."

"And you understand that the defendant was actually charged with a crime in this case?"

"Yes."

"And you have known that for how long?"

"Oh, I've been away, so I really didn't get all the particulars until maybe a year ago."

"And during the course of the last twelve months, you never once contacted law enforcement to tell them the information about Mr. Hernandez?"

"Well, I knew that Mr. Hernandez had finally met his just reward and was in the state prison, so I didn't say anything."

"That didn't answer my question. At no time did you ever contact law enforcement with that information?"

"No, I didn't."

"No further questions," Braden said.

After the deposition was read, the judge excused the jurors and requested that they return the next morning at 8:45 a.m.

Court was adjourned at 4:39 p.m.

On the drive home, Maria, Anna and I discussed the day's proceedings. Then we discussed our sore butts and agreed that the courtroom benches need padding.

CHAPTER 40

The truth is heavy; therefore few care to carry it.

—Winston Churchill

PEOPLE VERSUS ELAINE BARELA-PEREZ JURY TRIAL DAY THREE, JULY 10, 2008

Court convened at 8:49 a.m., and after the preliminary issues were discussed, the jury was brought in.

The next witness for the defense was Julie Perea. Julie was Elaine's home health care provider for a year and a half.

After Ms. Perea was sworn in, Mr. Berkshire asked her the preliminary questions then said, "Do you know Elaine Perez?"

"Yes, I do."

"How long? How do you know her?"

"I was her home health care provider for a year and a half."

"Was that after she was out of the hospital?"

"Yes."

"Did you know her before she went in the hospital?"

"I knew her, but not very close."

"And at this time, you're no longer working for or helping Ms. Perez?"

"No."

It was then established that Ms. Perea had known Frank for about seven years and met him through a mutual friend. "Did you ever help him financially?" Mr. Berkshire asked.

Ms. Perea explained that she bonded Frank out of jail prior to December 19, 2006, the day of the accident.

"Do you recall what happened that day?"

Ms. Perea explained that she received a phone call from St. Anthony Hospital explaining that there had been an accident. She was headed to work, and instead she drove directly to the hospital. When she arrived at the hospital, she went immediately to the emergency room where she saw Frank laying on a gurney while some nurses and doctors worked on him. She got close enough to ask Frank what happened, but before he could answer, a nurse quickly took him to get an x-ray of his chest because he was complaining that he was experiencing chest pain. When Frank returned from getting the x-ray, a police officer and another guy, whom she thought may be a detective, showed up and started asking Frank questions.

"I overheard Frank say that he was the passenger and that he remembered writing in his journal when he heard Elaine say, 'Huh.' He looked up, and the car just started flipping, and he could see something red go by, which he thought was a car that almost clipped them or something and Elaine was trying to avoid it." She then explained that right after Frank spoke to the officer and the detective, he told her something totally different.

"He said they were both in the car, Elaine and him, and they went to go pick up Andrew. Well, they parked over at another friend's house, which is maybe like five blocks away. It's on the other side of the golf course from where Andrew lives, or was staying with the other parent or grandparents. He said that Elaine left him there while she went and got Andrew."

"Did he say he drove there?"

"Yeah, yeah, 'cause he normally does drive. He doesn't like anybody else to drive. He drove to Sylvia's house. That's the lady where he was left at. Then Elaine took the vehicle and went and got Andrew. And when she came back to pick up Frank, she was still in the driver's seat. He got in the car. I guess she made a wrong turn to wherever they were going, and he got upset and said that he didn't like the way she was driving and told her to let him drive. So Elaine pulled over, and he drove."

In the cross-examination, Tim asked Ms. Perea in reference to Frank, "Did you ever post any of his bonds?"

"Yes."

"As a result of that, did you ever lose out on any money?"

"Yes."

"Approximately how much money?"

"Six thousand dollars."

"And you said that you were called basically the day this happened, referring to the accident?"

"Yes."

"And you wanted to know what happened right?"

"Correct."

"So you sat there as Mr. Hernandez explained to the police what had happened correct?"

"Yes."

"And then he went out for an x-ray at one point or some procedure and then came back."

"Yes."

"But you followed up with him and asked what happened."

"Yes."

"And then he tells you that he was driving."

"Yes."

"So sort of the substance of what he told you was that he was driving, he went to Sylvia's and stayed there, correct?"

"Yeah or outside of where she lives, yes."

"And then Elaine took the car and picked up Andrew."

"Yes."

"Then came back, he got in the car, they started to leave, but then he took over driving."

"Right."

"And that was the extent of the conversation."

"Yes."

"Now you said that after this happened, you basically ended up being the defendant's caretaker, right?"

"Yes."

"For a period of a year and a half."

"Correct."

"Were you aware that charges were filed against the defendant?"

"This was quite a ways down the road, but yes."

"So you brought her to court."

"Yes."

"And so there were occasions when you met with her attorneys? You were present when she was meeting with her attorneys?"

"Yes."

"So you knew that the accusation was that she was driving the car that day when this crash occurred."

"Could you repeat that again?"

"You were aware that what she was being charged with stemmed around this crash."

"That they were saying she was the driver, yes."

"And as a result of this, did you correct the police?"

"No."

"Did you call anybody and say, 'Hey, I know she wasn't the driver'?"

"No."

"Were you aware that the defendant, when she spoke with the police concerning this accident, admitted that she was driving?"

"Repeat that again."

"Were you aware that when Ms. Barela-Perez met with the police, she admitted to them that she was driving? Were you aware of that?"

"Just on the paperwork of when we, you know, talked to the attorneys."

"Thank you. No further questions."

After a brief redirect examination by Mr. Berkshire, "Your Honor, we don't have any further witnesses. We would ask that the stipulation be read to the jury," Mr. Berkshire said.

"Ladies and gentlemen, I'm going to read you a stipulation between the parties. Come now the parties and stipulate and agree that if Ron Gleeson were able to appear as a witness, he would testify as follows:

> On December 20, 2006, he learned Elaine Perez had been critically injured the previous day in a motor vehicle accident and visited her nearly every day from that point forward until she was released from the hospital on about January 30, 2007.
>
> The patient was in a coma when she arrived at the hospital on December 19, 2006. She did not awake from the coma for ten days or so and it was three weeks or more before she could communicate in a meaningful manner.
>
> He was at the hospital when the officers questioned Elaine on January 16, 2007. He was not allowed to be present at the questioning but was with Elaine for a long period of time after the officers left. Elaine was not very lucid when he visited with her following the police visit.

After the stipulation was read, the judge read the jury the instructions and closing arguments were read.

At 10:56 a.m. jury deliberations commenced. Oddly enough, in the middle of deliberations, a fire alarm went off, and everyone was made to leave the courthouse building. We spent over an hour waiting outside for the okay to return to the building.

Finally at around 4:00 p.m., the jury reached a verdict.

Court reconvened, and the judge said, "Back on the record in people versus Perez. The jury has advised they have a verdict, so I'm going to have them brought in at this time." The jury took their seats, and then the judge asked the rest of us to, "Please be seated." The judge turned to the jurors and said, "Ladies and gentlemen, I've been advised that you've reached a verdict, is that correct? And Ms. Meyer, are you the foreperson?"

"Yes, I am."

"Would you please give the verdict forms to my clerk?"

Anna, Maria, and I held hands, and our breath as the verdict was read.

"Jury verdict, count one, charge of child abuse. We, the jury, find the defendant, Elaine Barela-Perez, guilty of child abuse. Jury verdict, count two, charge of vehicular assault, victim Andrew Perez. We, the jury, find the defendant, Elaine Barela-Perez, guilty of vehicular assault, victim Andrew Perez. Jury verdict, count three, charge of vehicular assault, the victim Frank Hernandez. We, the jury, find the defendant, Elaine Barela-Perez guilty of vehicular assault, victim Frank Hernandez. Jury verdict, count four, charge of driving under the influence. We, the jury, find the defendant, Elaine Barela-Perez guilty of driving under the influence."

Tears welled up in my eyes as Maria and Anna threw their arms around me.

EPILOGUE

In the end everyone will hurt you. It's up to you to decide
who is worth the pain.

—unknown

HABITUAL TRIAL, AUGUST 11, 2008

$\mathscr{B}$ raden began by informing the court that the defendant,
Elaine Perez, was going to take the plea agreement
of a twenty-four-year sentence for the child abuse
charge in order to have the habitual trial vacated. Braden also
stated that the defendant's attorney plans on requesting a PSI
(presentence investigation).

At that moment, Mr. Berkshire stood up and advised that he
wanted to request a PSI as the defendant's dad, Mr. Gleeson, is
dying and also because the defendant has an appointment with
the child and family investigator (CFI) that's working on her
pending custody case.

I was confused by Elaine's reasoning for wanting a PSI, since
typically when there is a plea agreement a PSI isn't performed
as its purpose is basically to assist the court in determining an

appropriate sentence. So with Mr. Berkshires reasons (Mr. Gleeson is dying and Elaine has an appointment with the CFI) I had to believe that they were using the investigation to buy time allowing Elaine to remain at her current place of incarceration, which is close to home, for the time being.

The judge advised that it was the defendant's right to request a PSI and that the request is granted. Mr. Berkshire than asked if it would be possible for the defendant to attend her dad's funeral should it arise during the time she is incarcerated.

The judge denied the request, and Elaine began to cry. Sadly, that was the only time Elaine showed any emotion throughout the trial. The sentencing hearing was scheduled for October 2, 2008, and the hearing concluded.

SENTENCING HEARING OCTOBER 2, 2008

On October 2, 2008, Maria and I arrived at the Jefferson County Courthouse for Elaine's sentencing hearing. I noticed Kathy from victim/witness waiting for us as we passed through the metal detectors. She greeted Maria and me and said she would not be able to attend court with us but appointed someone else to sit with us. She asked that we meet that individual in the victim/witness office as she was expecting us, which we did prior to heading for the courtroom.

When we entered the courtroom, I noticed Elaine sitting in her wheelchair at the defendant's table. She had on an orange jumpsuit and looked healthier than the last time I saw her. Her hair had a shine to it, and she looked like she had picked up some much-needed weight.

Our designated victim/witness assistant and Maria and I all sat in the front row behind the prosecution's table hand in hand. Both Braden and Tim were present and acknowledged us with a smile and a wave, and then we waited while the judge tended to her other cases.

Anna arrived minutes later. I smiled at her while she took a seat next to me. We hugged then she took my hand and gave it a little squeeze for reassurance. "I'm glad you came," I said. "Well of course I came." She smiled warmly.

As we all sat nervously waiting I nearly jumped out of my skin when Elaine's name was finally called. We all scooted forward on our seats nervously glancing at one another while Elaine and her attorney took the stand.

The judge addressed Elaine, and handed down her sentence that would run concurrent (she will serve each sentence at the same time):

For child abuse, count one–the negotiated twenty-four-year sentence; for vehicular assault, count two–six years; for vehicular assault, count three–six years.

Of course I was aware of the twenty-four year sentence, but I just assumed that the vehicular assault charges would be dropped. So I was surprised when the judge tacked on two additional six year sentences, even though they were to run concurrent with her twenty four year sentence.

Even so, the time Elaine received wasn't important to me What was important, what I prayed for, was that she would take responsibility and even show a bit of remorse for hurting Andrew. Yet sadly, Elaine was not capable of accountability or remorse.

I left the courtroom that day under a cloud of immense grief because even though justice prevailed, in the end, only loss remains.